GEORGE ALBERT SMITH

George Albert Smith, about 1913,
wearing Sons of the American Revolution button

GEORGE ALBERT SMITH
Kind and Caring Christian, Prophet of God

Francis M. Gibbons

Deseret Book Company
Salt Lake City, Utah

Books by Francis M. Gibbons

Joseph Smith: Martyr, Prophet of God
Brigham Young: Modern Moses, Prophet of God
John Taylor: Mormon Philosopher, Prophet of God
Wilford Woodruff: Wondrous Worker, Prophet of God
Lorenzo Snow: Spiritual Giant, Prophet of God
Joseph F. Smith: Patriarch and Preacher, Prophet of God
Heber J. Grant: Man of Steel, Prophet of God
George Albert Smith: Kind and Caring Christian, Prophet of God
David O. McKay: Apostle to the World, Prophet of God

This is not an official publication of The Church of Jesus Christ of Latter-day Saints. The author, and he alone, is responsible for its contents.

All photographs used by permission of Church Archives, The Church of Jesus Christ of Latter-day Saints.

Library of Congress Cataloging-in-Publication Data

Gibbons, Francis M., 1921–
   George Albert Smith : kind and caring Christian, prophet of God / Francis M. Gibbons.
     p. cm.
   Includes bibliographical references.
   ISBN 0-87579-285-5
   1. Smith, George Albert, 1870–   . 2. Church of Jesus Christ of Latter-day Saints — Presidents — Biography. 3. Mormon Church — Presidents — Biography. I. Title.
BX8695.S518G52   1990
289.3'092 — dc20
[B]   89-29599
                                    CIP

Printed in the United States of America
10   9   8   7   6   5   4   3   2   1

To Judge Andrew Smith Gibbons
Honored father and counselor

Contents

Contents

Preface

This is the story of George Albert Smith, one of the greatest practitioners of Christian ethics known to The Church of Jesus Christ of Latter-day Saints. It traces his growth and development from a spindly boy, unsure of himself and struggling under the burden of his distinguished name, to the pinnacle of Church leadership. In the process, he endured physical disabilities and pain that repeatedly threatened his life and interfered with his apostolic duties. Notwithstanding, he maintained a positive, happy outlook, never complaining, always optimistic and consistent in trying to lift the burdens of others.

As a boy, he was identified as a future apostle of the Lord Jesus Christ and president of the Church through the prophetic blessing of an inspired patriarch. His long life thereafter was characterized by an effort to emulate his Lord, to observe the principles He taught, and to exhort others to do likewise.

The keystone of his behavior and teachings was love — love of God, which he demonstrated by keeping the commandments, and love of his fellow beings, which he demonstrated by repeated acts of kindness and caring concern. These were not empty gestures of generosity or glad handing but rather heartfelt expressions of interest in the welfare and happiness of others. Such were the purity of his motives and the genuineness of his conduct that his appeal to others was almost universal, crossing boundaries of creed, color, or nationality. People of every kind instinctively liked and trusted this man.

Two inherent qualities of character surface intermittently in the life of George Albert Smith that provide important insights into his motivations. The first was a fierce family loyalty and a pride of ancestry. In some, this quality manifests itself in a smug, complacent assumption of intrinsic superiority, bordering on arrogance or conceit. In George Albert Smith, however, it served chiefly as a goad to achievement and gave a sense of responsibility to measure up to his forebears, compensating through service to others for the advantages he had inherited through the accident of birth. With all this, he knew that he came from good stock and that in his body flowed the blood of prophets. Such knowledge, reinforced over the years through the words and examples of his ancestors, gave him poise and self-confidence in the presence of all people, including some whose physical and intellectual attributes and achievements overshadowed his own.

This love of ancestry was undoubtedly a major force that fueled his intense interest in historic monuments and markers and in the Sons of the American Revolution. He wanted the exploits and traditions of these ancestors to live on and to motivate those who would follow, in the same way he had been motivated.

The other inherent characteristic in George Albert Smith's makeup that propelled him toward superior achievement was a powerful competitive instinct. This may surprise some whose views of President Smith have been conditioned by the image of the benign, bearded, loving, and much-loved prophet he ultimately became. But beneath that exterior burned fierce fires of will, determination, and the desire to succeed, if not to excel. In the early years, this characteristic revealed itself in a love for debate and in competitive activities, whether in business or in sports. It was clearly evident in his battles against illness. One with less will and desire to conquer would have been crushed by the physical and emotional problems he faced. In his later years, this characteristic seems to have been muted into an internal drive, aimed toward self-improvement and the attainment of personal perfection rather than toward any demonstration of personal superiority or achievement over another.

It is easy to see in this characteristic why aspiring, energetic young people were attracted to him and were motivated by his admonitions for them to excel. "Don't be a scrub," he repeatedly told them, an admonition that says almost as much about the character of the speaker as it does about the message he delivered.

The sources necessary to write a biography of George Albert Smith are varied and extensive. His personal diaries, which he kept over the years, are an important original source. Also, his official and private correspondence and papers provide vital documentation. Many of these are housed in the archives of The Church of Jesus Christ of Latter-day Saints in Salt Lake City or in the Special Collections & Manuscripts section of the University of Utah Library. I am grateful to the personnel at these institutions, who were uniformly helpful and cordial in providing access to these important, basic sources. (I have used the abbreviation "GASC" in this book to refer to the George Albert Smith Collection at the University of Utah Library. Photos are used courtesy of LDS Church Historical Department.) Thanks also to Dr. Andrew S. Gibbons III and to Ruth Bay Stoneman, who provided important research assistance, and to many others, relatives or associates of President Smith, who provided valuable information, help, and counsel. Thanks too, as always, go to the Mentor.

Chapter One

A Child of Promise

H is name and pedigree were gold plated. George Albert Smith, born in Salt Lake City on April 4, 1870, was given the same name as his paternal grandfather, who was then the first counselor in the First Presidency of The Church of Jesus Christ of Latter-day Saints. His maternal grandfather, Lorin Farr, was the first mayor of nearby Ogden, Utah, and the first president of the Weber Stake. And the child's father, John Henry Smith, would later become the second counselor in the First Presidency. Moreover, his great-grandfather, John Smith, the uncle of the Prophet Joseph Smith, was the first president of the Salt Lake Stake and also the Patriarch to the Church when he died in 1854. If this were thought insufficient to establish his genealogical credentials, consider that eleven of the infant's pioneer ancestors trekked across the plains to Utah and six of his forebears were passengers on the Mayflower, one of whom, Edward Winslow, became governor of the Plymouth colony.

Such lineal distinction would serve both to buoy up

1

and to depress George Albert Smith throughout his life. While it lifted him to know he was descended from ancestors of worth and achievement, he was sometimes depressed wondering whether he measured up to them. A pivotal event in his life occurred in adulthood when his grandfather appeared in a dream to ask what he had done with the name *George Albert Smith*. The grandson answered with apparent relief that he had done nothing to dishonor or to sully it. Indeed, he added a luster to the name that outshone that given to it by the grandfather.

Aside from the prospect of coming distinction hinted at by his earthly lineage, spiritual incidents foreshadowed a famous future for this child. His mother had been told in a patriarchal blessing that none in Israel would excel her posterity. And a prophetic promise made to young George Albert Smith was more explicit. It came from a venerable old patriarch, Zebedee Coltrin, who was a confidant of the Prophet Joseph Smith and a charter member of the school of the prophets.

This enigmatic old man, who flits in and out of Church history like a firefly on a summer evening, appeared unexpectedly at the Smith home on January 16, 1884, announcing to Sarah Farr Smith that he wanted to bless her eldest son. This was George Albert, whose elder brother, John Henry, had died in infancy. Without preamble or explanation, and pressing Sarah into service as his scribe, the aged patriarch laid his hands on the boy's head and pronounced a blessing that was startling in its import: "Thou shalt become a mighty prophet in the midst of the sons of Zion," declared he. "Thou shalt become a mighty apostle in the church and kingdom of God upon the earth, for none of thy father's family shall have more power with God than thou shalt have, for none shall excel thee." (Copy of blessing in GASC, box 96, folder 13.)

To have predicted such a future for this thirteen-year-old boy required extraordinary spiritual sensitivity and audacity. The blessing meant nothing less than that the lad would ascend to the First Presidency as had his grandfather; and at most, it meant he would become the president of the Church, as his father's extended family included the Prophet Joseph Smith.

Other than the fact that he had been well born, there was little about this gangling boy to suggest that he would rise to such eminence. At that age, he had shown no unusual aptitude or distinction. He was just one of the children of one of the many polygamous families who lived in the neighborhood surrounding Temple Square in Salt Lake City. His home was on the northwest corner of the intersection of South Temple and West Temple, across the street from Temple Square and next door to the home of his grandfather President George A. Smith. In the middle of the block to the north was the home of President Wilford Woodruff; two blocks east were the homes of President Brigham Young; and two blocks north was the home of John Henry Smith's polygamous wife, Josephine Groesbeck. Nearby were the dwellings of other Church leaders and members, practically all of which were graced with an abundance of growing, exuberant children.

Large families were the rule at that day. George Albert's mother, Sarah Farr, ultimately gave birth to eleven children; and Josephine Groesbeck was the mother of eight. Amidst such a throng, it was easy to lose a sense of individuality and to have one's identity submerged in the general life of family and neighborhood. Therefore, to be singled out for special distinction, to be designated as a future apostle and prophet, affirmed, in a sense, the importance of the one and provided the boy with a powerful incentive.

To say that George Albert Smith had shown no special aptitudes at the time of his patriarchal blessing is only partially true. In fact, an appraisal of the boy's habits and personality reveal incipient qualities that emerged later as marks of his mature character. Despite a tendency toward physical frailty, he enjoyed the rigors of outdoor sports. A second cousin and childhood playmate, Richard R. Lyman, called the youthful George Albert "bold and daring."

And George Albert carried to his grave a long scar on the side of his forehead, the evidence of a terrible sledding accident. "The steeper the hills . . . the greater the thrill the young George Albert got when coasting on his sled," wrote Richard. The near-fatal accident occurred when the boy's sled slithered out of control on an icy hill and collided with an iron lamp post. "He was an equally enthusiastic horseback rider," noted this cousin, "and as a horseman, engaged in very active military drill." (*The Pioneer,* 3 [July 1951]: 2-B.) The mature George Albert Smith's almost obsessive interest in scouting, trekking, and trail marking seems but an echo of this youthful exuberance. Nor is it difficult to trace his theatrical interests as a young adult to boyhood pastimes he enjoyed within the shadows of temple square. "Remember the theatre that we used to stage at the back of our barn?" wrote George Albert to a boyhood friend, Charles J. Dwyer. "What a wonderful time we used to have, with our cap pistols and our masks and such costumes as we could rake up; the display we made was remarkable." (GASC, box 60, folder 15.) These juvenile theatrics were enriched with musical accompaniment as George Albert learned to play the Jew's harp and harmonica. And in later years he extended his musical skills to include the banjo and guitar.

During his boyhood, this future apostle showed no aptitude for business enterprise, a quality that emerged later. But he did show his inherent characteristic of helpfulness when a friend, Lewis Peck, sought his aid in carrying an early morning paper route. Since George Albert had no alarm clock, he was awakened by a creative Tom Sawyer device. Each morning, Lewis appeared at the Smith home to find a string dangling from an upstairs bedroom; the string was tied to one of his helper's big toes. Two or three jerks were usually enough to get him up and moving. Like most boys, George found it difficult to get up in the morning. In time, through discipline and repetition, he not only acquired the habit of early rising, but he also learned to enjoy it and to profit from it. We are left to speculate

4

whether this valuable habit, which gave George Albert a jump on the day and his competition, had its origin in a piece of string.

Life took on new meaning for this eldest Smith son when Lucy Woodruff came to live with her grandparents. Lucy's mother, the wife of Wilford Woodruff, Jr., died at an early age. And the little girl, pert and pretty, found a welcome home with her father's parents. George Albert was instinctively drawn to this newcomer and eagerly sought her friendship. But in his boyish awkwardness, he didn't quite know how to bring it off. He resorted to teasing and tormenting her, a ploy that understandably turned Lucy against him. She failed to see that he really liked her and was simply trying to get her attention. And he was blind to the fact that his romantic strategy had boomeranged.

This was the tattered state of their relationship when, at age twelve, George went to Provo to attend the Brigham Young Academy. There he lived with his grandmother's sister, whose home was near the tiny campus of the rural school, which, in time, would grown into a major university. Although the new scholar found a small student body at the academy, it included a disproportionate number of students who later attained distinction. Among them were George Sutherland, a future United States Supreme Court justice; Reed Smoot, who would become a member of the Twelve and a United States senator; Richard R. Lyman, another future member of the Twelve and a distinguished engineer; and Amy Brown Lyman, who became the general president of the Relief Society. George Albert was able to remain at the academy only one year. His father, who by this time was a member of the Twelve, had been called to serve another mission in England; and his eldest son was needed at home to help support the family. When George Albert Smith returned to West Temple Street in Salt Lake City, Lucy Woodruff found him to be changed person. Gone were the teasing and tormenting. In their place was

5

a courtliness and a gentility she had not seen before. One day after he had carried groceries home for her, tipping his hat as he left, Lucy, incredulous, said to her grandmother: "I just met George Smith. He's home from school, and he's decent."

Chapter Two

The Child Becomes a Man

W hat inner revolution transformed George Albert Smith from a child into a young man almost overnight? We may never know. But there are bits of evidence that enable us to make a reasoned guess. The absence of his father, leaving him as "the man of the house," surely had a maturing effect on him. And his experience away from home, exposed to the influence of students who were seriously seeking an education, undoubtedly left a mark of manhood on him. However, gauged by the frequency and fervor with which he mentioned it in later years, the most powerful influence for change exerted upon the future apostle during this period was that of an inspired teacher, Karl G. Maeser. This erudite convert, who had brought a love for learning and scholarship from his native Germany, had an unusual capacity to instill a thirst for knowledge in his students and to open their minds to truths of lasting value. "I love the memory of Brother Maeser," wrote Elder George Albert Smith on October 30, 1928, in a letter to Franklin S. Harris, the president of Brigham Young University. "I think I have spoken of him more than any other man, perhaps, among those who have contributed to my education." (GASC, box 54, folder 22.) The principal precept this student seems to have learned from his mentor is that thought is the father of action and that one is accountable for both his deeds and the thoughts that inspired them. "A thirteen year old boy, whose thoughts galloped around as mine did," Elder Smith once told a seminary graduating class, "couldn't understand why I should be held accountable for my thoughts. I was sure Dr. Maeser was a truthful man; but I couldn't understand how I could be charged for my thoughts because I couldn't control them." George Albert fretted over this idea, which stuck to him "like a burr," until one day it came to him "like a flash from the sky. . . . Of course you will be held accountable for your thoughts." (Ibid., box 124, scrapbook 1, p. 256.) Equally impressive to the student was Karl Maeser's frequent admonition, "Don't be a scrub."

Judging from his later actions and words, these ideas planted by Dr. Maeser grew to be a dominant force in the life of George Albert Smith. Thereafter he became more deliberate and thoughtful, more self-controlled, more inclined to set his own course and to be his own man. Notwithstanding this, he was still very young when he returned from the academy, unqualified for work other than the most rudimentary kind, to help care for his family. Job hunting took him to the ZCMI clothing factory, where the manager said he could not afford to hire more help. George reminded him he had not asked for money, only for a job, adding, "I know that if I'm worth anything, I'll get paid." Such chutzpah earned him employment punching buttonholes in overalls at two dollars and fifty cents a week. Later he was "promoted" to the cutting tables where, using a large, sharp knife, he cut fabrics according to patterns, guiding the knife along fissures in the table. Still later he was assigned to make packing boxes, which required more dexterity and initiative. This job revealed George Albert Smith's highly competitive nature, which was usually concealed by his gracious, gentle, and often self-deprecating manner. Learning that the other workers in the department made sixty boxes a day, he decided to and did excel them by making a hundred boxes a day. Such performance, added to his family's prominence, ultimately lifted him out of the clothing factory into ZCMI's sales force, where, in time, he directed the company's wholesale grocery sales in Salt Lake City.

During his struggling months in the factory, working for a mere pittance in jobs that required no special training and little intelligence, George became acutely aware of his menial status and of his family's poverty. So often had his father been called to church service away from home, and so meager was his income, that he had found it impossible to properly maintain two homes. So, they had fallen into disrepair and had taken on a somewhat seedy look. As a boy, George Albert had been oblivious to the unkempt appearance of his home. Now, however, as he grew toward manhood, he felt it important that it be improved. At the root of this desire lay the hope that improving the appearance of the Smith home would also improve his chances with Lucy Woodruff. The fact is that George Albert, though hardly out of puberty, loved Lucy and expected to marry her. Although she had shown an interest in him after the rough edges of his boyish doings had been smoothed over, it was not an undivided interest. There were other young men in the neighborhood to whom she seemed attracted, young men whose families stood much higher in the economic scale than the Smiths. These families, headed by men who had not been called to sacrifice their time and means for the Church to the extent George's father had, owned homes that were more pretentious than that of the Smiths, with more luxurious furnishings and well-manicured lawns.

To see the children of these families socializing together, enjoying lawn parties in a gracious setting, aroused a sense of inferiority in George Albert, as well as concern that Lucy's head would be turned away from him. In frus-

9

tration, he went to his mother, complaining about the run-down condition of the house and about the poverty of the family compared to their more affluent neighbors. Sarah first tried to console him by stressing the distinction of his lineage and the importance of the prophetic promises he had received. However, such intangibles, important as they were, could hardly compensate for a shabby yard in the mind of a teenager who was trying to impress a girl. The wise mother, realizing this, then suggested a remedy that immediately appealed to George. Fix up the yard! This launched a Smith family project to plant a lawn around the home. George Albert, who had the greatest stake in it, spearheaded this effort, which proved to be more difficult and time consuming than he had expected. The hard soil around the house had to be prepared with care for planting. Watering and weeding were constant demands. And a heavy rain after the grass had first taken root, and the run-off afterward, created havoc, almost making it necessary to start over. By degrees, however, the lawn shaped up, creating a new image of the Smith family in the neighborhood. At least, this was George Albert's view, and his labors were rewarded toward summer's end when he hosted Lucy and other friends at a lawn party.

But a good stand of grass was not the cure-all in George's quest for the affections of Lucy Woodruff. There were other suitors. One of them in particular, a handsome, vacuous dude from a wealthy family, was a tough opponent. This persistent young man, a smooth talker who lavished expensive gifts on the impressionable girl, pursued Lucy with astonishing single-mindedness for several years, creating a stressful triangle. As we shall see, Lucy ultimately traded show for substance in accepting the proposal of the man who was destined to become the president of the Church.

Once John Henry Smith returned from England, his eldest son was able to resume his studies. George Albert enrolled at the nearby University of Deseret, which, at the time, included secondary education. The campus of the

George Albert Smith (right), age sixteen

school, which later became the University of Utah, was then located on North Second West where Salt Lake City's West High School now stands. It lay within the boundaries of the seventeenth ward, where the Smith family lived, and was within easy walking distance from their home. George Albert proved to be a good student. But he found no teachers at Deseret who motivated him as had Karl G. Maeser, and no subjects that were of special interest. So, his time there passed in a routine way, almost like a stint punching buttonholes at the factory. At the end of the 1887–1888 academic year, he felt the need for a change from the grinding sameness of school. Besides, he needed money. So he took a job as an assistant on a surveying crew with the D&RGW railroad. The decision proved to be a costly one with far-reaching effects. While working on the western desert, in the glare of the summer sun, George Albert suffered permanent damage to his eyes. The injury ended his academic career and saddled him with a life-long disability. A decade later, he did enroll in a corres-

11

pondence law-school course, but after a short while he had to give it up because of his poor eyesight.

With no hope of completing his formal education, George turned to an occupation for which he was well suited by training and aptitude: his good track record at ZCMI earned him employment there as a traveling wholesale grocery salesman.

His territory extended from Salt Lake City south to St. George in Utah's Dixie. He was assigned first to work with an older companion named Jim Poulton, who took orders for shoes and clothing. The pair fitted up a rickety covered wagon loaded with food, bedding, personal effects, and samples and, pulled by two unlively nags, went on their way rejoicing.

With his personal effects, George Albert threw in his guitar, harmonica, and Jew's harp, along with a loud checkered suit, a garish bow tie, and a wide-brimmed hat. These were part of a comic act he had worked up over the years with which he entertained his friends. Jim brought along his flute, and George Albert had a set of dumbbells and Indian clubs that he used mainly to help stay trim; but he had become so expert with the Indian clubs that he occasionally gave exhibitions with them. Added to these things was George's fine baritone voice and a repertoire of funny songs he had learned.

This pair was undoubtedly a welcome addition to the groups of travelers, mostly salesmen, who congregated in the evenings at small hotels or rooming houses along the way. "Held a concert," George wrote on May 28, 1890. "Maynes singing; Jim singing and flute; I played guitar and harmonica." This entry was made in the little town of Holden, Utah, just a week after George Albert and his companion had started on their annual swing south. They usually timed their departure in May to take advantage of the good weather. On the day they left Salt Lake City, May 21, they were delayed three hours when the wagon broke down. But they made it to American Fork, where, in the evening, they teamed up in a guitar-flute duet. In the days that followed, George sold "bills of goods" at American Fork, Pleasant Grove, Provo, and Springville; and on May 28, when the impromptu concert was held in Holden, he had "sold two nice bills" at Scipio and Holden. Such success seemed to compensate for the Spartan accommodations. "Bed hard — room small," he wrote that night.

What George Albert experienced the first week of this trip was typical of what occurred during the next several months as he and Jim Poulton wended their way southward and back again. The journey became a wearisome yet fascinating succession of small Mormon villages, where they sold their wares, made new friends, and broke the monotony with almost daily musical sessions. Towns like Levan, Scipio, Meadow, Kanosh, and Minersville, which before had been merely names, now became realities, peopled with new-found friends and customers. More than that, most of these new acquaintances were members of the Church and were, therefore, brothers and sisters to the personable, gregarious son of Elder John Henry Smith.

Due to the prestige of George Albert's family, he was careful to avoid any conduct that would reflect unfavorably on them. "Beer drunk, but I refused," he wrote at one stop. And if ever the conversation turned to off-color stories during an evening, he would quietly excuse himself, saying he was tired. He did this in such an adroit way, however, never presuming to "preach" to his companions, that he retained their friendship. Nevertheless, his conduct made an eloquent statement about his principles and priorities that could not have failed to convey a message his words would have been powerless to do.

Despite the association with lively companions, the novelty of travel, and the satisfaction of success in selling, this was a lonely job. It took him away from his family and friends, whose companionship he missed and yearned for. More to the point, it took him away from Lucy, who by now had blossomed into a young woman of beauty and charm. Theirs had been a warm but troubled relationship,

13

agitated by the persistent pursuit of Lucy's other suitor. It was unsettling for George Albert to know that his absence had left the field wide open to his competitor. And Lucy's oscillating commitment to him was disconcerting. Given these circumstances, correspondence became a lifeline to the troubled traveler, whose spirits rose and fell with the regularity and content of his mail. "A man with the unusual name of Smith got two letters," George wrote jocularly on July 4, 1891, "one from Lizzie, one from Lucy. Pleased to know Lucy is better. I feel better myself now."

Meanwhile, there was more than selling and serenading to attract George's attention on the road. There were politics and religion as well. It was during his two years traveling for ZCMI that George Albert Smith first showed an interest in politics. And, judging from comments in his diary, this interest was more than academic. "Political argument on the street," he wrote while in Provo just a few days before receiving the welcome letter from Lucy. And three days later at Goshen, he "had a political discussion with a few young men." The comment that he "got the best of it" suggests that he enjoyed the confrontation and that he took pride in having bested the others in argument. Knowing this, it is not surprising that several years later he seriously considered a political career. Nor does it seem coincidental that it was about the same time he commenced studying law by correspondence. Effective as he may have been in political debate, George Albert Smith's chief skill as an advocate was in expounding the gospel and in defending the Church. Here he was on more familiar ground. Here he spoke with an authority and conviction he never demonstrated in political argument. That the patriarch told him he was destined for the apostleship implied that he was among the eminent leaders seen by Abraham in his vision of the premortal life. (Abraham 3:22–23.) His knowledge of that promise exerted a dominant influence on him throughout his life. Therefore, while music, droll entertainment, salesmanship, politics, and law intermittently claimed his attention, George Albert's overriding interest was in the Church. He demonstrated this in part while traveling by always attending church meetings when they were available. So, on June 15, 1890, at St. George, a community named in honor of his grandfather, he attended a stake conference where he was interested to find that wine instead of water was used in the sacrament. It was the first time he had ever seen this done. And he willingly responded to invitations to speak as he did at a sacrament meeting in Manti on July 5, 1891. His forthright, friendly style made him a favorite, especially of the young people. And while he was entertaining and jovial in the pulpit, there was an earnestness about him that carried conviction to his listeners. But, aside from his regularity in attending meetings and his effectiveness as a speaker, the best indication of his commitment to the Church was the way he lived. In his personal conduct, George Albert Smith exemplified the principles he taught. And chief among these were love for God, which he demonstrated by strictly observing the commandments, and love for people, shown by his unfailing kindness and consideration toward others. "Called at Groesbecks and saw the folks," or "Called at Grandma's and saw Aunt Lucy," or "Wish my friends would prepare themselves for the work to be done" are typical entries. They and many others demonstrate a genuine interest in family and friends that engendered a like response toward him. People loved him precisely because he loved them. As far as is known, no one ever disliked or envied George Albert Smith. It was this quality in him and his acquaintance with the people and communities in southern Utah that made Elder Smith ideal for the first significant Church calling he received.

Chapter Three

MIA Mission and Marriage

T
he call came from the First Presidency of the Church. It summoned George Albert to work in the Juab, Millard, Beaver, and Parowan stakes. Called at the same time to serve as his companion was William B. Dougall, Jr., a lifelong friend and a grandson of Brigham Young. Their charge was to activate and motivate the young people in these stakes who were members of the Young Men's and Young Women's Mutual Improvement Associations.

The pair left Salt Lake City on September 7, 1891, with only a vague idea about how to fulfill their missionary calling. Traveling by train to Nephi, they were made welcome in the home of the Juab stake president. Their first Sunday in the field, September 13, 1891, set a Sabbath day pattern that was followed with little variation during the two and half months of their service. In the morning, they attended Sunday school, where George Albert was called on to speak. "Only spoke a few words," he wrote. Later at Primary he did a little better; there he "had a nice time with the little ones" and "told them the story of the Savior's

16

birth and life." In the evening, they held a fireside meeting with the young people where both spoke, relating faith-promoting stories and bearing testimony. After watching his companion in action this day, Elder Dougall, who was the older of the two, decided to yield the leadership to George Albert. "I was surprised and much gratified," wrote Elder Smith, "that he felt to say to me that I was so much better qualified than he was that he desired to follow me in all of our labors."

When their destination was on the main line of the railroad and the distance was great, the missionaries traveled by train. Off the main line, they borrowed teams and wagons for transportation. Sometimes they walked. Usually, their food and lodgings were provided for by the members, who shared their abundance or their poverty. With youthful zest and without complaint, this jovial pair wended their way south to Parowan and back again, speaking, singing, and counseling while encouraging the young people to lift their sights and to increase their dedication to the principles of their religion.

This was also a time of development and self-improvement for the two young men. It gave them the opportunity to develop their skills in speaking and personal relations and to broaden their understanding of people and places. And during this period, George Albert made a conscious effort to improve his writing style. For the first time, lengthy entries of poetic beauty and descriptive power appear in his journal. "The sun was just setting," he wrote of an autumn scene on November 2, 1891, "casting its golden rays through the clouds that were resting on the mountain tops. Everything looked lovely—farms in every direction, as far as the eye could see. Fat cattle and horses grazing contentedly in the broad fields. . . . A rift in the clouds let the sun's rays fall on the upper half of the mountain, covering it with golden glory, as if giving it a good night kiss." And his description in an October 8 entry of a mismatched team of old nags, with their tattered gear and the decrepit wagon they pulled, is a classic. "The

17

harness was at one time leather," he wrote, "but it is patched with rope now and looks like hard times. The wagon . . . bed is twisted so that it looks like it is tipping off. We cut quite a grotesque figure, poking along with an umbrella over us, one horse willing to pull the load and the other horse willing that she should." And three days later, during a solitary walk up a canyon, moved by the beauty of his surroundings and the richness of the earth, he wrote, "I felt free here in the canyon and offered up a prayer in my heart to my Heavenly Father for his kindness to his people in every way."

It is difficult to appraise the success or the failure of the two elders or their perceptions of their work. It would have been out of character for Elder Smith to have commented favorably on their effectiveness as missionaries. However, given their enthusiasm, spirituality, and dedication, they doubtless had a positive, uplifting effect on the young people. The only negative comment found in his journal was the characterization of one dreary place as a "spiritual graveyard." And his journal and letters are devoid of descriptions about their living accommodations. It is assumed they ran the gamut from good to bad. We can infer the quality at the lower end of the scale from a statement that, following their stay in one place, George Albert counted eighty flea bites on one leg.

Because it was not a proselyting mission, these elders used devices unknown to conventional missionary work. George had taken along his outrageous checkered suit, and occasionally when the young people gathered in a social setting, he would put it on and, accompanying himself on the guitar, sing funny songs. A favorite was "Shut It," a song about a man with a big mouth. The chorus, "Shut it, shut it, don't open it quite so wide; Shut it, oh shut it, I don't want to get inside" always brought a good laugh. The young people at Beaver, Utah, were an especially appreciative audience, whose applause after George Albert had sung this song was "quite enough to take the roof off if it hadn't been fastened."

The comic quality in George Albert Smith's makeup, which was largely muted in later years, was occasionally exhibited off stage. "After supper at Brother Paxman's," he wrote on November 11, 1891, "I got a funny streak and the folks nearly died laughing at me. Sister Paxman nearly fainted and I had to stop."

George's joviality on this and other occasions during his mission often masked a deep uncertainty and gloom that clouded his interior world. Seldom if ever did these forebodings surface to the view of his companion or others. They were of such a personal and sensitive nature that he kept them locked within, except on the rare occasion when he confided limited glimpses of them to his journal or in his correspondence. "The letter that I looked for never came," he wrote cryptically on September 13, 1891, less than a week after leaving Salt Lake City. What he longed for arrived the next day—a letter from Lucy. But it did not bring the comfort he sought, only more turmoil. "Got LEW's letter," wrote he; "feel sorry that she is so ill." Lucy's illness was not physical. It was rooted in emotional stress over whether to marry her other suitor. That the man to whom she had once committed herself was then on a mission increased her agitation. George Albert learned indirectly that Lucy was actually planning her nuptials. Unwilling to abandon his mission, his only recourse was to convey his feelings by mail. Referring to Lucy's picture, he wrote from Nephi: "It recalled to me a time when I never knew what it was to be jealous; but it was a long time ago." Then followed a monologue that was more an expression of hope for Lucy's happiness than a plea for his own cause. "I then thought that I could live for you and you for me," he continued, "and we would always be happy. But it seems that such a thing was not to be, and maybe it is better so. . . . Be prayerful and humble; do not mistake the duty you owe to others. Your first duty is to yourself. I feel that you will be happy and my prayer is that you will."

There is a Solomon-like wisdom about this letter that

could not have failed to have a subtle, deterring effect on Lucy Woodruff. Here was a man who was willing to sacrifice his own desires in the interests of her happiness. Could there be any better evidence of genuine love than this? Whether it was this letter, some other factor, or a combination of them that brought it about, we do not know, but something occurred to halt her marriage plans.

Nevertheless, even after George Albert's release, she continued to oscillate in her affections for the two men. It was a difficult decision for a young woman to make. Both of them were clean in their habits and persons. And both of them shared Lucy's religious convictions. When she was with one of them, the attraction of the other faded into oblivion; but it soon returned when he came back into her presence. Realizing that her vacillation was causing needless pain to all three, she made a decision in late December 1891; on the last day of the year, she wrote a letter to the other suitor, informing him that she intended to marry George. Even then, however, the decision was not irrevocable, as her diary entry of that day implies: "I mailed my decision," she wrote, "and wished my heart was more at rest." (Copy of Lucy Woodruff's journal in GASC, box 138.)

As late as April 1892, Lucy was still seeing both young men and was still in turmoil. By this time, George Albert realized it was necessary that he take a firm position to bring the affair to a final conclusion. It was too painful for all concerned to be kept in a constant state of uncertainty. So on May 2, 1892, he wrote to Lucy about the need for her to make an unequivocal decision. The letter might even be interpreted as an ultimatum: "I will not encourage you any more," wrote he, "but will wait until you are strong again, and more able to realize the love I bear for you. When you, if ever, can come to me and tell me that you are not encouraging [sic], then can I feel that I am free to hope for your love without doing anyone on earth an injustice." (Ibid., box 124, folder 8.)

It is possible George Albert would not have written so

pointedly had it not been for an important letter he received May 2, 1892, from Box B calling him to serve a full-time mission in the southern states. Knowing he would be gone for two years, it was important that the matter be resolved before he left, freeing him to concentrate solely on his ministry. Whatever motivated the letter, it produced the desired result. Lucy finally terminated her relationship with the other man and began preparing for her wedding, which was scheduled to be performed in the Manti Temple on May 25, 1892.

Aside from the usual pressures accompanying the preparations for a wedding, Lucy was burdened with an unexpected one that caused her much mental turmoil. The disappointed suitor had reacted angrily to her decision, demanding that she return his gifts and advising her of his plan to go to Chicago, from where he hoped never to return alive. This veiled threat of suicide weighed heavily upon her, even to the day of the wedding, when, despite the excitement of the occasion and the beauty of the temple ceremony performed by George Albert's father, she was "frightened" as she "thought of him" and the possibility that he might take his own life. However, this threat proved to be as empty as the young man's head. Afterward, he returned whimpering to Salt Lake City and attempted to renew the relationship with Lucy during the days before she joined her husband in the mission field. Afterward, as she put the affair in perspective and saw that she had merely been infatuated with a handsome man who lacked substance, Lucy Woodruff Smith exclaimed again and again that she had "almost made a terrible mistake."

Chapter Four

Southern States Mission

The newlyweds had less than a month of married happiness before twenty-two-year-old George Albert left for the mission field. During that short period, they came to realize more fully the depth and sweetness of their love for each other. As symbols of that love, they exchanged gifts that each treasured throughout life. George Albert had given his wife a delicate, expensive brooch that she wore frequently and with pride. And Lucy's gift was one her husband was seldom seen without until the day of his death, except when he was dressed in work clothes or his out-of-doors gear. It was a gold locket with two pictures of herself, one as the pig-tailed girl he first knew and the other as the beautiful bride he married.

It was wrenching for the new bride to see her husband leave. "I would not detain him," Lucy wrote on June 22, the day before his departure, "but how can I stand it?" And the next day after he left, she wrote sadly, "He is gone, and I am left alone; not alone, but my very life seems gone with him."

While George Albert was lonely too, he had the preoc-
cupation of missionary work to divert his mind from their
separation. And en route to the mission headquarters in
Chattanooga, Tennessee, he had the excitement of seeing
the vastness and richness of America for the first time. He
had never before been outside Utah. So to see places he
had heard or read about all his life was enthralling. The
dreary expanses of Wyoming and western Nebraska were
a bleak reminder of the privations suffered by his pioneer
ancestors who had trekked the plains in wagons or afoot.
Omaha and the Missouri River called to mind stories of
the disease and death at Winter Quarters. And the verdure
and flourishing farms of Iowa and Illinois aroused thoughts
about the sadness yet resolution with which the Saints had
turned their backs on the beauty and wealth of Nauvoo to
face an uncertain future in the West. At Chicago, the missionary received his first view of a metropolitan city with
its bustle and noise and its contrasting opulence and squa-
lor.

As George Albert's train passed through Kentucky into
Tennessee, he entered the land where memories of the
Civil War were as fresh as yesterday and where Yankees
and westerners were regarded with deep suspicion by
some. During his stay there, he would often be made to
feel the sting of his alien status. Less than thirty years
before, Confederate and Union soldiers had fought the
famous Battle Above the Clouds on Lookout Mountain
near Chattanooga. There were families in town whose relatives had given their lives in that fierce struggle; and the
mountain, whose summit affords a sweeping view of
nearby Georgia, stood as a mute reminder of the carnage
that some could not or would not forget. Yet there were
many in Tennessee and the neighboring southern states
who were unprejudiced toward strangers and who had
attempted to bury the bitter memories of the Civil War.
These, and the genial rays of southern hospitality that
over-shone all, added to the rich rewards of missionary

service, were to make Elder Smith's two-year service there a highlight of his life.

The president of the Southern States Mission at the time was thirty-nine-year-old J. Golden Kimball, who less than three months before had been sustained as a member of the First Council of the Seventy. One of the sons of Heber C. Kimball, this friendly, forthright man, whose comedic candor later made him a legend among the General Authorities of the Church, would become one of George Albert Smith's most loyal friends and admirers. The president promptly assigned the new missionary to the Middle Tennessee District, where he was to get some seasoning in the field before assuming his duties as the mission secretary, a position that would place him second in charge of the work. The original plan was that Elder Smith would return to the mission office in August and that Lucy would join him at that time. Only three days after George Albert left Salt Lake City for the mission field, the new bride wrote to her husband, telling of her hope that their separation would be a short one. "Ever so many of the girls have smiled at my eagerness to join you," she wrote on June 26, 1892, "but I don't care; it doesn't plague me. I like them to know that I miss you." (GASC, box 65, folder 2.)

A few weeks after Elder Smith arrived in the field, President J. Golden Kimball went to Salt Lake City on business. Lucy assumed she would be able to accompany him when he returned in August. So certain of this was Elder Smith that he had arranged to rent a house and was negotiating to obtain furniture for it. He and Lucy became anxious when President Kimball decided it was necessary to postpone the reunion because he felt George Albert needed more training in the field. And they were almost panicked when their leader indicated that Lucy might not go at all. "Was nearly used up by the information that Lucy could not come," the disappointed missionary confided to his journal on August 29. (Ibid., box 67, book 1.) And Lucy wrote on October 7, "I believe it would break my heart to remain here now after living on the thought that I was coming to you." (Ibid., box 65, folder 7.) Whether through the intervention of Providence or John Henry Smith we know not, but for some reason President Kimball changed his mind, and in early November the young and now happy bride arrived in Chattanooga to join her husband.

Lucy had received a formal call to work in the mission office. And she occasionally teamed up with her husband in regular missionary work. However, the supervisory nature of George Albert's assignment often made it necessary for him to travel throughout the mission, either with the mission president or with other missionaries. At that time, the Southern States Mission included all or parts of the states of Kentucky, Tennessee, Mississippi, Alabama, Georgia, North and South Carolina, and Florida. With more than a hundred missionaries to supervise and with numerous branches throughout this vast area, there were constant demands on President Kimball and his young assistant.

Missionary work in the South at that time bore little resemblance to the intensive work performed by missionaries today. Tracting, cottage meetings, street meetings, and testimony bearing then constituted the entire inventory of a missionary's proselyting arsenal. While missionaries did not travel without purse or scrip, they often depended on the hospitality of strangers for food and shelter. And after converts were baptized, they were left with only their testimonies and some Church literature to sustain them spiritually. In time, there would be a sufficient clustering of members to justify the organization of a branch. And these small units would then be serviced and shepherded by the itinerant missionaries until there was sufficient local strength to enable them to be self-sufficient.

It was in this setting, then, that the future president of the Church obtained his first training in Church administration and in the dynamics of Church growth. And it was here, on the street corners and in the homes and halls of the South, that George Albert Smith developed the speaking style that became a trademark during the years of his apostolic ministry. It was a style marked by natural eloquence, vigor, and adaptability to the demands of the moment. George Albert Smith was a superb extemporaneous speaker. Only seldom did he prepare a talk. But he always filled his mind with ideas, scriptures, and apt stories. He then depended on the inspiration of the moment to draw out of him what was needed by his listeners. His nephew, Robert Farr Smith, once saw a remarkable example of this. The incident occurred at a meeting in Orlando, Florida, in 1941 while George Albert was touring the Southern States Mission with the mission president, William P. Whitaker. The nephew, who drove the car, urged his uncle before the meeting to abbreviate his remarks because of his age and the fatigue he had suffered earlier. The apostle said he would follow this good advice, but then he spoke for an hour and twenty minutes. Asked about it later, he said, "Bob, I tried to [stop]. But somehow the congregation would not let me." (Statement of RFS in possession of author.) Convinced of the need for speakers to be led by spiritual promptings, President Smith often would say, "Give the Lord a chance" as he counseled young people about public speaking.

The peaceful environment George Albert Smith found in the Southern States in 1941 stood in stark contrast to the one he found in the early 1890s. Then the Church was much maligned, its members were often objects of scorn, and its missionaries were occasionally abused and sometimes killed. Elder Smith had heard reports of such mistreatment, but he had to experience it personally before it had real meaning. The reality came to him on November 5, 1893, in southern Alabama after he and J. Golden Kimball had retired in the log cabin of some investigators. Their preaching in the neighborhood had aroused bitter opposition, which this night turned violent. About midnight, the cabin was surrounded by an angry mob whose leader pounded on the door, demanding in vulgar and profane language that the elders come out or "they were going to shoot them." When they refused to obey, the mob commenced to fire into the corners of the cabin. "Splinters were flying over our heads in every direction," Elder Smith wrote of the incident. "There were a few moments of quiet, then another volley of shots was fired and more splinters flew." He was interested in his reaction to what he considered to be "one of the most horrible events" in his life. "I was very calm as I lay there," the missionary wrote later, "but I was sure that as long as I was preaching the word of God and following his teachings that the Lord would protect me, and he did." The next morning when the elders stepped outside, they found a bundle of heavy hickory sticks of the kind that had been used to beat other missionaries in the south. (*Improvement Era,* March 1932.)

The feeling George Albert had during this frightening experience that God would protect him was one that became a constant source of assurance. He had the faith that God would protect him from harm, and therefore he lived from day to day without worry or fear. Yet he experienced feelings akin to fear when he learned later how the blessings of the Lord had protected him from death. Such an instance occurred while he worked temporarily with Elder H. E. Stout. The two were caught in a rainstorm after dark as they hiked over a mountain toward the home of a friend, Joseph McKee. Unable to see, they inched along, groping their way by feeling the wall of the mountain. At one point, George Albert removed his hand from the wall and took several steps along what he thought was a diverging trail. Suddenly, the Spirit whispered to him to stop. Obeying, he called to Elder Stout who was leading the way, and, following the sound of his voice, turned toward him. Soon after, as they climbed over a pole fence, George's valise fell open, scattering his gear on the ground. The next morning at McKee's, he discovered that his comb and brush were missing. Returning along the trail, he found them at the pole fence. He also found by tracing his footprints in the soft mud that he had wandered in the darkness to the very edge of the cliff. One more step would have hurled him into the gorge below. "I felt very ill when I realized how close I had come to death," he wrote later. "I also was very grateful to my Heavenly Father for protecting me." (Ibid.)

Elder Smith learned afterward about another instance when Providence shielded him from danger and perhaps death. It occurred when an armed mob waited in concealment to assault George Albert and his companion, who had stopped to visit a family of investigators at their isolated farmhouse. After refreshments, the elders sang several hymns, including "Do What is Right." As the strains of the singing drifted through the woods, the members of the mob were touched. Said their leader who later joined the Church: "We have made a mistake. These are not the kind of men we thought they were. Wicked men can't sing like angels; and these men sing like angels." (*Conference Report,* October 1945, p. 116.)

Complications at home made it necessary for J. Golden Kimball to return to Salt Lake City in November 1892. What was intended as a short stay stretched into a nine-month absence. And less than three months after returning to Tennessee, he had to go home again. This time he remained for seven months. So, for sixteen months of his two-year mission, George Albert Smith was virtually in charge of all proselyting and administrative work in the Southern States. The only restraint on him during this time was through the periodic letters from his leader. "I feel more anxious, having absented myself so long," President Kimball wrote on March 13, 1893. "Your counsel to the Elders to be cautious and make no changes is in harmony with my feelings. Keep giving them counsel and when you think you have them fully educated, you can commence urging them to push out into new fields." (GASC, box 66, folder 8.)

The depressed economic conditions during the panic of 1893 brought about a temporary change in the Church policy encouraging new converts to emigrate to the western United States. "If people emigrate to Utah or Arizona under existing circumstances, it will result seriously," Elder Kimball wrote to his assistant on July 18, 1893. "They cannot get employment of any kind. Discourage the elders and people. It will be folly for them to come out until we direct them to do so." (Ibid., folder 12.)

Some mobbings of elders during the late spring of 1893 also put a brake on the work. Writing on June 3, President Kimball asked his assistant to tell the missionaries to discontinue proselyting during the summer, restricting their activity to visiting members and friends. "Never before have I fully sensed what it would mean if elders were killed," wrote an anxious mission president. Concerned that George Albert had been away from Chattanooga for a while, he added: "How thankful I am that you have returned. I solemnly declare that the office assistant must not leave again unless I am there to take his place." (Ibid., folder 11.) Later, afraid that his outspoken comments might have offended Elder Smith, he wrote a conciliatory letter, saying: "Always let this one idea stand uppermost; that I appreciate your labor, zeal and good spirit. . . . If any of my letters read too bluntly, remember the character of the person." (Ibid., letter of June 30, 1893.)

George Albert reciprocated the good feelings shown toward him by his mission president. Through the years of their association as General Authorities, they often reflected on their service together in the mission field, expressing thoughts of mutual love and respect. "J. Golden Kimball was my mission president in the south," wrote Elder Smith many years later. "I learned to love him for his courage and kindness. His sense of humor drew men to him and his testimony of the divinity of the Gospel of Jesus Christ inspired them." (Claude Richards, *J. Golden Kimball* [Salt Lake City: Bookcraft, 1966], p. 114.) And in a letter to Lucy written during her convalescence from a serious illness, Elder Kimball expressed similar sentiments: "My missionary experience and close association with you and your good husband . . . was one of peace, unity, con-

29

tentment and happiness. We were as one family, united in brotherly and sisterly love, to uplift and encourage the elders in preaching the gospel of Jesus Christ." (Ibid., box 134, folder 6.)

The Smiths were released in June 1894. The severance of missionary ties caused both pain and elation. It was wrenching to leave the friends and work they loved. But it was exhilarating to think of creating a home for the children they expected to have, and of carving a niche for themselves in the religious and cultural life of Salt Lake City. They took the long way home via Niagara Falls, where they enjoyed a belated honeymoon. The three-day train ride across the continent provided the first opportunity since their marriage for long, uninterrupted conversation and reflection about the past and future. An inventory of their physical assets was easy and somewhat discouraging to compile. Essentially, it consisted of the clothes they wore or carried in their bags and a few personal effects they had left at home. But the lack of material things was not a matter of real concern to them, nor would it ever be. They had the simple faith that the necessary doors would be opened to enable them to live comfortably, notwithstanding the depressed economic conditions. These, incidentally, were pointedly drawn to their attention in Chicago, where the bitter Pullman strike smoldered. There they were forced to lie down on the floor to avoid sniper fire as the train passed through the brawling giant of a city.

Any concern the young couple had as they toted up their assets and liabilities did not relate to whether or how they would live but rather to the quality of their lives. Two things troubled them: the husband's health and their childlessness. George Albert continued to have eye problems, which were a constant annoyance and inconvenience. And the frailty of his physique, characterized by a latent nervousness, was a concern. Yet, he learned to live with these disabilities and did not allow them to sour or dominate his life. As to their lack of children, the Smiths had occasional doubts about whether they would ever be parents, especially Lucy, whose diaries reveal an anxious impatience for motherhood. But, given the short time they had been married, this was not a major concern, although it was unsettling.

Against these negatives, however, was a host of positive things that augered well for a happy and successful future. They loved each other; they were optimistic and forward looking; and they had supportive families and loyal friends. Moreover, their experience in the mission field had strengthened their religious convictions, broadened their understanding of Church doctrine and procedure, and increased their awareness of the problems and needs of others. As for George Albert personally, two years of service on the cutting edge of the Church had provided invaluable insights into the apostolic process of preaching, proselyting, and conversion. It was the first essential step in his quest for the credentials and credibility necessary to put a foundation under the patriarch's promises.

Chapter Five

The Maturing of a Prophet

George Albert and Lucy Smith lost little time in becoming established in the mainstream of the religious, business, social, and political life of Salt Lake City. Their deep family roots on the street where they first met prompted them to rent a house at 125 North Temple. It was within sight of the towering and towered temple, which had been dedicated in their absence, and near the main business district. Lucy's grandfather, Wilford Woodruff, the president of the Church, continued to own a home on West Temple, and George Albert's father still maintained his two family homes there. Moreover, for a time George and Lucy shared their home with Lucy's father and part of his family. Living in such close proximity to both the Smith and Woodruff families, whose prominence and influence at the time were perhaps as great as any other two families in the Church, gave the newlyweds an unusual sense of security and belonging. This feeling was heightened by their warm acceptance into the Seventeenth Ward, whose stately chapel, with its vaulted ceiling and beautiful stained-glass window, was just through the block.

Beyond the prominence of their families, the young couple had much to offer this large and thriving ward. Their teaching and people skills, honed during their mission, and the husband's ability as an entertainer soon led them to leadership positions in the auxiliary organizations of the ward and stake. And George Albert's priesthood potential was promptly recognized by his call to serve in the presidency of the third quorum of seventy. These high-profile positions, added to their happy and gregarious personalities, also caught the Smiths up in the active social life of the ward and stake, whose organizations then provided many of the entertainment and leisure activities now dominated by television, radio, and the movies.

Despite the pinched economic conditions at the time, George Albert had no difficulty in finding good employment. His selling skills, sharpened by two years of missionary service, and his good track record at ZCMI readily earned him a position on its sales force. There, in not too long a time, hard work, skill, and a wide range of acquaintances brought him financial success in an occupation that rewards the productive salesperson. Indications of this financial success are seen in his construction of a new home for Lucy—on West Temple Street, of course, next to his father's home—and in the fact that on one occasion John Henry borrowed several hundred dollars from his son to pay taxes.

The missing ingredient in George Albert and Lucy's formula for complete happiness was the lack of children. Both had been reared in and around large families, and both yearned to have many children. Their religion taught that the greatest joy in time or eternity derives from parenthood. And they saw in the perpetuation of their seed the potential for the kind of fruitful regeneration experienced by Abraham and Sarah; they too wanted and hoped for a progeny as numerous as the sands on the seashore. But when, after almost three years of marriage, Lucy had not conceived, she was assailed with doubt and began to fret that she would be barren. Such were her feelings when

*Emily (age eight) and
Edith (age four)
running to their father*

in the spring of 1895 she was visited by her grandfather,
President Wilford Woodruff, who asked about her children. In telling him she had none, the young wife burst
into tears, pouring out her grief and worry to the aged
prophet, who was more like a father than a grandfather
to her. After speaking words of comfort, he had Lucy sit
on a chair and, placing his hands on her head, gave her
a prophetic blessing, promising that she would bear children. On November 19, 1895, less than a year later, Lucy
gave birth to her first child, a daughter named Emily. Four
years later, on November 10, 1899, she gave birth to a
second daughter named Edith. These two girls were a
study in contrasts. The elder girl, Emily, was so active and
aggressive and filled with self-confidence, it was said of
her later that had she been a boy, she surely would have
risen to the presidency of General Motors or some other

major enterprise. Edith, on the other hand, was quiet, shy, demure, and retiring. The observant father captured the essence of their contrasting personalities in diary entries made during their childhood. "It is Emily's birthday," Elder Smith wrote on November 19, 1907, while he was in Hunt, Arizona. "She is twelve years old. She is such an active, strong-willed child. I pray that the Lord will protect her and make her a woman of strength and ability. She has a keen intellect and makes splendid progress in school." And a year later, on November 10, 1908, after helping his wife entertain forty-five children who had been invited to Edith's ninth birthday party, he wrote this about his youngest daughter: "Edith was very happy and seemed much pleased with several little presents she received. Edith is a quiet, lovable child and is very solicitous for her mother." Such marked differences in character never seemed to create controversy or antagonism between the two girls. In their adulthood, they and their husbands owned homes near each other and their parents, and they and their families lived together in harmony. And whatever personality differences they had were swallowed up in their love and loyalty toward their parents and, after the mother passed away, toward their father alone. After Lucy died, Emily and Edith collaborated as hostesses for Elder Smith during all his years as both the president of the Twelve and the president of the Church.

The third and last child of the Smiths, George Albert, Jr., was born on September 10, 1905. In his childhood, George, as he was called, seemed to share the temperament of the younger daughter, Edith. "A most lovable and obedient child," the father said of him during his growing-up years. And the mother, in a letter written to her husband when the son was seven, said: "My boy is certainly a gift from God. He is just about as perfect as his father." But, as he matured, George showed many of the leadership and scholastic qualities of the elder sister as seen in his graduation from the Harvard graduate school of business, where he served as student-body president and later became a full professor and an administrative dean.

George Albert and his son were joined in a bond of love and admiration. They were frequent hiking or camping companions, and sometimes the apostle took George with him on Church assignments. After Elder Smith became the president of the Church, when he was confronted with complicated problems affecting the growth of an international organization, he was heard to say, "I need my boy," as he thought of George's special skills in corporate organization and management.

This filial companionship and interdependence is a significant trait of the Smith family. A manifestation of it is seen in the way the Smiths clustered together on West Temple Street and how, later, George Albert and his family clustered together around Yale Avenue and Thirteenth East Street in Salt Lake City. And another manifestation of it appears in the bond between George Albert and his father, John Henry Smith. As George Albert's stature grew as the head of a family, as a businessman, and as a church leader, he became a close confidant of his father. This was especially true when the son built his new home next door to his father and Sarah's home on West Temple. Then they were in almost daily contact, discussing matters pertaining not only to the family but to the Church, to business, and to politics as well.

Shortly after George Albert returned from the South in the summer of 1894, his interest and involvement in practical politics began. In July of that year, only a month after he and Lucy were released from their mission, the United States Congress passed the Utah Enabling Act, which authorized the call of a convention to draft a constitution prior to statehood. John Henry was chosen to preside over this convention, whose work produced a document that was overwhelmingly ratified by the voters. In the convention, John Henry became accustomed to dealing with leaders of different religious and political beliefs in an effort to arrive at a consensus. He was known for his fairness in trying to understand and accommodate the views of others. At the same time, he was known for his fairness in advocating his own views on issues involving matters of conscience or principle. Such qualities, which are essential for success in the democratic process of give and take, brought John Henry Smith a high reputation among all classes of people. And these qualities were learned or inherited by the son, George Albert, who idolized and sought to emulate his father.

An indication that George Albert's political involvement had moved from arguing on the street (as he did while selling in Southern Utah) to a practical application of his views is that he now joined his father and fourteen other men in organizing the Republican Party in Utah. While this means little today to those accustomed to seeing Church leaders in the ranks of the Republican Party, it was revolutionary at the time. For decades the Republican Party had been anathema to most Latter-day Saints because it had been the author of the antipolygamy laws. But in the early 1890s, after the Manifesto, when influential Democrats began to oppose statehood for Utah, many Church leaders transferred their allegiance to the Republican Party, as did John Henry and his son.

The father's prominence and George Albert's industry, eloquence, and friendliness were significant factors in the rise of the Republican Party in Utah. "My father did more to establish the Republican Party in Utah than any other man," wrote George Albert to his friend H. Clay Evans on March 16, 1897. "He devoted his time and means to accomplish the desired end. I did all I could, going out on the stump, and helping the unpopular cause along." (Copy in GASC, letterpress book 1.)

In time, the Smiths' interest in politics turned from organizational matters and the support of others to an active effort to win elective office for themselves. In doing this, their purpose was to make sure that voices in support of Latter-day interests were heard in the halls of government. And, in the pursuit of office, they showed a keen understanding of political reality and an admirable adroitness in steering toward the goal. "There seems to be a boom on to run me for congress as representative," John Henry wrote to George Albert on September 1, 1898. The father reported that this was an obvious effort to sidetrack him from the senate, an office he then sought. "You will take a decided stand against this matter," John Henry instructed his son, "in conversation with men and also in the convention when it convenes." He also directed George Albert to obtain the names of the chairmen of the county Republican committees and to "have letters written to them saying I intend to be a candidate for the senate, all being well." (Ibid., box 17, folder 32.)

Two years later, after his try for the senate failed, John Henry encouraged his son to seek office. "Lay your plans to get to congress after a time," he counseled George Albert in a letter dated January 30, 1900. (Ibid., box 18, folder 18.) And two days later he explained, "If a good, live Republican Mormon Monogamist can be elected, it will do more to restore quiet than anything else." (Ibid.)

This effort also failed, ending the overt attempts of the father and son to gain elective office. However, in 1902 a strong ground swell of support developed for George Albert to run for the U.S. Senate. He declined because he had previously told his friend Reed Smoot, who wanted the office, that he would not run. How this decision changed the scenario of "what might have been" is seen in a letter dated March 25, 1929, from C. P. Overfield to Major W. I. Lincoln Adams about approaching Elder Smith to use his influence with Reed Smoot to obtain an ambassadorship for the major. "Mr. Smith is in a position to do this with great power and effect," read the letter, "for had he not thrown his strength behind Mr. Smoot in 1902 for the United States Senatorship, it would have been Senator Smith instead of Senator Smoot during all of these intervening years. We who are on the inside know the true situation in this regard, and it was a wonderfully unselfish action on the part of George Albert Smith to do what he did at that time." (Ibid., box 57, folder 2–.)

It was through the prominence of John Henry Smith and his son in the Republican Party that George Albert was appointed receiver of public monies and disbursing agent in the United States Land Office for Utah in January 1898. The appointment was made by President William McKinley. The Smiths first attempted to obtain the Salt Lake Postmastership for George Albert because of its greater permanence. They reasoned correctly that the position of receiver would decline in importance in the years ahead and perhaps even disappear as the public lands were disposed of. But the postmastership went to Governor Arthur L. Thomas, a non-Mormon. So George Albert accepted the alternate appointment uncomplainingly. It represented one of the first major U.S. appointments given to a Latter-day Saint after statehood. In 1902, this appointment was renewed by President Theodore Roosevelt, who was a personal friend of the Smiths. George Albert was a member of the Rough Rider's party that toured Utah and Idaho during the 1900 presidential campaign. He met the president again in September 1901 at the Pan-American Exposition in Buffalo, New York, when he spent an afternoon with him in the home of Anthony Wilcox. This was the day before Roosevelt became the president following the assassination of President McKinley, who was killed while visiting the exposition. George Albert heard the shot that killed McKinley.

Following his call to the Twelve in October 1903, Elder Smith's involvement in politics waned but did not disappear. During the 1904 presidential campaign, for instance, when a faction in the party attempted to prevent the nomination of Theodore Roosevelt, he gave the president a strong letter of endorsement in which he also said he did not wish to be reappointed to his position in the land office. And to prove that his support was genuine, he later took a leave of absence from the land office to campaign for the president.

This seems to have ended George Albert Smith's overt activity in politics, although he continued intermittently to play a role behind the scenes. So, when George Sutherland mounted a campaign to unseat Senator Thomas Kearns, Elder Smith wrote the senator to express dismay that his support among the Latter-day Saints was being seriously eroded because of the bitter attacks on the Church and its leaders by the Kearns family newspaper. "Every member of the Mormon church has been repeatedly insulted in the columns of the paper you are reputed to be interested in," wrote the apostle, "and the democrats of the state are not slow to see an opportunity to prejudice the people thus abused against anyone who will support the owners of the paper." He warned that unless the senator could stop these "vile attacks," his chances for re-election were "very slim indeed."

During the years George Albert was gaining stature in business and political circles, he was also building his reputation as a man of broad interests and activities. He became, among other things, an officer in the Kanab Cattle Company, chairman of the Latter-day Saints University finance committee, a cavalry officer in the Utah National Guard, and a commissioner representing Utah at the Tennessee Centennial. In the last capacity, he and the other commissioners were charged with preparing an exhibit to display Utah's industrial, agricultural, and other resources.

But all these activities, while absorbing much of his time, were not the main focus of the life of George Albert Smith. As always, his family took precedence. And next to the family in his scale of commitment stood the Church. During these early years, he gained prominence in Church circles through his call as an assistant in the superintendency of the Young Men's Mutual Improvement Association of the Salt Lake Stake. The other two members of this trio, Richard R. Lyman, superintendent, and Joseph F. Merrill, first assistant, were professors at the University of Utah. With George Albert, they were destined to become members of the Twelve. Since the Salt Lake Stake then encompassed the entire city, its MIA was a showcase for the whole Church during an era when the auxiliary organizations were beginning to exert an influence on the Latter-day Saints worldwide. These three creative young men introduced innovations in the MIA that were ultimately adopted throughout the Church. Chief among these were a broadened activity program, featuring oratorical and other competitions, and leadership training. Later, George Albert was called to served as the superintendent of this organization. In this position, he assumed the responsibility to train prospective missionaries. Since during all George Albert's years of service in the Salt Lake Stake MIA superintendency, Wilford Woodruff, Lorenzo Snow, or Joseph F. Smith had been the general superintendent of this auxiliary, the young man worked under the watchful eye of the president of the Church. Here his leadership skills, his commitment, and his spirituality were scrutinized by the man who held final earthly authority in calls to the apostleship.

Chapter Six

Call to the Twelve

George Albert Smith abhorred nepotism and was overly sensitive about the large number of Smiths who occupied positions of authority in the Church. In October 1903, Joseph F. Smith was the president; John Henry Smith and Hyrum Mack Smith were members of the Twelve; and John Smith was the patriarch. At the lower levels, in the Salt Lake Stake and its wards, members of the prolific Smith clan were prominent participants in every aspect of the work. That this was so is not surprising, given the large size of the family and the ability and dedication that characterized its members. Yet, some unthinking persons were inclined to criticize and to make slighting remarks when still another Smith was called to service. At a Salt Lake Stake conference where several Smiths had been presented for a sustaining vote, George whispered uneasily to a companion that if one more Smith were named, he intended to walk out. It was then that his own name was presented as the new superintendent of the stake YWMIA. That he had not been consulted in advance about the call was not unusual for

42

that day. The practice was a carry-over from the pioneer era, when Brigham Young often read names at general conference of those called to foreign missionary service though they had not been advised beforehand.

Little did George Albert know that the same surprise tactic would be used in his call to the Twelve. On October 6, 1903, he returned home from the land office in mid-afternoon, intending to take his family to the fair. On arrival, he found the house crowded with neighbors who, with Lucy, were sharing some joyous event. He was incredulous to learn the cause for celebration: he had just been sustained as a member of the Twelve. The messenger of good news was a neighbor, Nellie Taylor, who abruptly left the Tabernacle after the sustaining of officers and rushed across the street to congratulate the family. George Albert assured his friend she was mistaken as he knew nothing about the call and that the new apostle had to be some other Smith. Embarrassed and apologetic, Nellie returned to the Tabernacle, where others confirmed that the name presented was indeed George Albert Smith. With an air of triumph and with several following in her wake, she hurried back to advise that she had heard it right. George Albert was "completely dumfounded." Although he had faith in Zebedee Coltrin's promise, it was difficult to believe that the time had arrived. He was only thirty-three years old and was without experience as a line officer of the Church, except for brief service as one of seven presidents of a seventy's quorum. But he had never been a bishop or stake president where he presided directly over a congregation. Yet, as a member of the second governing body of the Church, he would now be expected to give direction to many who had figuratively worn out their lives in the yoke of direct priesthood leadership. This was an intimidating calling, especially to one as sensitive as was Elder Smith to the perception of nepotism that his call would have conveyed to some. It meant that almost one out of every five of the General Authorities was a Smith. And the odds went up four years later when another son of President Joseph F. Smith became a General Authority—David Asael Smith, who was called as a counselor in the Presiding Bishopric in December 1907.

Knowing of George Albert's strong feelings about nepotism, John Henry's first words to his son when he saw him after the conference session were, "George, I didn't have anything to do with it." While this statement is true, it does not mean that John Henry, like his son, was ignorant of the call until it was announced in the Tabernacle. Indeed, President Joseph F. Smith had consulted with the father two days before, telling him, "The mind of the spirit is that your son George Albert should fill the vacancy in the Apostles," a vacancy created by the death of Brigham Young, Jr. John Henry had answered that were it a political appointment, he would have advised against it because of the appearances. "But," he added, "I cannot stand in the way of the suggestions of the spirit to you." (John Henry Smith journal, book 25, p. 710.)

Elder George Albert Smith's strong feelings about this subject probably contributed to the debilitating nervousness with which he was afflicted a few years later. To a person as able, as intelligent, and as spiritually sensitive as he was, it was doubtless a galling thing to have anyone imply that his call to the Twelve was a consequence of family influence and not of spiritual promptings or his own worthiness and competence. We have already seen that he had keen competitive instincts. And the normal reaction of a competitor who is challenged is to accelerate his efforts, which in turn exerts greater physical and emotional stress on his system. While we cannot enter the mind of another to report the forces that motivate, deter, or debilitate, we can draw reasonable inferences from known facts. And the facts suggest that Elder Smith's concern about nepotism had almost become an obsession that, more than likely, exerted a continuing negative influence on the perception he had of his call to the Twelve and his apostolic role. And, as we shall see later, he drove himself unmercifully in performing his duties in an apparent attempt to fulfill every expectation of those who either supported or maligned him.

The new member of the Twelve was ordained and set apart in the upper room of the temple on October 8, 1903. Before going there, he had prayed silently that his ordination would be by the one who had initiated the call. It was a source of comfort and confirmation that Joseph F. Smith, the Prophet, was voice in ordaining him both a high priest and an apostle and in setting him apart as a member of the Quorum of the Twelve. However, his father was asked to give the customary apostolic charge, which underscored the historical significance of the fact that never before had a father and son served simultaneously in this quorum, nor has it occurred since. In his response, the new member of the Twelve committed himself to the call, expressing what might be regarded as the creed that governed his years of apostolic service: "I desire to do all the good I can," he said, "to keep the faith, and do the will of my Heavenly Father, and to assist you, my brethren, in every way possible in carrying on the work."

The new apostle had no time to savor the spiritual significance of his call. It was decided that he would retain his land-office appointment until it expired in 1906. Meanwhile, it was expected he would fulfill the customary duties of a General Authority, which, in addition to headquarters assignments, included frequent stake conference appointments and mission tours. So, the day after his ordination, a Friday, he spent a full day at the land office; and the following weekend found him in nearby Provo on his first stake conference assignment. The Saints who assembled in the Provo Tabernacle on Sunday October 11, 1903, heard the voice and the fervent testimony that would be sounded in similar meetings for the next forty-two years. During that time, which spanned Elder Smith's service as a member of the Twelve, he was constantly on the move, except during periods of illness or occasional vacations, training, counseling, and admonishing the leaders and members of the Church. And the so-called vacations frequently consisted of a few days here and there sandwiched between official assignments.

In the first year of his apostolic service, Elder Smith's conference assignments were close to home, making it possible to discharge his land-office duties on weekdays without difficulty. So, during that time, the Saints in Ogden, Alpine, Coalville, Nebo, Richmond, and other nearby stakes had the opportunity to hear the new member of the Twelve and to gauge the depth of his character and competence. What they found was an eloquent, energetic, and entertaining speaker who conveyed meanings beyond his words. The appraisal of many who heard George Albert Smith speak is that often he imparted a spiritual message unrelated to his discourse. A typical reaction to his impact on an audience was expressed by Elder Boyd K. Packer who, as a child, once heard Elder Smith speak. "In my little boy's mind," said Elder Packer at the rededication of the Box Elder Tabernacle in Brigham City, "came a thought that there stood an Apostle of Jesus Christ." (*Ensign,* July 1987, p. 75.)

By September 1904, Elder Smith had accumulated enough leave to enable him to get away from the land office for a month. In consultation with the Brethren, he decided to make a busman's holiday out of his vacation by touring the Northern States, Central States, and Southern States missions. Taking Lucy and Edith along, he left by train on September 1. Traveling via Denver, they went first to the Kansas City–Independence area, where they spent two days visiting important sites of early Church history—the temple lot, Far West, Gallatin, and Adamondi-Ahman. At Montrose, Iowa, Lucy was pleased to be able to take a picture of the old army barracks where her father, Wilford Woodruff, Jr., was born. Crossing the river, they visited places of interest in Western Illinois, especially grandfather Wilford Woodruff's two-story brick home in Nauvoo and the old jail in Carthage where the Prophet Joseph Smith and his brother Hyrum were martyred.

Along the way, Elder Smith held meetings with missionaries and members. At Chicago, his most memorable one was a street meeting held with mission president German E. Ellsworth and several elders. In the midst of it, they were interrupted by a policeman who made them stop because they lacked a permit. "He also advised me to move up or he would do business with me," George Albert wrote of the unfriendly cop.

Going south, the party stopped in St. Louis to see the World's Fair, then in progress. On September 15, the second day of their visit, over forty thousand were admitted to the fair, the largest daily attendance to that date.

The balance of the tour was a trip into nostalgia for George Albert and Lucy. Joining mission president Ben E. Rich, they toured the southern states. Visits to Chattanooga, Nashville, Atlanta, and other Southern cities aroused memories of their own missionary service, which were intensified by contact with the young elders then in the field. They found some softening of attitudes toward the Church. But, the work was slow and sometimes tedious as the missionaries sought to tear down the walls of prejudice against the Latter-day Saints and to overcome the human inertia and fear that impeded their progress. With his forward-looking attitudes and his understanding of the challenges they faced, Elder Smith was able to motivate the missionaries and to infuse them with new energy and resolve.

The travelers arrived home shortly before the October general conference, which marked the first anniversary of Elder Smith's call to the Twelve. He had now been in office just long enough to grasp the magnitude of the responsibility he bore and the personal limitations he brought to the task. To think that he and his apostolic brethren shouldered the burden of carrying the message of the gospel to all the world was intimidating. And, it was a burden he could never really lay down. Wherever he went, the mantle went with him. And whatever he did seemed not to diminish the task. If he were instrumental today in bringing one person into the fold, his work was merely multiplied by the birth that day of scores of others outside the fold. Any attempt to view his responsibilities and the likelihood of success from a strictly human point of view was overwhelming. The only relief from a sense of futility at the magnitude of the task was to recognize his subordinate status. In the final analysis, it was not his work; it was the Lord's work. George Albert Smith was an agent or representative, not a principal. It was not his own agenda he was following, but the agenda of the head of the Church, Jesus Christ, whose witness and disciple he was. Put in this perspective, Elder Smith's role was clear and relatively simple. When acting in his official capacity, he needed only to find out what the Lord would have him do. This then became the sole criterion that governed his actions in Church administration. A significant example occurred in May 1905 at the reorganization of the Box Elder stake presidency. Customarily two members of the Twelve traveled and worked together to effect a reorganization. On this occasion, Elder Smith's companion was Charles W. Penrose, the junior member of the Twelve, who had been called the previous July. It was the first time Elder Smith had served as the senior apostle in attending to a stake reorganization. In conducting the usual interviews with local leaders, twenty able brethren were identified as possible successors to the outgoing stake president, none of whom was known to the two apostles. As they weighed the relative strengths of these candidates, they were "unable to determine which man was best." At length, the choice seemed to narrow to two men, although there was still much uncertainty. In these circumstances, the two apostles decided to leave the decision until the next morning. "I awoke feeling the assurance Oleen Stohl is the man for president," wrote Elder Smith on May 28, 1905. "I have prayed about the matter and am now quite satisfied. I met Bro. Penrose, and he felt as I do."

With variations, the experience Elder Smith had at Brigham City was repeated often during the years of his ministry. It was not uncommon for revelation about his work to come instantaneously, showing him in a moment what he should do. In other instances, however, as in the call of President Stohl, answers came only after careful analysis and fervent prayer. But by whatever means it came, the result was the same, a result that brought comfort to the apostle in the knowledge that the ultimate decision did not rest with him but came through the veil, either by dictation or confirmation.

The frequency of Elder Smith's stake conference, mission tours, and other assignments kept him on the move almost constantly. Whenever possible, he traveled by train, which simplified and expedited his work. Often, however, he was assigned to isolated places that lacked railroad facilities. Since in those early days the automobile was still largely a manufacturer's dream, travel away from the railroad routes was on horseback, by wagon or coach, or on foot. A few months after attending the conference in Brigham City, Elder Smith was assigned to Woodruff, Utah, in the northeast corner of the state. To get there, he had to travel by train to Evanston, Wyoming, and then to ride for three hours in an open wagon over a rutted road. Any inconvenience in getting there was offset by the enthusiasm with which he was welcomed by the Woodruff Saints. Named after Lucy's grandfather, President Wilford Woodruff, who was the president of the Church at the time, this stake was organized in June 1898, only seven years before Elder Smith's visit. He found here the durable, persistent kind of people who inhabited other Latter-day Saint communities throughout the western United States and extending north and south into Canada and Mexico. They were mostly ranchers and farmers sent to this remote place by the leaders of the Church. George Albert Smith loved these friendly, genuine people—his people. And here in Woodruff, and wherever he went throughout the Church, the Saints reciprocated these feelings for the man who to them stood as a link to the origins of the Church. In him they were reminded of the chosen lineage through which the restoration of the gospel had taken place.

While Elder Smith's travel schedule was rigorous and often wearing, it was occasionally interspersed with interesting diversions. At Morgan, Utah, for instance, less than a month after George Albert's visit to Woodruff, the local brethren persuaded him to test their fishing waters. The results were most satisfactory. Half in jest and half in seriousness, the delighted apostle had Daniel Heiner, John H. Rich, and Moroni Heiner sign the following statement in his journal on September 23, 1905: "This is to certify that today while fishing in the East Canyon Reservoir, we saw George Albert Smith catch and land in the boat a trout weighing 5 5/8 pounds, same being weighed at the drug store in Morgan." To dispel any disbelief of his fish story at home, he had the trout iced and expressed to Lucy.

Three months after the Morgan conference, Elder Smith received an unusual and rewarding assignment. He and Lucy were invited by the president of the Church to accompany a group from Salt Lake City to Windsor County, Vermont, where a monument honoring Joseph Smith was to be unveiled and dedicated on December 23, 1905, the hundredth anniversary of the Prophet's birth. The party consisted of Church leaders and their companions, including the other members of the Smith family who were General Authorities. Since George Albert was the junior member of the clan in length of service, he was appointed to supervise all physical arrangements before and during the trip.

His task was simplified by chartering several Pullman cars, which avoided the inconvenience of checking and transferring baggage. His main duty, therefore, was to see that the pantry on board was well stocked with provisions and to oversee the work of two porters, Seth Young and Bud Price, who had been assigned by the railroad to prepare and serve the meals and to take care of the other personal needs of the passengers.

The train left the Salt Lake City depot on December 19 for the three-day transcontinental trip. En route, the party followed a relaxed routine. Singing, visiting, sight-seeing, and religious discussions were interspersed with checker playing, President Joseph F. Smith's favorite diversion.

On December 22, the party arrived at South Royalton, where it found a typical white and frigid Vermont winter. Horse-drawn sleighs took the travelers to nearby Tunbridge, where they were able to check the town records for genealogical data about the Smith and Mack families before attending an evening reception at the quaint Tunbridge hotel. Here they were welcomed by civic officials and assorted residents who were curious to meet the leaders of the Church whose founder had bestowed such vicarious fame on their community. For months they had watched with interest as the 38 1/2-foot granite shaft had been put in place on the old Solomon Mack farm. It marked the site where Joseph Smith was born a hundred years before, and its height was symbolic of his short but action-filled life span of 38 1/2 years.

Early on December 23, the visitors, whose breathing etched miniature clouds on the icy air, loaded into sleighs to be driven to the farm site. There, in brief services, the monument, standing stark and tall against the rock-ribbed Vermont hills, was dedicated in memory of the Prophet Joseph Smith.

In returning home, the party stopped in Massachusetts so the Smith clan could trace and savor their family roots. At Topsfield, they visited the ancestral home of Asael Smith, the father of Joseph Smith, Sr., and Uncle John. At the town cemetery, they paid homage at the gravesite of Robert Smith, the first member of the clan to reach American soil. There they also found a monument erected in 1873 to the memory of Robert Smith and the first and second Samuel Smith. What unexpected distinction had come to the progeny of these three who bore such an undistinguished name!

From Massachusetts the chartered train traveled to Palmyra, New York, where the passengers visited the farm once owned by Joseph Smith, Sr., whose son and namesake had received the remarkable vision that opened the drama of the Restoration. A meeting was later held at the nearby Hill Cumorah, where President Joseph F. Smith offered a prayer of gratitude and benediction. Contacts made during this visit with Avery Chapman, the owner of the Joseph Smith, Sr., farm, and Pliny T. Sexton, the owner of the Hill Cumorah, culminated eventually in the Church's purchase of both of these historic properties. George Albert Smith would later play a key role in these acquisitions.

The last stop on the traveler's itinerary was at Kirtland, Ohio, where they visited the temple and the homes of Joseph and Hyrum Smith. Four days later, on December 31, as they sped across the plains of Nebraska, the travelers held a service aboard the chartered train. Each member of the party bore testimony about the reality and goodness of God and the joys of the trip then coming to an end. Following this meeting, "a resolution was passed," wrote George Albert in his diary, "thanking me for my care in looking after the party. It was signed by every member of the party." Elder Smith's official duties ended the following day when, after seeing that his friends were safely off the train with their luggage he tipped the porters thirty dollars each for their attentive service.

Because of the acquaintances he had made at Palmyra and his friendly skills in dealing with people, George Albert Smith was later appointed by the First Presidency to negotiate for the purchase of the Joseph Smith, Sr., farm and the Hill Cumorah. Accompanied by Lucy, he left Salt Lake City in early June, 1907 for this purpose. Sewn into Lucy's skirt was $20,000 in cash for use in the negotiations. His first priority was to buy the Hill Cumorah. But he found Mr. Sexton unwilling to sell. Nevertheless, the owner was friendly, showed the apostle all around the property, and commented that it "would likely come to the church some day." That day was over twenty years in coming, however, as the purchase of the hill was not completed until February 18, 1928, when it was acquired from the estate of Mr. Sexton, who had died in the meantime. The ease with which it was purchased at that time and the favorable terms were due in no small part to the good relations Elder Smith developed with Pliny Sexton and his family over the years. The apostle seldom if ever passed through this area without contacting his friend and renewing acquaintances.

When, during his 1907 visit, George Albert found Mr. Sexton unwilling to sell, he turned his attention to Mr. Chapman and the Joseph Smith, Sr., property. Here he found a more encouraging response; after friendly negotiations, the owner deeded the hundred-acre farm to the Church for the $20,000 which Lucy retrieved from its hiding place.

During a week's stay in the Palmyra area at the time of this purchase, Elder Smith became imbued with the importance of events and places in early Church history in arousing reverential appreciation for the past. He visited the old homes of Martin Harris and Peter Whitmer and the building where E. B. Grandin printed the first edition of the Book of Mormon. He was also shown the printer's copy of the first edition and was introduced to the Robinson brothers, the descendants of Robert Robinson who owned the Hill Cumorah at the time Joseph Smith obtained the plates from the Angel Moroni. The later purchase of the Whitmer and Harris homes and other acquisitions by the Church in this area can be traced in large part to the enthusiasm of George Albert Smith for historic sites and artifacts and to his influence in the leading councils of the Church.

From Palmyra, Elder Smith and Lucy took a side trip into Maine to visit members of the Carter family, relatives of Lucy's Grandmother Woodruff. En route home they held meetings with the missionaries in the Central States Mission at Independence, Missouri, and the Western States missionaries at Denver, Colorado. And soon after returning to Salt Lake City, Elder Smith took a long, tiring trip into Canada for a series of meetings with the Saints in and around Cardston, Alberta.

At the October 1907 general conference, George Albert

Smith marked the end of his fourth year as a member of the Twelve. By now, he had severed his connection with the land office and was, therefore, free to travel more extensively than he had in the past. And being a junior member of the Twelve and still in his thirties, he was assigned more frequently to fill the assignments a long distance from Church headquarters. So a month after the conference, he headed south for Mexico, where he was scheduled to hold conferences with the Latter-day Saints in Colonia Dublan, Colonia Juarez, and Colonia Diaz. On the way, he held meetings in northern Arizona along the Little Colorado River, in the Salt River Valley at Phoenix and Mesa, and at Thatcher in the Gila River Valley. He found Phoenix to be "a pretty little city"; and at Thatcher, he stayed in the home of stake president Andrew Kimball, whose large family included a new deacon, twelve-year-old Spencer W. Kimball, a future president of the Church.

These communities, and the ones the apostle found in Mexico, were still struggling pioneer villages. They lacked the amenities to which he had become accustomed in Salt Lake City. Most of the homes he stayed in were small and crowded; the streets were unpaved and dusty, and the meeting houses were cramped and always filled to overflowing. Elder Smith was fastidious in his grooming and cleanliness, and, because of frail health, he was exceedingly careful about his diet. At home, for instance, he insisted on having separate towels for his face, feet, and body; and a whole wheat concoction was an essential item in his usual breakfast menu. He was also sensitive about odors, and he often carried breath sweeteners to make sure he was not offensive to others. It was difficult to accommodate habits such as these to the realities of frontier living, where running water was considered the ultimate in personal luxury and where bathrooms were a rarity. George Albert's unfailing courtesy and consideration for the feelings of others prevented him from complaining about the facilities or food provided by his hosts, who

54

always offered the best they had. Nor did he attempt to dictate menus or to insist on special treatment in sleeping or other arrangements. He merely accepted what was offered, expressing genuine thanks for the kindnesses shown to him.

But such diplomacy did not prevent Elder Smith from attempting to lift the standards and habits of the Saints. He did this through his public discourses, which enabled him to call attention to deficiencies without personalizing them. So, on this trip, as he did at other times, he alluded to the lack of good ventilation in the public meetings, which opened the door for general comments about personal hygiene and cleanliness. His sermons were also sprinkled with other items of personal counsel and admonition, such as the need to get out of debt and the need for "retrenchment" in personal living, which was then a popular theme among the General Authorities.

The traveler spent a week and a half touring the Mormon colonies in Mexico, where he found the living conditions similar to those north of the border. But the transportation was less efficient, which made it necessary to travel to some remote places on horseback. Here his host and guide was fifty-five-year-old stake president Anthony W. Ivins, a prosperous rancher, who had been called as a member of the Twelve at the general conference two months before. Elder Ivins was then winding up his affairs prior to moving to Church headquarters in Salt Lake City.

Elder Smith did not feel well while he toured the Mexican colonies. The combination of sun, dust, and jolting horseback ride on December 6 caused a throbbing pain in his right eye all day. This distressing experience occurred sporadically after the eye was injured while he worked on the railroad. And it occurred intermittently throughout the remainder of his life, attested to by occasional cryptic diary entries: "Eyes bothering me"; "Eyes bleary"; "My eyes are weak"; and "My eyes have been quite distressing today" are illustrative. (See diary entries of March 16, 1923; April 16, 1940; December 3, 1942; and September 28, 1945.)

Only seven months before the long trip to Mexico, Elder Smith underwent surgery to straighten his left eye, which until then focused outward. While the surgery was successful, it produced an altered focus that required a long period of adjustment. This annoyance further disturbed Elder Smith's peace of mind and aggravated the nervousness that had troubled him since childhood.

Recrossing the border, the apostle boarded a train for Los Angeles, California, where he arrived on December 15, 1907. There, in addition to meetings with missionaries and members, he enjoyed a first-in-a-lifetime experience when he was given a seventy-six-mile automobile tour of the area. "A delightful experience," was his reaction. The novelty of the horseless carriage had not yet worn off, so that each ride was an event worthy of historic comment.

From Los Angeles, Elder Smith traveled up the coast to San Francisco, where he first saw the devastation caused by the 1906 earthquake and the industrious efforts to restore the city. "What a terrible wreck the earthquake made," he wrote on December 18, 1907. "The city is building fast." As he had done elsewhere during this tour, he held meetings with missionaries and members while he was in San Francisco.

The frenetic pace of travel and meetings was interrupted temporarily in the summer of 1908 when George Albert enjoyed a leisurely three-week tour through the Pacific northwest and California as a guest of President Joseph F. Smith. Impressed, perhaps, with the efficient way he had managed the trip to Vermont in 1905, or sensing a need for the intense young apostle to ease off temporarily from his arduous schedule, President Smith invited George Albert to accompany President Smith and a small party, which included the Prophet's first counselor, John R. Winder. "I had stocked the Broiler Car Merlin with a bill of groceries and fruit for the journey," wrote Elder Smith on June 26, 1908, "and we left the depot in good spirits."

Traveling through Idaho into Oregon, the party visited

LaGrande, the Hood River, and Portland. Independence Day found them at Seaside. "We hung out a new flag at the end of our car," wrote George Albert, "and joined the populace in strolling on the beach and shooting firecrackers." Moving on to California, the vacationers visited San Francisco, Pacific Grove, Los Angeles, Long Beach, and San Diego. At Los Angeles, they left the train to sail to Catalina Island, where they marveled at the throngs of vacationers and sun worshipers and sampled the delicious marine cuisine of the island's restaurants.

On the last day of this enjoyable outing, July 17, 1908, the travelers "spent the evening visiting and testifying of the pleasures of the trip and appreciation of each other's kindness."

Elder Smith ended the year with another lengthy tour of the Southern States Mission. En route there, he traveled through New York to learn whether the attitude of Pliny T. Sexton toward selling the Hill Cumorah had changed. He found his friend still unwilling to sell; but the apostle seemed satisfied that he had increased the reservoir of good will toward himself and the Church.

George Albert was met at Lynchburg, Virginia, by the Southern States mission president, forty-three-year-old Charles A. Callis. This short, dynamic convert, whose slight Irish brogue betrayed his Dublin origins, would join Elder Smith in the apostleship twenty-five years after the tour, which took the pair through North and South Carolina, Florida, Alabama, Georgia, and Tennessee. The two-week marathon, marked by the customary meetings with members and missionaries, ended at Memphis, Tennessee, on December 20. "Brother Callis and the brethren have been very kind and thoughtful during my visit," wrote Elder Smith on that date, "and I appreciate it."

Despite the solicitous attention the apostle was always given as he traveled, and despite the efforts of everyone involved to care for his every need, these trips sapped his strength and increased his nervous tension, which was building to an explosive level. The irregularity and unpredictability of his meals, the crowded itinerary, the upset of a different bed every night, and the demands of members and missionaries who sought spiritual uplift and guidance were rapidly exhausting George Albert Smith's shrinking residue of stamina.

He was able to relax for a few days during the Christmas holidays; and he was free from travel assignments during the following January, although he was under the pressure of his continuing assignments at headquarters. And he mourned the passing of his maternal grandfather, Lorin Farr, who died at age eighty-eight and who was buried in Ogden on January 17, 1909.

By February 1, Elder Smith was on the road again. This time the purpose was personal. Since his modest living allowance was insufficient to fill all the needs of his family, George Albert had become interested in the Danielson Plow Company as a means of supplementing his income. So on this occasion, he traveled to the company's factory and headquarters in Independence, Missouri, to "try to figure out how to make the plow business go." It was hardly something to lift the spirits of an apostle; but it was a necessary diversion from duty, like Paul's occasional stints at tent making.

George Albert returned home to find Salt Lake City locked in a controversy that divided the community along religious lines. It involved the great debate over the sale and use of liquor, which ended years later with the enactment of the eighteenth amendment to the U.S. constitution. Elder Smith became actively involved in this debate. He believed the consumption of liquor had a destructive effect on society generally and caused countless personal tragedies. Because of the Word of Wisdom, the debate stirred up bitterness in Latter-day Saint communities that did not exist elsewhere. Since most Church members shared George Albert's views about booze and were outspoken in opposing it, many non-Mormons saw this as an attempt to impose the Church's religious beliefs on them through law. Such were the lingering resentments caused by several decades of controversy between the Mormon and non-Mormon populations in Utah that the root issue of liquor was overshadowed in the debate by the issue of alleged overreaching by the dominant church. This was especially stressful to George Albert Smith, who had attempted to create bridges of understanding with nonmembers. Yet, he was unwilling to sacrifice principle for peace. So, he was vigorous and outspoken in the debate, ignoring the consequences.

Shortly after returning from Missouri, he attended a prohibition meeting at the Salt Lake Theatre. There he spoke at length to a packed audience, which was largely sympathetic to his views but which included powerful and outspoken opponents. He retired that night, February 24, 1909, "feeling quite used up." Sleep failed to calm his frazzled nerves. The next day, Elder Smith suffered a general collapse and was unable to rise from his bed. The accumulated pressures of a hectic life-style on a weakened physique had taken its terrible toll.

Chapter Seven

Trial and Trauma

February 24, 1909, opened the door to several years of trial and trauma for Elder George Albert Smith. During this long period, he was unable to perform his apostolic duties fully. Like an injured athlete, he struggled now and then to re-enter the game, to compete as he had before. But, the stamina was gone. The meager reserves of energy had been used up. Yet, the desire to serve, the compelling urge to be up and about the Lord's business, burned with undiminished intensity. Herein lay the most dreadful aspect of his illness—the inability of an infirm body to rise to the demands of a driving, determined spirit.

Had he been more heedful of the danger signs, the apostle might have avoided the general collapse that took him temporarily out of the game. More than anyone else, he was aware of his physical limitations. And this knowledge dictated the need for extreme care in conserving his energies. But, he generally ignored this dictation, even when the alarm bells rang loudly. "My heart seems to be weak this morning," he wrote on January 24, 1909, only a week before leaving for Independence. "I don't know what to make of it. I am afraid I have over-done during the past year." A medical checkup at the time revealed that his heart was sound. Nevertheless, his doctor prescribed a long rest. The patient's response was to leave almost immediately for Independence to try to get the plow business going. On returning from the east, he developed respiratory problems, later diagnosed by Doctor Gamble as La Grippe, the most elite — by name at least — among the several strains of influenza. Elder Smith's remedy for La Grippe was to continue working at an undiminished pace and to enter the arena in the fight for prohibition. The results of this imprudence have already been noted.

Once he was down, help came from every quarter. His priesthood brethren blessed him with several administrations. The best doctors available probed, punched, and diagnosed him. And Lucy hovered over him with anxious concern as group prayers were offered in his behalf. The consensus of all except George Albert seemed to be that it was a classic case of nervous exhaustion, aggravated by La Grippe. Complete bed rest over a long period was prescribed as the remedy. The patient was obedient for eight days, but then he decided enough was enough. "I am sitting up today and dictating my first letter since I went to bed about a week ago," he wrote on March 4 in a letter to George B. Lowrie. "This is the fifth time I have had lagrippe, and I believe it has been the hardest siege of all." (GASC, letterpress book 2.)

To brush aside his collapse as a bad case of the flu was an obvious self-deception. He wished fervently it were so. And he acted on this wish for over a month, interspersing rest with work, impatiently awaiting the time when he could labor at full speed again. But when April general conference came and went with no improvement in his condition, Elder Smith finally faced the reality. A severe nervous disorder and not La Grippe lay at the root of his illness. Only then did he agree that a long vacation at a

*George Albert Smith
with son George Albert,
Jr., 1909*

lower elevation and away from the pressures of Church responsibilities was necessary.

Emily and Edith were in school, and Lucy needed to be with them and four-year-old Albert, so the Smith family decided George Albert would go to Southern California without them. Lucy's aunt and uncle, John and Lucy Acomb, accompanied him, for companionship and to help with housekeeping. On April 13, 1909, the trio arrived in Ocean Park, California, where they rented a modest bungalow near the beach for twenty-five dollars a month. Here the patient settled into an unhurried routine of sleeping, walking along the beach, splashing in the surf, and fishing, interspersed with periodic trips to a medical specialist in Los Angeles. The doctor probed for physical causes to explain the nervousness. George Albert told him about chronic stomach disorders, a lame back, pain in his side, weak eyesight, and constant fatigue. After mulling these facts over, the doctor prescribed a remedy that by now was well known to the patient—rest and relaxation. Neither this doctor, however, nor any other George Albert had consulted could tell the patient *how* to rest and relax. Long hours in bed, beach combing, and idle recreations were not calculated to ease the tensions of one burdened with an exaggerated sense of duty, a gnawing feeling of inadequacy, and a crushing load of responsibility. Indeed, the remedy may have postponed the cure. But, the patient could have done little else under the circumstances, except, of course, to continue to seek divine relief. And this he did by frequent, fervent prayers and by administrations at the hands of priesthood brethren. He was also built up in his feelings by frequent communications of love and support from family, friends, and associates. "Last night I had such a comforting influence come to me," wrote Lucy on April 28, 1909, "which told me that you were to use wisdom in the care of yourself; and I know you will." (Ibid., box 27, folder 11.) His father wrote about the same time, urging him to take "just as much care of yourself as you can." And a week before that, his mother, hardly able to realize that her boy had grown into a man, admonished: "I hope you are where you are having the sunshine. Now my dear boy, I want you to do everything you can to regain your health. Don't be afraid to tell Aunt Lucy your wants." (Letter of April 13, 1909, ibid., box 27, folder 11.)

The concerned parents came to visit soon after to make certain everything possible was being done to make their son comfortable and to speed his recovery. And after school was out and the parents and the Acombs had returned to Salt Lake City, Lucy and the children joined him for the summer.

The arrival of his family was a tonic for the patient. Most important was to have Lucy at his side, comforting him with her sunny disposition and quiet efficiency. And the presence of the children seemed to tap a hidden reservoir of energy. The father supervised a kite-flying party on the beach, introduced the three of them to the excite-

Lucy Woodruff Smith
with daughters Edith
and Emily, 1909

ment of the surf in the "big plunge," and took them and
Lucy to the auto races at Santa Monica. But though Elder
Smith was careful and deliberate on these occasions, acting
mostly as a benign spectator, they invariably sapped his
strength and were at odds with the purpose of his retreat
and the advice of his physicians. And a later illness of
Emily divided Lucy's attention and introduced an unwanted tension into the daily routine of a man who was
still teetering on the edge of nervous prostration.

As August wound down and as the time approached
for the children to re-enter school, the Smiths began to
prepare for the trip home. On August 21, a week before
leaving, George Albert almost drowned. He went alone to

the beach, ventured out too far, was upended by a gigantic wave, and then was caught in the powerful undertow. Confused and frightened, he struggled to regain his balance but was overwhelmed by the churning surf and was carried seaward in the rip tide. What followed remained a blur in his memory. Choked and blinded by the sea water, he called frantically for help between gasps and tried to swim toward shore. The emergency summoned up strength he would not ordinarily have had, and he managed to reach the pilings of the Bristol Pier. While continuing to cry for help, he struggled from pile to pile, clinging to them despite the pain from the barnacles that tore at his flesh. At last, a man on the beach heard his cries and came to George Albert's aid.

This frightening experience cooled Elder Smith's ardor for swimming in the ocean. During the balance of his stay at Ocean Park and at other times in the future, he was content merely to walk on the beach or to sit and gaze at the sea and the surf, which held a hypnotic fascination for him.

The apostle and his family arrived in Salt Lake City on August 28, 1909, where they were met at the train depot by Brothers Nicholas and Winslow Smith and Uncle John Acomb. Because of George Albert's nervousness and his need for a quieter environment, he decided to stay temporarily with the Acombs. And because his doctor, following an apparent trend of the day in diagnostic medicine, had decreed that he should have more fresh air and should discontinue sleeping indoors, the Acombs set up a tent in their backyard for him. The doctor concluded, following an examination on September 13, that the patient's heart muscle "was badly strained" and that he "must take a year of absolute rest."

This prospect was discouraging. George Albert had already tried the rest cure and found it wanting. To do nothing eroded his self-confidence, created feelings of worthlessness, and aggravated his nervous tensions. But what was the alternative? He could reject the doctor's advice and go back to work. The apostle seems to have toyed with this idea for a while. He attended a few meetings with his brethren but would then do penance by sleeping in his tent at night. When the recently installed president of the United States, William Howard Taft, visited Salt Lake City in late September, Elder Smith attended an organ recital in his honor at the Tabernacle. Afterward, he shook hands with the great man, whose goodly girth and walrus mustache were already becoming his trademarks. And during the October general conference, the apostle decided to test his durability further by speaking. It proved to be a disaster. Although he spoke well and felt all right while standing at the pulpit, when he sat down, he began to tremble and perspire heavily.

This incident seems to have sealed his decision to follow the doctor's advice. Soon after, he began arranging for a place where he could try the rest cure again. His near drowning and the long distance from home seem to have tipped the scales against another stay at Ocean Park. St. George in Utah's Dixie was finally selected because of its proximity to home and its warm, dry climate.

The Smith family moved to St. George on November 10, 1909. With them was George Albert's twenty-six-year-old brother, Nathaniel, a skilled carpenter and loyal friend, fondly called "Than" by the family. Here, Lucy and the children occupied the "Rose Jarvis cottage." So that the patient could follow Doctor Pike's prescription for fresh air, Than set up a tent fifteen feet east of the kitchen door. It had a wooden floor and sides and was well ventilated, even when the tent flaps were closed during times of cold or storm. The family installed a wood-burning stove in the tent to remove the chill during cold weather, and they set up an extra bed for Than, who spent the nights there so as to be near should his brother need help. Here George Albert spent almost six months, never once dressing in street clothes. Lucy nursed him during the day, preparing meals and caring for his every need. And each night, Than

*Lucy Woodruff Smith
with son George Albert,
Jr., 1909*

gave him a good massage to preserve muscle tone and to prevent atrophy.

The entire community, which was predominantly Latter-day Saint, adopted the famous patient as their own. The neighbors plied the family with food, flowers, and friendship. Priesthood brethren called frequently to inquire about the apostle's condition and to administer to him as requested. Workers from the temple came often to cheer him up. And get-well letters and messages of love poured in from all parts of the world. Yet, amid all this attention and care, and with his family and friends near, George was depressed and discouraged. His impaired eyesight made it impossible for him to read for any length of time, even had the light in the tent been adequate. And the rustic accommodations were such as to discourage writing. Lucy's heavy nursing duties and care of the children made it impossible for her to spend much time reading to him or serving as his secretary. But, the fact is, Elder Smith had no real interest in reading or writing during this period, or in anything else, for that matter. He was so weak at times that the slight exertion of arranging his bed covers caused a nervous chill. Occasionally he suffered "sinking spells" when his whole system seemed to cease functioning. And one day, he fainted twice during a series of these attacks, losing consciousness completely. As the winter wore on, the patient's confidence level plummeted. He could detect no improvement in his condition. Unlike the stay at Ocean Park, where he was dilatory in following instructions, in St. George he had meticulously done what the doctor prescribed. Yet, nothing had changed. He was as weak as ever, as nervous as ever, and as incapable of working as ever. And there appeared to be no viable prospect that conditions would change.

In these circumstances, feelings of hopelessness and uselessness gradually began to dominate his thoughts. That his illness imposed a heavier burden on his brethren was an added source of concern, as was the knowledge that, while he lived, no one could replace him in the Quorum of the Twelve. Such musings led to the resolve to ask the Lord to release him through death if his recovery were not possible, provided this coincided with the Lord's will. When he asked Lucy to join him in such a prayer, she balked. The idea was repugnant to her at first, as it seemed to imply a complaint about the burden of care of her husband's illness imposed on the family, or to imply a desire on her part to be relieved of that burden. At length, however, when George Albert explained the reason for his request and the great frustrations he suffered, she relented. After the couple prayed together in this way, peace came to them, and this was a turning point in Elder Smith's battle with illness. Because he prayed with fervency and faith, the continuation of his life was a comforting indication that work remained for him to do on earth, despite his infirmities. And while he suffered many months of illness and inertia before he could take his place in the harness again beside his brethren, the hopelessness that had almost overwhelmed him seemed to have dissipated.

Two other incidents at St. George held out hope for the future. The first was the vivid dream, already referred to, in which his grandfather, George A. Smith, appeared to him. The setting was in a beautiful forest near a placid lake. At first, George Albert was alone and felt that he had finished his "work in mortality and had gone home." Soon he found a clearly marked but seldom-used trail, which he began to explore. After he had walked some distance through the forest, he saw "a very large man" coming toward him whom he recognized as his grandfather. George Albert hurried to approach him. As he drew near, however, the grandfather stopped, looked at him earnestly, and said, "I would like to know what you have done with my name." That question caused the whole panorama of the grandson's life to pass before him, "as though it were a flying picture on a screen." He then replied, "I have never done anything with your name of which you need be ashamed." With that, the powerful grandfather, who weighed over three hundred pounds in life, took the frail grandson in his arms. "As he did so," reported Elder Smith, "I became conscious again of my earthly surroundings. My pillow was wet as though water had been poured on it—wet with tears of gratitude that I could answer unashamed." (See "Your Good Name," *Improvement Era*, March 1947, p. 139.)

Of the many spiritual experiences George Albert had during his life, this one seems to stand out above the others in the positive influence it exerted on him. It seemed to be a seal approving his previous conduct. And later, judging by the frequency with which he mentioned it, the dream was a constant motivation, reminding him who he was and how he should act.

The other incident that encouraged Elder Smith was a letter dated April 9, 1910, from his father, who had been sustained as the second counselor in the First Presidency at the April general conference. After telling him how he was loved and missed by the Brethren and the Saints, John Henry admonished his son, "Keep up good fortitude and good faith; don't waiver in your determination to live." Then followed a prophetic statement that could not have failed to inspire the son in his illness. "The bitter experience through which you are going," wrote his father, "is but designed for your purification and uplifting and qualification for an extended life work." (GASC, box 29, folder 6.)

As May approached, preparations were made to move the patient and his family back to Salt Lake City to avoid the heat of a St. George summer. Efficient Than stowed the tent. Lucy boxed up the family's personal gear, and all was loaded on a wagon in which a bed had been prepared for the patient. Amid the good-byes and well wishes of their many friends, the Smiths commenced the two-day journey to Modena, the nearest town, located on the railroad line. On the first day, Elder Smith was exhausted by the jolting of the wagon and the dust kicked up by a stiff northwest wind. But he arose refreshed the second day and enjoyed the ride as the wind died down, happy to be in the open and away from the cramped quarters of his tent. At Modena, the party boarded the train, where a comfortable drawing room awaited them.

Once home, a bed was made up for the patient on the back porch of the Smith home, where he slept well "when the dogs and cats would allow." On the recommendation of doctors Allen and Middleton, his stomach was washed out every other day with a salt solution, which helped to relieve the gas that had troubled him.

By now, Elder Smith was showing some signs of improvement. He was able to move around without becoming exhausted, so much so that in mid-June he accompanied Dr. S. H. Allen and a party of three others to see the birds on an island in the Great Salt Lake. They were gone for two days, during which they went swimming in the buoyant waters of the lake. George Albert found this so invigorating that Dr. Allen recommended that he stay at the lake so he could swim every day. A large room at the end of the north pier was cleaned up and furnished sparsely with beds and other necessities. The patient moved in on June 18 and stayed there most of the summer, often bathing in the lake several times a day. Uncle John Acomb stayed with him for a week. But later George Albert was so improved that it was unnecessary for someone to be with him constantly. So Lucy and the girls began to alternate staying with him at night, commuting on the Salt Air Train, which ran regularly between the city and the lake.

This was home to George Albert Smith for three months. It was an environment unlike anything he had experienced before. There was a midway on the main pier south of his quarters to which vacationers thronged during the summer, giving the place a carnival atmosphere. But, this was not unpleasant to the apostle. He was gregarious by nature, and to see children enjoying the excitement of Saltair's famed fun house, the Ferris wheel, the roller coaster, and other midway attractions was a source of pleasure to him. Saltair employees and other regulars at the resort soon became aware of the presence of the famous tenant and sought to help him when necessary and to shield him from unwanted intrusions by the curious. The days he spent there were wholly unstructured. He lived by the sun, sleeping as long and as often as he wished, bobbing around in the lake whenever he had the urge to do so, reading and writing to the extent his weakened eyesight would allow, and visiting with family and friends as they came to see him.

As summer waned and as the patient's daily swims became less pleasant, it was decided to provide him with treatment in a well-staffed and equipped clinic where his diet and exercise would be controlled and where professional assistance would be constantly available. The clinic selected was Gray's Sanitarium, where he received daily hand and electric massage treatments to alleviate the nervousness and the intermittent dizzy spells he suffered. During the five weeks he stayed at Gray's, George Albert gained fifteen pounds, bringing his weight up to 160, almost ideal for his height and spare bone structure.

The apostle left Gray's in late November, returning to Acomb's fresh-air tent, although he went home daily for at least one meal with the family. At this time, Elder Smith's doctors shifted their prescription from rest to exercise and decreed that he should walk as much as possible each day. With no apparent questioning or criticism about this professional about-face, the patient obediently complied, reporting on November 28, 1910, "Weak—but walked two miles." Within three weeks, he tripled his daily distance to six miles. We can gauge the effectiveness of this new regimen by a journal entry on December 19, 1910: "Nerves quite unsteady," he wrote. "I can't talk or visit without discomfort."

Although his nerves were still unsettled, Elder Smith began to attend quorum meetings again in January 1911; and on March 4 he moved back home, vacating the Acomb tent. "They were so kind to me," he wrote of this benign couple. "I can never repay them."

Those who believe adversity comes in clusters of three might claim support for their superstition in the plight of the Smith family during the first months of 1911. George Albert was still unwell. Lucy, who had suffered a bout with La Grippe in January, developed complications that required hospitalization and surgery in March, less than two weeks after her husband returned home. And in early April, during general conference, John Henry suffered severe bleeding of the lungs, an attack that almost took his life and that foreshadowed his death six months later from the same cause.

Despite their infirmities, the father and son left Salt Lake City on May 31 for a three-week trip to several state capitals in the east, including faraway Augusta, Maine.

Their purpose was to inspect the capitol buildings of these states as part of John Henry's duties as a member of the Utah State Capitol Commission. Appointed by the governor, this commission was to gather data for Utah's capitol building, which was then being planned. While the trip was without pressure, it was tiring for the two men, whose reserves of stamina were meager and dwindling.

During this period, George Albert was troubled by a problem that was disheartening and humiliating. For several years he had managed the financial affairs of Annie D. Watson, overseeing her stock portfolio without fee. Although the value of these assets had increased substantially under the apostle's stewardship, and although he had kept meticulous records, a suspicious relative of Auntie Watson charged him with mismanagement, touching off embarrassing audits by two separate attorneys. Elder Smith was vindicated by a report that the trust was in good order and had been honestly and efficiently managed. Yet, he was deeply hurt to think anyone would question his integrity or competence.

However, the stressful emotions stirred up by these events hardly equalled those he experienced at the death of his father on October 13, 1911. "Our blessed father was called home by the Lord," wrote George Albert on that day. "It was a terrible shock to me. . . . No more generous or kind parent could live than he was." But John Henry Smith was more than a loving father to his son. He was also a friend, counselor, confidant, and exemplar. In every emergency, the powerful and wise man had been near to provide support and direction. And now, when the son needed the father more than ever, he was gone.

The funeral was held October 17, 1911. As George Albert was the eldest of the fifteen surviving children, everyone, including the two wives, looked to him for leadership in settling the estate. A search of John Henry's papers revealed he died without leaving a will. This, coupled with the nebulous legal status of the polygamous wife, Josephine, and her children, posed potentially explosive problems. Since the intestate statute decreed how property was to be distributed to the legal heirs, dissent by Sarah or her children about any distributions to Josephine or her children would have snarled the affairs of the estate and created animosity in the family. But, this was not to be. There was harmony as George Albert, serving as the administrator of the estate, worked out an equitable plan for distributing the property, regardless of the mandate of the statute. This example of unity was satisfying to Elder Smith, who looked on it as a fitting tribute to his father. "It is over two years ago," he wrote to Laura Badger on January 28, 1914, about matters pertaining to the estate, "and I have yet to hear an unkind word or complaint of any kind from any one of them. In fact, I believe they have acted in this matter with a full desire that if father could know of their actions, he would pleased with them and proud of his family." (Ibid., box 36, folder 2.)

Elder Smith's responsibility to administer the estate was only one facet of the changes in his status caused by the father's death. He now felt a responsibility to lead in every aspect of the family's affairs. When his brother Winslow had brought word that the father was dead, George Albert had responded, "Well, I better get out of this bed and look after the family." There followed a new surge of activity in other family matters, and also in his ecclesiastical responsibilities.

Early December found the apostle in San Francisco, California, where he held a series of meetings. On the night of December 2, following a busy day, he had a vivid dream involving his father and other relatives. In it he saw himself, his father, and President Joseph F. Smith together. As George Albert approached him in the dream, the president held out a "good sized package" that apparently contained something George wanted. While this went on, John Henry "sat smiling" but did not speak and "seemed much interested in what was transpiring." In the same dream, Elder Smith saw his grandfather, Lorin Farr. So vivid was the dream that he described in detail what the grandfather wore (a gray pepper-and-salt business suit with a soft hat) and how he looked and acted (twenty years younger than when he died, walking like a young man). As they met, the grandfather shook George Albert's hand and talked with him about the family. In commenting on the experience, the grandson was struck by the fact that he could feel the warmth of his grandfather's hand and detected that he had a body of flesh and bones. Elder Smith made no effort to interpret the meaning of the dream or to explain its impact on him other than to note that "it was a great comfort to me."

Since he referred to them throughout his life, Elder Smith obviously attached spiritual significance to this dream and to the one he had in St. George when President George A. Smith appeared to him. They were unlike certain confused dreams he had had, caused by indigestion or emotional upset. These were clear and logical and conveyed messages of love and hope from the deceased ancestors most interested in his welfare, his father and two grandfathers. And they came during his long illness when he was most in need of encouragement.

The rush of activity following his father's death rapidly drained Elder Smith's meager reservoir of energy. "I gave out," he recorded on January 5, 1912. "Attended too many meetings." A few days later he was "out of commission." Convinced that he was still a sick man, unable to fulfill his responsibilities, Elder Smith arranged to return to Ocean Park. Because of complications with their schooling, the children remained in Salt Lake City with Lucy. On February 13, 1912, George Albert left for the coast, where, except for occasional trips in California and to Utah and Arizona, he stayed for sixteen months.

At Ocean Park, he resumed the casual routine he had followed before, sleeping and resting each day as long as he wished. And he walked on the beach and fished off the pier when he felt strong enough. Significantly, he did not go swimming. In April, he traveled to Tucson, Arizona, where he spent several weeks at the Pueblo Club as the guest of John Mets. The dry desert air seemed to agree with him. This and the ample meals served at the club enabled George Albert to build his weight back to 158 pounds.

When school was out, the Smiths leased their Salt Lake City home to the Reynolds family for a year, and they, in turn, leased the Evangeline Cottage in Ocean Park at 129 Hart Avenue. They settled down there to a semblance of family life with the children attending school in California the following year.

Occasionally during this period, Elder Smith was able to fill minor Church assignments. He laid the cornerstone for a chapel in Los Angeles, went to Oakland to negotiate for the purchase of some property, and visited the Latter-day Saint communities in the Salt River Valley of Arizona. Also, he attended the October general conference in 1912 and spoke for five minutes, the first time he had spoken in the Tabernacle in three years.

He went to Salt Lake City several weeks before the conference to transact some business and to meet with his brethren. Following a usual custom, he wrote letters of encouragement to his family while away. As the children were entering strange schools for the first time, he had special words of counsel for them. "As soon as you find any of your companions have bad habits," he cautioned Emily who was in high school, "avoid those habits and set them a good example." (Letter of September 21, 1912, ibid., box 33, folder 15.)

In a letter to Edith the same day, he counseled: "If the children kind of look at you funny because you are a Mormon, just be proud of it. . . . To be a Mormon is greater than anything else if you are a good one." (Ibid.) And the day before, he had written to seven-year-old Albert: "I am glad you are looking after the garden," he told the future Harvard professor. "Get more tomatoes not flea bites. Kiss Mamma and the girls for me. Papa is pleased with his little man." (Ibid., folder 12.) A special burden of Elder Smith's long illness was the frequent separation from his children and the inability to provide the personal attention he would otherwise have given them. Such unavoidable neglect did not create a schism in their relationship, however, nor did it seem to arouse resentment in the children. On the contrary, they never manifested anything but love and loyalty toward him and submission to his counsel.

Elder Smith received a Christmas greeting from his mission president, J. Golden Kimball; the greeting asked, "Who knows what is the future for a good, clean, pure, honest, faithful man like you are?" He then answered his own question: "You are being molded and fashioned into a vessel of honor." (Letter of December 24, 1912, ibid., box 32, folder 14.) The following year, 1913, would witness the end of this molding process and Elder Smith's return to his apostolic duties.

Chapter Eight

Back in the Swim

T o say George Albert Smith's health had been restored would be an unwarranted exaggeration. During the remainder of his life, he was frail and subject to occasional sieges of illness. But 1913 saw a definite improvement in his condition and a return to relative normalcy.

The family moved back to Salt Lake City in late May, and by July the apostle was busily involved in his official duties once more. His first assignment was to accompany the president of his quorum, Francis M. Lyman, to a conference in the Benson stake. This seventy-year-old kinsman, the father of George Albert's boyhood friend Richard R. Lyman, was like a father to him. Ordained to the apostleship on the same day, Elder Lyman and John Henry Smith had sat side by side in the council meeting of the Twelve for thirty years. And being the one responsible to make assignments to the members of the Twelve, President Lyman apparently wanted to make certain that the son of his cousin and long-time associate was well enough to resume his apostolic duties. What the president found seemed to convince him that his colleague was ready to go to work.

Not long after returning from the Benson Stake conference, George Albert was assigned to go to the eastern
states mission, headquartered in New York City. On the
way, he stopped in Washington, D.C., where he visited
with fellow apostle Reed Smoot, who, according to Elder
Smith, was making a "splendid record" as a United States
senator. In New York City, he found mission president
Ben E. Rich very ill, so much so that Elder Smith set apart
Laurence W. Richards as the temporary president of the
mission. Fondly called Uncle Ben, President Rich, whose
reputation for independence and straight talk was legendary, had literally worn out his life in missionary service in
the eastern and southern states.

After holding the usual meetings with members and
missionaries in New York City, and after conferring with
Isaac Russell about a Church historical film, Elder Smith
traveled to New England. There, he interspersed meetings
and consultations with visits to some of the Smith ancestral
shrines, which seemed to nourish his sense of destiny.

On the return trip, traveling through western New
York, George Albert made the predictable stop in Palmyra
to check with Pliny T. Sexton about the Hill Cumorah. His
friend was not ready to sell yet, but prospects for the future
looked encouraging. At Chicago, the apostle rendezvoused
with his brother Nicholas G. Smith, who, accompanied by
his family, was en route to South Africa, where he had
been assigned to serve as the mission president. The joy
of this reunion was marred by news from New York that
Uncle Ben was dead. In conferring with Salt Lake City,
George Albert was instructed to return to New York to
assist President Rich's family and to reorganize the mission, which he did. He arrived back in Salt Lake City September 29, 1913, after forty days on the road.

Following the October general conference, during
which he spoke for ten minutes without difficulty, George
Albert began serving as an administrative assistant to President Joseph F. Smith. The Prophet apparently was impressed with his cousin's efficiency in handling travel ar-

rangements during the trip to Vermont in 1905 and the later trip to the Pacific Northwest and California. And so he began to use him in the office of the First Presidency to arrange for and to accompany him on his trips and for other administrative purposes. The first trip George Albert planned in this capacity was to the Midwest. The pair left Salt Lake City in late October 1913 for Chicago, where President Smith dedicated two chapels. They returned home via Missouri, where at Independence the two Salt Lake Smiths held a meeting with the Saints and visited their cousin, Joseph Smith III, the president of the Reorganized Church. Depsite their differences in religious doctrine and practice, Joseph F. and George Albert retained a close relationship with this son of the Prophet Joseph Smith who at the time of this historic meeting was nearly blind and deaf. The visit was historic in that it is the only known instance when the sons of Joseph and Hyrum Smith sat in council with a direct descendant of Uncle John Smith.

The visitors traveled north from Independence to Far West, where they inspected the abandoned temple site where the Twelve had commenced their heralded mission to the British Isles in the early 1840s. Of equal and perhaps greater interest to President Joseph F. Smith was a vacant lot across the street from the temple site where he had been born seventy-five years before, on November 13, 1838. All evidence of the humble home had been obliterated. But vividly alive in memory were the stories his mother had related about the terrible persecutions his family and other Saints had endured at Far West and elsewhere in Missouri. Such were the emotions aroused by these bitter memories that members of the Smith family in Utah, descendants of Hyrum and Uncle John alike, harbored ill feelings toward Missouri for the indignities heaped upon their ancestors, and they were little inclined to do or say anything for its benefit.

Soon after returning from Missouri, George Albert began preparing for two other trips with the Prophet. The first was in early November to Los Angeles, where another chapel was dedicated; and soon after, they traveled through Arizona, where still other chapels were dedicated and where they visited the Grand Canyon.

Elder Smith enjoyed these trips immensely. It was pleasant to have the close companionship of the President of the Church, a relative who helped to fill the void created by the death of his father. And to engage in lengthy, unhurried conversation with this man, the son of the Patriarch and the nephew of the Prophet, who could remember with clarity having seen the corpses of the two martyrs laid out in the Mansion House in Nauvoo, provided an almost encyclopedic briefing on the early history of the Church. More important, however, was the fact that this intimate association with a seasoned leader provided this future president of the Church with an important role model.

However, serving President Smith in this way was not an unmixed blessing. It required George Albert to subordinate himself completely to the wishes of his leader and to be constantly on call. The difficulty here was not that President Smith was overly demanding or unreasonable. But the mere possibility he might need help at any moment restricted Elder Smith in his own actions. Moreover, this close relationship created uneasiness in George Albert because of the perception of nepotism it might convey to others. These feelings surfaced in a letter he wrote to Samuel O. Bennion, president of the Central States Mission, about the Prophet's plans to dedicate a new chapel in Independence, Missouri, in October 1914. George Albert expressed the wish that President Smith would give other brethren the opportunity to travel with him. Yet, he made it clear that he enjoyed and appreciated the privilege. (GASC, box 36, folder 4.)

The increased tempo of Elder Smith's Church activities during this period was paralleled by a host of new nonecclesiastical responsibilities. In 1914, for instance, he attended the International Irrigation Congress in Calgary, Alberta, Canada, where he was elected fifth vice-president of the congress. This was the first in a long series of official assignments he received in organizations pertaining to irrigation and reclamation, subjects of vital concern to the Latter-day Saints, most of whom lived in arid areas of the western United States. The next year, he was elected second vice-president of the congress at a convention in Sacramento, California. And in 1916, he became the international president of this organization during a meeting held in El Paso, Texas. In September 1917, at a meeting of the International Dry Farm Congress in Peoria, Illinois, he was also elected president of that organization. And finally, a year later at a joint meeting in Kansas City, Missouri, the two congresses voted to merge, and George Albert Smith became the first president of the combined groups. Because of his leadership in these organizations, Utah's Governor Bamberger appointed Elder Smith as a member of the committee on the reclamation of lands in the Colorado River drainage basin. His high profile in the causes of irrigation and reclamation and his natural eloquence made him a favorite as a speaker for organizations involved in related activities. So, in 1923, he was the featured speaker at a combined meeting of the Forestry Reclamation and Home Making conference in New Orleans, Louisiana.

The qualities that Elder Smith exhibited in his work with these organizations were commented on by a long-time associate, Franklin S. Harris, one-time president of Brigham Young University. "His leadership," wrote Dr. Harris, "his broad human sympathies and his understanding of the problems of the west, led workers from all parts of the country to rally to his support and to follow his capable leadership." And as to the moral influence Elder Smith brought to bear in his leadership, President Harris noted: "In the presence of George Albert Smith, no one ever thought of expressing anything but the highest sentiments of which he was capable. No one would think of telling a low or vulgar story or doing anything that was not on the highest plane." (Unpublished manuscript, Ibid., box 100.)

During the years George Albert was gaining prominence in irrigation and reclamation circles, he was also extending his influence and interest into other secular activities. In January 1915, he was elected a director of both the LDS Hospital and the Utah Savings and Trust Company. The following year, he became a vice-president of the bank, a position in which he served actively for several years. And about the same time, his old employer, ZCMI, summoned him to its board of directors, as did the Mutual Creamery Company. In later years, as his seniority in the councils of the Church increased and as his experience and judgment in business matters matured, his involvements in commercial enterprises multiplied. He became a director, vice-president, and later president of the Utah–Idaho Sugar Company; president of the Libby Investment Company; president of ZCMI; director and later president of the Heber J. Grant Insurance Company; director and later president of the Utah First National Bank; and director of the Decker Wholesale Jewelry Company. While Elder Smith lacked the time to become deeply involved in the daily management of these companies, his judgment, integrity, and vision, his diplomacy and his knack for getting things done, made him a valuable asset to them and contributed significantly to their success.

During the years following his illness, George Albert also extended his interests and influence into various civic and social activities. He became affiliated with the Utah chapter of the Sons of the American Revolution and in 1917 was elected its president. Soon after, he represented his chapter at a national SAR convention held in Rochester, New York. About the same time, he was elected as a Utah delegate to attend a congress of the League to Enforce Peace, held in Philadelphia, where former President William Howard Taft presided. The object of this group was to hasten the end of the war in Europe and to lay the groundwork for an organization that would help secure peace in the future. Before this, Elder Smith had been involved in various activities to support the United States' effort in the war. He was a member of the security committee of the National Defense Council; participated in Red Cross and War Bond drives; and was a member of a committee to select army chaplains.

As the war neared its end, an apocalyptic wave of disease swept over the world, carrying tens of thousands to the grave. Elder Smith was in Kansas City attending sessions of the International Irrigation and Dry Farming Congresses when the government ordered the cancellation of all public meetings. At home, he found that, obedient to this decree, all church gatherings had been canceled, including stake conferences. This provided a temporary respite from his heavy travel and speaking schedule. His family retreated to the seclusion of their home, venturing out only when urgent matters required them to leave it. One such occasion occurred on November 12, the day following the tumultuous celebration of the Armistice, when George Albert and his cousin, Joseph Fielding Smith, were called to administer to the president of the Church, who lay gravely ill in the Beehive House. The Prophet had been stricken with influenza, which had been aggravated by mourning over the recent death of his son Hyrum Mack Smith. The venerable leader passed away on November 19, 1918, six days after his eightieth birthday. His death severed the one remaining link between the General Authorities of the Church and its early leaders. He was six years old when his father, Hyrum, and the Prophet Joseph Smith were murdered, and therefore he had a clear memory of their appearance and demeanor. The man who would succeed him, Heber J. Grant, the ranking apostle, was born nine years after the exodus and therefore had only secondhand knowledge about the two martyrs and the early days of the Church.

Elder Smith and two new members of the Twelve, Stephen L Richards and Richard R. Lyman, were appointed to coordinate the funeral arrangements with President Smith's family. Because of the flu epidemic that still raged, only graveside services were held. The Prophet was laid to rest on the north bench of the Salt Lake Valley, not far from the burial site of Elder Smith's father.

The passing of these two powerful men effected no change in the ecclesiastical status of George Albert Smith, other than that it ended the intimate relationship he had had with the president of the Church and the First Presidency. During the fifteen years of his service in the Quorum of the Twelve, his close kinsman had been the head of the Church; and during most of that time, his father had either been a ranking member of the Twelve or a member of the First Presidency. These relationships, while not giving him any added authority or official status, had enhanced his prestige and opened many doors that otherwise would have been closed to him. With their passing, however, these advantages ended. Elder Smith would have been the first to acknowledge that he had not only missed these two relatives personally, but that he also missed the perquisites he had enjoyed because of them. Yet, their passing relieved him of the concerns he had had about the perceptions of nepotism that their relationship had created.

A few days after the funeral, George Albert and Lucy hosted several relatives at a Thanksgiving dinner. "It was the most pleasant day we have spent in the new home," Elder Smith wrote of the occasion. The "new home" was located at 1302 Yale Avenue, on Salt Lake City's east bench. The Smith's had purchased this large, brick bungalow from Isaac Hancock and had moved into it a few months before. It would be home to them the rest of their lives. Several years before, they had talked of building a new home. The neighborhood near Temple Square where they then lived was rapidly losing its residential character as the city's business area continued to grow. The east bench was also attractive because its higher elevation avoided much of the coal smoke that was concentrated in the downtown area during the winter months. And new schools there were an added inducement to these parents of growing children. So, several years before purchasing the Hancock home, the Smiths had taken positive steps toward relocating. Elder Smith had purchased a lot on Fifteenth East and Twentieth South Streets that Lucy did not particularly like. It was within a block of the old penitentiary and was some distance from the schools the children would attend. So, with money she had inherited, Lucy purchased a choice lot astride Red Butte Creek near Thirteenth East. George Albert jokingly told friends he wanted to live on Fifteenth East and Lucy wanted to live on Thirteenth East, so they compromised on Thirteenth East.

In reality, Elder Smith promptly recognized the superiority of Lucy's choice and wholeheartedly agreed this was where they should establish their new home. A major attraction was the creek, which was far below the level of the street and whose banks were covered with trees. The bottom of the canyon afforded seclusion and a sense of remoteness, as if it were a mountain retreat far from civilization. Several years before moving to the area, the family built a small, rustic cabin near the stream that became a favorite place for summer outings. Here the family could enjoy cookouts; or Elder Smith and Albert could camp overnight as if they were far away in the wilderness. But, the feature of the property that most attracted George Albert was its size. It was large enough for the construction of three homes, for the creation of a new Smith compound. There was room enough for each of the children to build a home near the parents. Elder Smith's hope for such an arrangement was only partially realized. When Emily married, she and her husband, Robert Murray Stewart, a prominent Salt Lake attorney, built a home across the creek to the south. And Edith and her husband, George Elliot, built a home on the same side of the creek as the parents. However, there was a vacant area between these two houses, earmarked as the place where Albert could build his home, creating the same kind of side-by-side living arrangement as had existed between George A. and John Henry; and between John Henry and George Albert. But, this fond hope was never realized as Albert remained in the East

*George Albert Smith,
wearing outdoor clothes
and leaning on an ax*

after completing his schooling at Harvard. The site where
he could have built his home remained vacant throughout
his father's life and became a garden area, where, as the
president of the Twelve and later as the president of the
Church, George Albert Smith could entertain large groups
of people in an outdoor setting.

In a sense, Elder Smith compensated for the failure of
Albert to establish his home next door when he invited
the widow and two children of his brother, Nathaniel, to
move into an apartment across the creek near Emily. He
became a surrogate father to the niece and nephew, Robert
Farr Smith, who loved and idolized his uncle even to the
extent of growing a mustache and beard exactly like those
of the uncle.

A few days before the Smiths enjoyed their first thanksgiving banquet in the Yale Avenue home, George Albert attended a special meeting of the Quorum of the Twelve in the upper room of the Salt Lake Temple. There on November 23, 1918, Heber J. Grant was ordained and set apart as the seventh president of the Church. At the same time, Anthon H. Lund and Charles W. Penrose were set apart as President Grant's first and second counselors, the positions they had held in serving President Joseph F. Smith. Since he was the ranking apostle next to President Grant, President Lund was also set apart as the president of the Quorum of Twelve.

This was the first time Elder Smith had participated in the historical process of selecting and ordaining a new president of the Church. All of the apostles present on that occasion gathered in a circle around President Grant and, laying their hands on his head, and with President Lund acting as voice, ordained him as the prophet, seer, and revelator and the president of The Church of Jesus Christ of Latter-day Saints. All of the keys, powers, and authority necessary to direct the Church were then conferred upon him. These had been given to him in an inchoate form when he was ordained an apostle and set apart as a member of the Twelve on October 16, 1882. But, they now became fully operative. The only other time Elder Smith participated in this solemn and sacred procedure was twenty-seven years later when he was ordained and set apart as the eighth president of the Church in the same manner, with George F. Richards acting as voice.

Chapter Nine

President of the
European Mission

Elder Smith had known President Grant since child-hood. At the time of George Albert's birth in 1870, "Hebe" Grant was a fourteen-year-old teenager who lived three and a half blocks from the Smith home and who aspired to become a great baseball pitcher. He tried to put a foundation under his dream by endlessly throwing a ball at Bishop Woolley's barn. This annoying practice prompted the bishop to label him the laziest boy in the Thirteenth Ward. On learning why the boy battered his barn so — how at a young age he cared for his widowed mother, and how at age twenty-four he became a stake president and at age twenty-six an apostle, the bishop changed his mind. Then he became one of Heber J. Grant's strong supporters, of whom there were many, including George Albert Smith. "There is a unanimous feeling of satisfaction in the reorganization of the presidency," Elder Smith wrote to his new leader on December 11, 1918. "I am grateful indeed to be associated with you." In the same letter, he told the new Church president, "I want you to know that, day or night, it will afford me pleasure to do anything you desire me to do that will be of assistance to you and that will further the interests of the work of the Lord." (GASC, box 39.)

President Grant's response to this offer was swift and surprising, as on January 27, 1919, he privately told Elder Smith to prepare to go to England to preside over the European Mission. George Albert's positive response was equally prompt. But Lucy and other members of the family were reticent. They wondered whether his health was robust enough to withstand the rigors of cold and damp Liverpool, where his headquarters would be located, and the pressure of overseeing the work in all the British Isles and Western Europe. And there was concern about Edith's ill health, for she was scheduled to go abroad with her parents. "I am pleased to hear that your daughter Edith is improving," wrote President Grant, "and I believe the climate in the old world will be beneficial to her and to you." There followed a statement that proved to be prophetic: "Am convinced that a mission abroad will prolong your life." (Ibid., box 41, folder 12.)

Obtaining visas and arranging personal affairs took several months. In the meantime, Elder Smith continued to fill the customary assignments, including a lengthy trip in May that took him to Montreal in eastern Canada. After a round of farewells, including one hosted by President Grant in the Beehive House, the new mission president was ready to go. He left Salt Lake City on June 4, 1919, in company with Lucy, Edith, and Albert. He was forty-nine years old. Emily and her husband, Robert Murray Stewart, who had been married the previous February, remained at home, taking up residence in the Yale Avenue place. Also included in the traveling party were Elders Lon J. Haddock, Virgil Stallings, and Thomas M. Wheeler, who would serve as missionaries in England.

The travelers retraced the route followed in May by Elder Smith to Montreal, their port of embarkation. It was the second trip abroad for George Albert and Lucy, who, several years before, had sailed to England on a combined business and pleasure trip. But it was the maiden voyage for twenty-year-old Edith and her fourteen-year-old brother. Their excitement over the novelty of sea travel added a special enjoyment for the parents.

On June 25, the family stepped ashore at Liverpool, England, where they were greeted by Elder George F. Richards, whom Elder Smith would replace as the European mission president. After the passengers had cleared customs and had collected their baggage, they were driven in cabs to Durham House at 295 Edge Lane, which the Smiths would call home for the next two years.

This imposing old mansion served both as a residence and an office for the mission president. In its basement were the equipment and materials used to publish the *Millennial Star,* the oldest Church periodical then in existence. Elder Smith would become the editor in chief of this paper, which had been established almost eighty years before and whose first editor was Parley P. Pratt. The Durham House, which had a private section for the mission president and his family, also served as the quarters for some of the elders working in the mission office, as a way station for various missionaries and other members passing through Liverpool, and as a place of worship for some of the local Saints. The age of the mansion, the heavy use it had received, and the scarcity of materials and furnishings created by the war had given the once-proud building a dowdy, used-up appearance. Thinking, perhaps, of the comforts and privacy of the family's new Yale Avenue home, Elder Smith confided to his journal: "It isn't like home, but we hope to get used to it." In time, Lucy's homemaking skills and the availability of materials and equipment transformed the mansion into a place of beauty and comfort.

Elder Richards remained in Liverpool only long enough to give his successor a general overview of his responsibilities and then left for Salt Lake City with his family. What George Albert had inherited was a job that would have challenged the capacities of someone in the bloom of health. He not only had overall charge of Church affairs in Great Britain and Western Europe, but he also had direct responsibility for all ecclesiastical and temporal matters in the British Mission. This entailed the supervision of struggling branches of the Church scattered throughout Great Britain and the deployment, direction, and motivation of missionaries. But, Elder Smith was not in robust health, and his condition during the first year after arriving in Liverpool cast doubt on the accuracy of President Grant's prediction. "Brother George Albert Smith came to preside over the European Mission a practical invalid," wrote one of his missionaries, James Gunn McKay. "He had to be carried to and from means of transportation in order that he might fulfill his appointments." (Ibid., box 100, folder 8.) When Elder McKay returned home and reported incidents such as this, there was speculation that George Albert would be called home. Son-in-law Robert Murray Stewart reported this in a letter to Elder Smith, who responded: "He has seen me break down two or three times and I think it gave him a scare, but the fact is, I am just about as well as I was when I left home." (Ibid., box 173, folder 9.)

A principal problem the new mission president faced was a shortage of missionaries to help carry on the work. During his first months in England, he supervised no more than twelve Americans. His goal was to increase this number to the same complement that had been allowed before the war. There were two main obstacles to attaining this goal. First, food shortages caused by the war had prompted government officials to severely curtail visitors visas. And, second, lurid stories in the press had given the Latter-day Saints a bad reputation. The perception of a Mormon missionary as a lustful polygamist, intent on enticing young women to join him in a life of debauchery in America, had seeped into the consciousness of British society. George Albert learned of this only a few weeks after arriving in Liverpool. "When the girls are taken to Utah by the elders," the son Albert wrote to Emily in a letter dated July 14,

1919, telling of a lecture he had attended, "they are given
to the authorities who use them for a vile purpose and
then they cut their throats to save their souls." (Ibid., box
173, folder 5.) In the same letter, he told his sister how his
"blood just boiled" when the speaker called Joseph Fielding Smith "Dirty Joe" and said he had six wives.

Elder Smith's reaction to slanderous accusations about
the Church was typical of his character. Instead of striking
back in anger and frustration, he attempted to reason with
those who attacked him or the Church. Once on a train
he met a protestant minister, who at first was friendly.
Then he learned George Albert was a Latter-day Saint.
"Aren't you ashamed to belong to such a group?" the
minister asked bluntly. In the most pleasant but positive
way, Elder Smith answered that he would be ashamed not
to belong to it, knowing what he did about the Latter-day
Saints. Taking another tack, the minister thought it was
presumptuous for the Mormon Elders to proselyte in England rather than in the "heathen" nations. When the minister defined a heathen as one who does not believe in the
God of Abraham, Isaac, and Jacob, and conceded there
were heathen in England under the definition, George
Albert responded good-naturedly, "Surely you are not
going to complain at me and my associates, if you have
not converted them, if we come over here and help you."
Silenced by such logic, and attracted by the friendly charm
of the stranger, the minister listened patiently as Elder
Smith made a statement that over the years has become a
stock answer used by Latter-day Saints to explain why the
Church proselytes agressively in so-called Christian nations: "We are asking you to keep all the truth you have
acquired in your church," he began; "then let us sit down
and share with you some of the things that have not yet
come into your life that have enriched our lives and made
us happy. We offer you these things without money and
without price. All we ask you to do is hear what we have
to say, and if it appeals to you, accept it freely. If it does
not, then we will go our way to somebody else that we

hope will be more fortunate." (Sermon in Washington, D.C., November 4, 1945, ibid.)

Conversations such as this one were common with Elder Smith during his many travels. He seemed determined to follow the scriptural charge to "open your mouth" and not to be reluctant to share the gospel with others. "Talked Mormonism all the way home and exhausted myself," he wrote on July 21, 1919. This entry was made following his first trip to London after arriving in England. He and Albert had left Liverpool six days earlier with the aim of trying to break the logjam on visas for American missionaries. Since both Albert and Edith had also been set apart as missionaries before leaving Salt Lake City, Albert accompanied his father on this and many other trips as a missionary companion. The experience was choice for both of them and helped solidify the same kind of relationship between them as had existed between George Albert and his father, John Henry Smith.

Except for any gospel seeds the pair may have planted during occasional conversations with strangers, this trip was essentially unproductive. The difficulty was that their arrival in London coincided with an elaborate Peace Day celebration. The holiday mood that pervaded the city smothered any inclination to transact business. The centerpiece of the festivities, which commemorated the end of the First World War, was a giant parade that impressed the strangers from Utah. "A great sight," wrote the apostle. "The papers pronounced it the greatest of all London pageants." And at night, there were brilliant fireworks that outshone by far those the pair had seen at Saltair back in Salt Lake City. Among the dignitaries present was general John J. Pershing, commander of American forces during the war. At a reception at the famed Savoy Hotel, Elder Smith and Albert were able to shake hands with the old warrior.

Three months later, Elder Smith traveled to London again in another try for more missionary visas. This time, he was accompanied by Elder Junius F. Wells. Armed with a letter of introduction from Ambassador Davis, the pair called on Sir Robert Stevenson Horne, Britain's minister of labor. A scheduled five-minute ceremonial interview lengthened into an hour-and-a-half conversation. The discussion ranged from Britain's labor woes to the history and doctrines of the Church. Finally, it centered on the purpose of the visit—Elder Smith's request for additional missionary visas. "When told we wanted the privilege of recruiting our missionary forces up to two hundred and fifty, the same as before the war," he wrote to Emily on October 14, 1919, "he said it would afford him pleasure to issue instructions to his department to allow that number to land as fast as they should arrive." (Ibid., box 172, folder 7.) Sir Robert's favorable response was based not only on the friendliness and persuasion of his American visitors but also on George Albert's assurance that the missionaries would be self-sustaining and would not enter Britain's overcrowded labor force.

Pleased as Elder Smith was by this interview, he was not blind to the obstacles that still remained before the missionaries could return in large number. "Of course, we are not out of the woods yet," he told Emily, "as the anti-Mormons in England are very active and bitter. It is hardly possible to get the papers to publish our statements in most cases, and if they do, somebody writes a contradicting statement that most people prefer to believe." (Ibid.) But, aside from the public opposition, which was bitter and constant, there was another hurdle that was even more difficult. It later appeared that the minister of labor lacked the broad authority to admit the missionaries. This entailed further bureaucratic delays and several additional trips to London. The pressure exerted by these delays and other burdens of office wore heavily on the apostle so that on New Years Day, 1920, he suffered a "breakdown" and was confined to bed for three weeks. But, England's verdant spring brought good news and some relief from the persistent pressures he labored under when, on May 31, 1920, an order was entered permitting the missionaries to come in.

During the time the visa problem was on hold, Elder Smith was exceedingly busy in becoming acquainted with the members and missionaries in Great Britain. Within six weeks, beginning on August 19, 1919, he traveled successively to Nottingham, Sheffield, Birmingham, and Hull England, as well as Cardiff and Bristol Wales; Dublin, Ireland; and Glasgow, Scotland, accompanied by members of his family or by elders Junius F. Wells and Lon J. Haddock. Lucy and the children and Elder Haddock accompanied him to Dublin in late September, when they experienced a "stormy passage" in crossing the Irish Sea. Two weeks later, while en route to Glasgow, the apostle experienced an "attack of nervousness and extreme weakness." He managed to hold the scheduled meetings despite his illness; but on returning home, he was confined to bed for two days, thereby missing a conference in Liverpool. Then followed trips to Manchester, West Hartelford, and Newcastle for additional meetings. During this period, he also made hurried trips to London to check on the status of the visas. There he usually stayed at "Deseret," a facility the Church occupied in London, where he also held meetings with members and investigators.

In his travels, Elder Smith often met with business, professional, and government leaders to foster goodwill toward the Church. Because of the flood of libelous trash about the Latter-day Saints that poured from the British press, he curried the favor of newspaper editors and journalists. So at Newcastle, on October 26, 1919, he went from a session of conference to the office of editor W. D. Black to thank him for an article favorable to the Church that had appeared in his paper. George Albert was astounded that this had been done voluntarily, a thing of such rarity as to receive special comment in his journal.

Five days later, he was again in London. At the train depot, he saw the king of England welcome the shah of Persia. The two monarchs, dressed in royal elegance, approached each other deliberately, almost in slow motion. The imperial greeting consisted of half bows, a handshake, and brief comments, unheard by the onlookers. All around were liveried attendants whose bright uniforms were accented by white horses harnessed to ornate carriages, or mounted by the military honor guard. "Quite a display," wrote Elder Smith, whose simple tastes and democratic ways were at odds with such style and glitter.

Obtaining passports from the French and Swiss consulates, the apostle left the next day for his first trip to the continent. With him were Albert and Elder Wells. Crossing the channel, the trio traveled by train to Paris, where they registered at the Grand Hotel. They spent a day sightseeing in the French capital, which boasted some of the world's most famous historic sites — the Jena Bridge, built for Napoleon Bonaparte in 1814; the Eiffel Tower; the Cathedral of Notre Dame; the Louvre; the Tuileries Gardens; the Arch of Triumph; and the National Art Center. Leaving this ancient center of culture and refinement, a monument to human intelligence, they toured the battlefields of the recent war, Arras, Lens, and Vimy Ridge, a monument to human stupidity. "The destruction was beyond description," wrote Elder Smith. "Miles and miles of what used to be fertile, fruitful territory is so pitted and shot to pieces that it looks like the Great American Desert." He added the now failed hope that this "lesson of war will postpone another for a long time." (Ibid., box 173, folder 7.)

Amid the splendor of a golden autumn, the three Americans traveled into Switzerland, where they held meetings with small branches in Basel, Zurich, and Bern. At Basel, they were joined by mission president Angus J. Cannon and by Scott Taggart. And at Bern, Elder Smith paid a courtesy call on the United States minister, who accompanied him to a meeting with the Swiss minister of foreign affairs, Dr. Charles R. Paravicini. This bit of diplomacy later prompted Dr. Paravicini to request all Swiss Cantons to open their doors to the Mormon missionaries.

After a rough crossing of the channel, the travelers

arrived in London in time to witness another display of royal pageantry. The occasion was the reception for a Spanish prince, a young boy. Present were the queen of England, the queen of Spain, and their royal entourages. "What a fuss they make over royalty, even a child," wrote Elder Smith with ill-concealed disdain.

The apostle commenced his first trip to Scandinavia on June 22, 1920. Again his companions were Albert and Elder Junius F. Wells, who was then serving as the associate editor of the *Millennial Star*. During a period of five weeks, the travelers visited Norway, Sweden, Denmark, Holland, Germany, and Belgium, holding numerous meetings with Church members in the major cities. "It was the first time many of them had ever seen one of the general authorities," wrote Albert of the trip, "and it was the first time any of them had seen one for many years." (Ibid., box 24.) At most meetings along the way, Elder Smith had his son speak through an interpreter. "Albert did very well," he wrote following a meeting held in Copenhagen on July 8, 1920. It was a source of joy for the father to see this teenage boy developing in his understanding of Church doctrine and in his ability to expound it extemporaneously. For his part, the son stood in awe of his eloquent and Christ-like father, whom he honored and sought to emulate. Aside from the solid grounding in Church fundamentals this close association afforded him, the extensive travels and personal contact with people in many foreign lands gave young Albert a depth of understanding enjoyed by few of his age. Bergen, Stockholm, Goteborg, Copenhagen, Hamburg, Rotterdam, Utrecht, Amsterdam, and Brussels were not merely names to him but were real places whose mention called up mental images of their streets and buildings and the people who inhabited them. And the mention of Brussels, the last stop on the tour, would always arouse a memory in the minds of both father and son that time could not erase. It was there, at the urging of Elder Wells, they decided to fly to London. The day was July 24. Perhaps this infused them with the pioneering spirit their adventure required. And, it was an adventure. Their pilot was a daring young RAF veteran. The plane was a single-engine air force cast-off with two open cockpits. Elder Smith and Albert shared one of these. By the father's computation, they took exactly three hours and ten minutes to make the 240-mile hop. "The machine jumped around a good deal," he wrote in a letter to Murray Stewart, adding that "about two thirds of [the flight] was quite pleasant." (Letter of August 2, 1920, ibid., box 124, folder 10.) Some inkling of the effect of the other third is gained from a letter Elder Smith wrote to his friend Clarence Howard five years after the event. "When we arrived in the big city and were walking from the field," he wrote on August 8, 1926, "my son Albert asked me how I liked the trip and I said 'Fine, but the next time I do a trick like that, I'm going to keep one foot on the ground all the way.' " (Ibid., box 52, folder 23.)

At "Deseret" in London, George Albert learned that eleven new elders had arrived from the United States during his absence. This was the first fruit of his year-long effort to increase the complement of missionaries in Great Britain. It signaled a new day for the work there and was a tangible and gratifying evidence to Elder Smith that his efforts had not been useless.

The apostle made his last trip to the continent a few weeks after returning from the Scandinavian tour. Lucy and the two children went with him. After holding meetings in Bern and Basel, the party accompanied President Angus J. Cannon on a tour of Germany. During stops in Frankfurt, Dresden, Leipzig, Berlin, and other German cities, the Saints and elders were built up by Elder Smith's teaching and counseling. At Berlin, Lucy and Edith left the party to go to Norway. Traveling to Christiana (now Oslo), Lucy attended meetings of the International Council of Women representing the Young Women's Mutual Improvement Association.

By this time, Elder Smith had the work under control. The flow of new missionaries was constant; the proselyting work was thriving; the branches were growing; and public attitudes toward the Latter-day Saints were improving. But much remained to be done. When, therefore, a letter arrived from President Heber J. Grant in November 1920, authorizing George Albert to return home for the winter, George Albert declined with thanks. "The work here is just getting on its feet," he wrote, "and I think a few months longer will not hurt me; and, I prefer to remain until things here are in better condition."

Because of his success in solving the visa problem for British missionaries, Elder Smith was asked to help a mission president obtain visas for himself and family. J. Wyley Sessions, called to preside over the South Africa Mission, had been unable to obtain visas for a year from British officials in the United States. After President Sessions arrived in Liverpool in January 1921, Elder Smith accompanied him to London. The British passport office turned a deaf ear but referred them to the high commissioner for South Africa, who summarily turned down the request because the applicant was a missionary. But Elder Smith persisted with questions until he learned the concern was that President Sessions would be merely an itinerant preacher. When it was made clear he would preside over an existing congregation and would have a permanent residence in Capetown, the application was approved.

Shortly before going to London with Wyley Sessions, Elder Smith wrote a loving letter to his mother, who had been ill. "I feel I am needed for a while longer," he wrote on January 3, 1921, "but if you want us to come home this spring, we can do so as President Grant has already said I could have my release at any time. . . . I am praying that the Lord will heal you and give you joy in contemplating the reunion of your family in your little home. . . . I feel better since visiting with you on paper and will rejoice when I can put my arms around you and tell you how much I love you and how grateful I am that you are mine and I am yours." (Ibid., box 15, folder 4.) This letter, which conveys the tender feelings George Albert always had for his mother, was the last one he wrote to her. She died peacefully on February 4, 1921, at the comparatively young age of seventy-one. The long distance that separated them prevented the son from attending the funeral. Sarah was eulogized by Richard R. Lyman of the Twelve and by Anthon H. Lund of the First Presidency, who passed away less than a month afterward.

Death came close to the Smith family again shortly after the mother's funeral when Albert's close friend, James Willis, was killed. The two boys were riding their bicycles when a truck ran over James, killing him instantly. The effect of the accident on Albert was profound. It not only deprived him of the association of one of the few friends in Liverpool his own age, but it was a sobering reminder of the fleeting nature of life. How quickly the end could come without warning! And three months later, the family mourned once more when word came that Lucy's father had passed on. The sad news arrived while George Albert was away from Liverpool. Lucy advised him in a letter, reminiscing about her father's long and eventful life, which began near the dawn of Church history. Speculating about the length of their own lives, she wrote: "You and I are getting old and I do hope nothing will keep us apart too much. I depend on you and love you so much." (Ibid., box 42, folder 22.)

The apostle's absence from Durham House on this occasion was unrelated to his Church assignment. He had been asked by his old employer, ZCMI, to accompany a group of business executives, sponsored by the British Drapers Chamber of Trades, on a tour of England and Scotland. With him at the beginning of the month's tour were Edith, and Emily, who had come for a visit before the family returned home. Later Albert and Lucy alternated as the apostle's traveling companion. The itinerary took the party to most of the major cities of England and Scotland, where its members inspected clothing factories and retail outlets and were exposed to the rich cultural heritage of Great Britain. In London, Westminster Abbey, the Brit-

101

ish Museum, and the National Gallery were favorite sights. In the Midlands, Warwick Castle and Stratford-upon-Avon were principal attractions. At the birthplace of the Bard, they stayed at the Shakespeare Hotel; and after dinner they attended a performance of *A Midsummer Night's Dream*. At Chalfont, England, they visited John Milton's cottage, where the famed author had written *Paradise Lost*; and at Bobby Burns' cottage, Elder Smith was asked to eulogize Scotland's favorite poet.

To tour these ancient lands, so rich in history and tradition, was a revelation to one whose birthplace counted longevity in terms of decades, not centuries. And to see the buildings and landscape used and enjoyed by ancestors of long ago aroused feelings of kinship with the dead that George Albert had not experienced before. It was a once-in-a-lifetime opportunity, almost perfect in its enjoyment — but not quite. The thing that marred the occasion was an obnoxious Englishman who persisted in needling Elder Smith, belittling him and the Mormon Church within hearing of others. For a while, the apostle bore these insults without complaint, even though they caused feelings of coolness toward him by other members of the group. But when the man offended Edith with a tasteless comment, her father complained to the tour chairman, offering to withdraw if that would heal the rift that had been created. The chairman, Mr. Eastman, pleaded with George Albert not to leave and promptly took steps to muzzle the critic and to put to rest the negative feelings toward the Smiths his conduct had aroused. This succeeded in toning him down and restoring peace — for a while. Later, however, he reverted to form during a two-day stay at Gordon Selfridge's High Cliffe Castle. One evening as George Albert entered the great hall of the castle for a formal dinner, this dolt, his coat adorned with a flashy array of ribbons and medals, approached him to say in a loud, pompous voice, "I say, Mr. Smith, just what does that funny little button you always wear represent?" flicking the Sons of the American Revolution lapel button George Albert frequently wore. "I'll tell you, my friend," he answered politely; "that represents the time that my great-grandfather licked your great-grandfather." (Letter of Emily Smith Stewart to T. Earl Pardoe, ibid., box 96, folder 1.) This proved to be the ultimate put-down, as those within hearing laughed loudly while some applauded. The incident abruptly ended any further attempts to embarrass Elder Smith or members of his family by the little man who later became an object of ridicule.

Although this trip did not afford opportunities for conventional proselyting, it opened many doors of influence and friendship that proved beneficial to the Church and to George Albert's success in the future. He met British government, professional, and business leaders at receptions at Lancaster House; at the home of Lady Astor, who was a member of parliament; and at the country estate of Viscount Burnham. He was also introduced to educational leaders at Harrow and Eaton and at Oxford, where the group was entertained by the mayor. In all of these contacts, Elder Smith's gracious and cordial manner created a reservoir of goodwill for the Church and helped to break down the prejudices and misconceptions that had hindered the work in Great Britain for so long.

After returning to Liverpool, George Albert received a long letter from President Heber J. Grant commending him for his effective service and especially his wise advice to the British Saints not to emigrate to the United States but to remain in their homes to help build up the Church there. He also repeated his previous counsel that Elder Smith stay in England only as long as he felt it would be in the best interest of the work. However, he expressed concern for Lucy, who, it had been reported, was suffering from respiratory problems caused by the damp climate.

It was a combination of Lucy's poor health and her husband's feeling that he had accomplished his mission that caused President Grant to call Orson F. Whitney as the president of the European Mission to replace Elder Smith. Elder Whitney and his wife and several elders arrived in Liverpool on June 12, 1921. The Smiths remained in England another month, sharing the accommodations of the Durham House with the Whitneys while George Albert tutored his successor in the duties of his new office. With that task completed, the Smiths packed up and, with a mountain of luggage, were accompanied to the Mersey River Pierhead in Liverpool by the Whitneys and the office elders. There, on July 15, 1921, they boarded the *Melita* for the Atlantic crossing to Montreal. The week's voyage, free of all responsibilities, provided Elder Smith with a much-needed interlude of rest and reflection. And like their return to Salt Lake City from Chattanooga following their mission to the Southern States, it also afforded George Albert and Lucy the opportunity to quietly recap their experiences of the previous two years and to lay plans for the future.

Given Elder Smith's recurring frailties, Lucy's battle with England's damp climate, and Edith's intermittent bouts with eczema, this was not the easiest time of their lives. In fact, it was one of the most difficult. Yet out of that difficulty emerged a sense of satisfaction and achievement hardly matched during any other period. They had responded to the call of the president of the Church without question, leaving behind their new, comfortable home and not knowing how the change in climate and the rigors of George Albert's assignment would affect him. But he had survived and succeeded against all odds. And his years in England had provided Elder Smith with training and experiences that would be vital in his later service in the Twelve and as the president of the Church. He could not have failed to recall that every president since Joseph Smith—Brigham Young, John Taylor, Wilford Woodruff, Lorenzo Snow, and Heber J. Grant—had served for a time in Great Britain. And that tradition would be perpetuated in himself and David O. McKay, who had served a British mission as a young man and who would succeed Orson F. Whitney as the president of the European Mission.

Unlike their return from the Southern States, George Albert and Lucy knew precisely what to expect on arriving in Salt Lake City. Their new home awaited them as did Elder Smith's continuing duties in the Twelve. It was, therefore, with a sense of anticipation and excitement that they landed at Montreal to commence the last leg of their journey. But, there was to be a detour. President Grant and a group of dignitaries from Salt Lake City had planned to celebrate Pioneer Day, July 24, at the birthplace of the Prophet Joseph Smith in Vermont and had invited Elder Smith and his family to join them. There George Albert was greeted by the tall, bearded Prophet, who embraced him and commended him for his faithful and effective service in England. And during the day's festivities, at the site of the granite monument erected in memory of the first president of the Church, Elder Smith was moved to reflection about the origins of the Church, about his relationship to the Prophet Joseph Smith, and about his previous visit there in 1905. So much had happened since then. And so much lay ahead.

After leaving the monument, Elder Smith took his family to Palmyra, New York, to visit the Joseph Smith, Sr., farm and the nearby Hill Cumorah. Pliny Sexton was not yet ready to sell the hill. But not too many years remained before the Church would acquire it, fulfilling the dream of George Albert Smith.

Leaving Palmyra, the Smiths traveled by train to Chicago, Illinois, where they spent three days with George Albert's brother Winslow, who was then serving as the president of the Northern States Mission. It was only the second time in two years the apostle had enjoyed the opportunity to visit with one of his brothers. The other occurred in Liverpool a few months before when Nicolas and his family stopped there on the way home from South Africa, where Nicolas had served as the mission president for seven years. These occasions were cherished by the Smith family when the members could reminisce about their ancestry and the shared experiences of the past. It

105

was always a source of satisfaction to these three brothers that they had served simultaneously as mission presidents. And still another, son, Glen, would be called later as a mission president.

George Albert and his family arrived in Salt Lake City on August 3, 1921, after an absence of twenty-six months. Some of the apostle's brethren and members of the family were at the Union Pacific depot to welcome them. As the family traveled east on South Temple, they were excited to see the familiar sights, the old neighborhood on West Temple, the buildings on Temple Square, the Hotel Utah, the Church Administration Building, the Brigham Young homes, and the dignified mansions along East South Temple that reflected a picture-postcard beauty with their luxuriant shade trees and well-manicured lawns. And when they turned south on Thirteenth East, passing the University of Utah, East High School, and the rows of substantial homes, reaching at last Yale Avenue, the Smiths knew they were *home*. Lucy was especially grateful to reach the comfort and seclusion of this haven, as she was the only member of the family who was not more fit than when she left. After carefully inspecting everything— the house, the grounds, and the rustic cabin in the bottom of the canyon, Elder Smith wrote with an obvious sense of satisfaction: "Our property is in good condition and we will soon be settled and comfortable. Our Heavenly Father has been good to us and I am very thankful to him for his watchcare and the preservation of our lives. We are all better than when we left except Lucy who has suffered from asthma, and is not well."

Once the Smiths were comfortably settled in their home and had regained their bearings after such a long absence, George Albert began to project his future activities. His Church assignments, he knew, were beyond his power to control and would come to him either from the president of the quorum, Rudger Clawson, or from the First Presidency. Beyond his formal Church assignments, however, was a wide variety of activities that lay within his discretion to pick and choose. From these he would select a few that were relevant to his apostolic or personal responsibilities and of special importance to him. These selections, which reflected his interest in people, history, business, and government, would claim much of his time during the remainder of his life, a life filled with triumph and defeat, happiness and sorrow, and always with surprises.

Chapter Ten

Headquarters Duties Resumed — The YMMIA

W hen the Brethren learned George Albert Smith's health was sound, they heaped his plate high with work. President Clawson gave him numerous stake conference assignments during the remainder of 1921, and these frequently took him away from home. Members of the Church in the Panguitch, Kanab, Logan, Blackfoot St. Johns, Snowflake, Mesa, St. Joseph, and Juarez stakes enjoyed George Albert's uplifting influence. His experiences abroad had magnified him before the people and enriched his native eloquence. While these conference assignments were temporary, he also received from the First Presidency a surprise appointment that lasted more than thirteen years. On September 21, President Grant and his counselors called George Albert Smith as the general superintendent of the Young Men's Mutual Improvement Association. Organized at the direction of President Brigham Young in 1875, this auxiliary aimed to build testimony in young men; to train them in social relations, athletics, and public speaking; and to help develop their talents. Since 1880, when

Wilford Woodruff became the general superintendent, the YMMIA had been led by a member of the Twelve or the president of the Church. The last superintendent before September 1921 was President Joseph F. Smith, whose counselor Anthony W. Ivins had continued to lead after the Prophet's death until George Albert was set apart. The release of Elder Ivins was triggered by his call as a counselor to President Heber J. Grant in March 1921, a few months before Elder Smith returned from England.

The call to head the YMMIA was the most challenging assignment George Albert Smith had received as a General Authority. He was to lead the young men of the Church toward self-improvement and personal excellence. He brought impressive credentials to the assignment. First was a love for youth. There was nothing artificial about his frequent expressions of love for young people. As the eldest child in a large family, he always showed concern for his younger brothers and sisters, both Sarah's and Aunt Josephine's. The MIA mission to Southern Utah and his service in the Salt Lake Stake YMMIA superintendency and as the European Mission President had honed his talent in leading young people. And his long battle with illness had given him compassion for those who were weak, handicapped, or insecure. These qualities, added to his fiery eloquence, his apostolic stature, and his surprising flair for organization, equipped him well for the assignment.

Over the years, Elder Smith's organizational ability had been hidden beneath a gregarious and jovial nature. One thought of him chiefly as a gifted salesman, entertainer, or speaker. But his appointment as YMMIA superintendent revealed a knack for building an organization and infusing it with his personality and objectives. The first step was his selection of his two counselors. Richard R. Lyman, the first counselor, was an experienced youth leader, well acquainted with the MIA from his service as the Salt Lake Stake superintendent. His role as a university professor had also given him good insight into young people. Melvin J. Ballard, the second counselor, had a special appeal to youth because of his deep spirituality and rare eloquence. His years as a mission president had also developed skill in motivating and directing young men. Both counselors were members of the Twelve, which added significant weight to the superintendency.

The second step was the selection of a general board. Here George Albert assembled a group of high-profile leaders skilled as educators, professionals, and business executives. They had attained stature in their fields, were independent in thought, and were accustomed to expressing their views openly. All of them had good moral character, but a few were unorthodox in some of their religious views. Since the MIA was oriented toward activities and not religious instruction, this was not deemed a problem.

The third step was to provide a framework within which these talented people could make their best contributions. George Albert did this by streamlining board meetings to conserve time and by creating numerous task committees and delegating broadly to them. This released the energies of his associates, who responded with creative suggestions for programs to achieve the aims of the YMMIA. Under the guiding hand of Elder Smith, these were altered and polished to bring them into harmony with the objectives of the Church; then they were implemented throughout the stakes and missions. The result was a strong emphasis on youth activities, for both young men and young women. Soon after George Albert became the general superintendent, he initiated frequent contacts with the young women leaders. These became almost weekly conferences where the aims and procedures of the two organizations were coordinated. During this period, the M-Men basketball program was developed. It was stimulated by stake and regional competitions, leading to the all-Church tournament that showcased athletic skills and sportsmanship. The youth organizations jointly sponsored music and dance festivals, leading to the gala events staged for years at Saltair and later in the stadium at the University of Utah.

Through the cooperation between the young men and young women organizations Elder Smith had fostered, the *Young Women's Journal* was combined with the *Improvement Era* in 1929, which increased their unity and effected many economies. George Albert was conscious of the need to conserve the limited resources of the Church, and he searched for ways to reduce expenses without sacrificing the needs of Church members. When he became the YMMIA superintendent, the apostle found that the organization was mired in debt. Through inefficient distribution, manuals and other instructional materials had piled up in Salt Lake City, draining the liquid assets while creating a paper glut. New procedures were adopted by the ZCMI alumnus, who knew about the need to keep inventory at a reasonable level and to maintain a consistent cash flow. Soon, the materials were moving to the field, where they were needed, and the money generated was used to pay the debt. These and other efficiencies Elder Smith introduced revolutionized the finances of the YMMIA. "Not only did the work grow in efficiency and the interest in it on the part of the young all over the church increase continuously," wrote his first counselor after George Albert had been released, "but the funds in the treasury kept growing higher and higher until we were able to turn over to our successors a great fortune." (Letter of R. R. Lyman to GAS, March 2, 1937, ibid., box 67, folder 1.)

But the efficiency and solvency of the organization was merely incidental to Elder Smith's main purpose. He was primarily interested in building character and testimony in young people. The ingredient that guided the organization to this end was his genuine love for people. "Yours is a leadership of love," wrote Elder Lyman. "It was love that tied you and your assistants in the superintendency and the members of the board with such unity and tightness." (Ibid.) And this love emanated from the leadership to the members of the YMMIA throughout the Church.

111

Elder Smith's devotion to Scouts and Scouting best illustrates how an abstract principle like love was translated into a force for good in the lives of young men. "There is nothing dearer to my heart than the welfare of the boys in our church and in our neighborhood," wrote Elder Smith to his friend Dr. W. W. Henderson. "And there is perhaps no other factor in our Mutual Improvement program which is being used more effectively for making fine manhood of boys than in this program of the Boy Scouts of America." (Letter of December 14, 1926, Ibid., box 52, folder 24.)

Elder Smith's involvement in Scouting began long before he became the general superintendent. When Scouting was officially organized in the United States in 1910, he was an advisor to the YMMIA. A year later, scattered Scout troops in the Church were organized as the MIA Scouts. And in 1912, Elder Smith and others recommended that Scouting be adopted officially by the Church, and they submitted an application for a national charter. The next year, after Congress had granted Scouting a national charter, the Boys Scouts of America sought to bring the Church's Scouting program under its umbrella. After negotiations, Elder Smith and the other Church representatives agreed, on condition that the officials of Latter-day Saint troops would be appointed by priesthood authority and that the Church could change the policies of the national organization to harmonize with Mormon doctrine and goals. From that time, Scouting was an official program of the Church. Six years later, in 1919, local Scout councils were organized. At that time, George Albert Smith became a charter member of the executive board of the Salt Lake Council, a position he held until his death.

From this background, the responsibility for Scouting in the Church was naturally given to the YMMIA when George Albert became its general superintendent. And among Elder Smith's many duties, Scouting soon took a preferential place. George Albert loved young men and recognized their potential. He subscribed to the aims of Scouting to foster loyalty to God and country and to de-

George Albert Smith
with Boy Scout trophy

velop physical, mental, and moral strength. And he saw in the Scout goal of doing one good deed each day a strong incentive for Christian living.

No one was more diligent in performing daily good deeds than George Albert Smith. His acts of kindness and helpfulness are legendary. In driving to his office, he never passed up a pedestrian if there was room in his car. He never denied anyone who sought his help; indeed, he went out of his way to find those in need and to assist them. The residents on and near Yale Avenue became accustomed to the bearded Saint who roamed the neighborhood, giving words of hope and encouragement, inquiring about the health of parents and children and blessing them when asked to do so. It would be impossible to count the legions who received letters of congratulations or condolence from him, or inscribed pamphlets or booklets, which he gave away by the gross. When money was needed to help finance a missionary from his ward or stake, Elder Smith was one of the first to donate. And when the Boy Scouts

113

launched their annual drive for funds, the apostle not only contributed liberally, but he also became an enthusiastic agent in soliciting contributions from others. Many business and professional leaders found an appeal for funds from a jovial George Albert Smith irresistible. His mere presence in their offices shed a genial ray of liberality that made it impossible to decline his requests to help his boys.

Ordinarily when Elder Smith engaged in Scouting activities, he wore his Scout uniform, displaying with pride the insignia of achievement he was entitled to wear. And when he went into the field for jamborees, campouts, cookouts, or trail marking or trekking, he ordinarily wore his knee-high boots. To see George Albert decked out in full regalia left no uncertainty about his commitment to Scouting nor about his genuine enjoyment of the key role he played in it.

Aside from his executive responsibilities in Scouting, Elder Smith took a personal interest in the troop in his own neighborhood, Troop 41 of the Yale Ward, originally part of the Liberty Stake and later a unit in the Bonneville Stake in Salt Lake City. On Independence Day in 1930, for instance, he accompanied twenty-two Scouts from Troop 41, with other Scouts from troops in Cache Valley and Idaho Falls, on a caravan trek to Wyoming. They camped first at Fort Bridger, where, around a crackling fire, the bearded apostle joined enthusiastically in singing songs and recounting stories of the hardships endured by the Mormon pioneers. The next day, they reached Independence Rock, a lonely sentinel in the Wyoming badlands, which was always a welcome sight to weary travelers headed West. There the camp routine was altered when, after the customary singing and story-telling, Elder Smith dedicated the place in memory of the rugged ancestors who had passed that way almost a century before. A year later, he would participate in the formal dedication of this site and the placing of a monument that was foreshadowed by this visit in 1930. On the way home, the Scouts joined Elder Smith in placing markers at the Rock Creek crossing, another pioneer landmark, and at the common grave of fifteen members of a pioneer company who were the victims of an early autumn storm.

Such outings were always an exhilarating though tiring experience for Elder Smith. He enjoyed the youthful exuberance of the boys and marveled at their boundless energy and their intense interest in camping and the outdoors. He soon realized, however, that as boys matured they took less interest in such things. This realization led to the development of the Vanguard program for boys ages fifteen to seventeen and the M-Men program for young men ages seventeen to twenty-four. Writing about typical fifteen-year-old boys, Elder Smith noted: "They are not satisfied to follow the commands of others, but aspire to leadership themselves and feel very much superior to their smaller brothers and acquaintances. The first novelty of scouting has worn off, and they crave something new." (*Improvement Era,* April 1930, p. 389.) Vanguards were given less supervision than the younger boys and had discretion to select projects of their own liking. Emphasis was given to career paths and to special activities that provided new experiences and broadened perspectives. The M-Men were also permitted to elect their own officers, and all members were encouraged to participate in one of the organization's five standing committees. The program developed by Elder Smith and his associates offered a wide variety of activities in athletics, music, dance, and drama, as well as academic opportunities.

Because of the success of these programs in filling the needs of older boys and young men, the Boy Scouts of America requested permission to adopt them for use in other churches. "We are very grateful for the permission extended in your very kind letter of August 8, 1934," wrote James E. West, the chief Scout executive, to Elder Smith, "to use your church programs in scouting, and especially that phase of it which has to do with the program of the Vanguards." Mr. West noted that "the curriculum planning committee of the protestant churches will have real appreciation for the practical working plan offered in the Vanguards." He concluded, "We are therefore hopeful that you will see, after a few years, the fruits of your labors in a very much wider field developed by the Christian Churches generally." (*Improvement Era,* April 1950, p. 290.)

Not only did the Church receive wide acclaim for its efforts to train and motivate the youth, but the Church's chief executive of Scouting and other youth activities, George Albert Smith, received national recognition for his leadership. His roles included the vice-presidency of the executive committee of the Salt Lake Council and membership on the executive committee of the Twelfth Region, which included California, Nevada, Arizona, and Utah. By 1926, this region led all others in the United States in the number of Scouts enrolled and in the quality of its program; and Utah led all other states in the region. In 1932, Elder Smith's status as a Scout leader was further enhanced by his election to the National Executive Council of the Boy Scouts of America, the first Utahn so recognized. For several years, he served as the chairman of the prestigious Program and Resolutions Committee of the National Council. The position brought him into frequent contact with leaders around the country, creating goodwill toward the Church and wide recognition of his leadership qualities. This resulted in his receiving the two highest Scouting awards in the United States, the Silver Beaver, awarded by the Twelfth Region, and the Silver Buffalo, awarded by the national committee. The citation that accompanied the Silver Buffalo award acknowledged his "indefatigable" service and his "enthusiasm" for Scouting as largely accounting for "the fact that Utah stands above all other states in the percentage of boys who are scouts." (GASC, box 89, folder 3.)

Elder Smith's leadership skills were not one dimensional. While he exerted profound influence on the youth, his influence on adults was equally pronounced, and precisely for the same reason. The element in his character that attracted people and caused them to follow him was his unqualified love for everyone. On his sixty-second birthday, the members of his board surprised him with a party. They gave him a specially prepared picture book and spoke about the accomplishments of their leader. The thread that ran throughout their remarks was the charity and kindness that typified Elder Smith's leadership. "We know of no man in whose heart the milk of human kindness is more abundant than in you," said his second counselor, Melvin J. Ballard. And Dr. E. E. Ericksen, a professor of philosophy at the University of Utah who, admittedly, was often outspoken and critical, said that Elder Smith "was always so kind and sweet in replying to me, that I more than once was made ashamed of myself." Dr. Ericksen added that had it not been for his membership on the board and Elder Smith's style of leadership, his own life "may have been quite a different story." (Ibid., box 100, folder 8.) Similar remarks were made at the time of Elder Smith's release in January 1935. The first counselor, Richard R. Lyman, said that the general superintendent had always led "with affection and never with fear," and that no member of the board had "ever felt suppressed in the slightest degree." And Bishop Heber C. Iverson expressed the feelings of other board members in saying: "A more lovable man . . . I cannot name. He is human no doubt. . . . Unquestionably he has failings, but I want to say that my love has blinded me to every fault. If he has any I have never discovered them." (Ibid., box 76.)

What emerges from these statements and many others like them is the image of a man who was without guile, who genuinely loved everyone around him, and who had such self-confidence and self-esteem that he did not feel intimidated or threatened by anyone regardless of his station or achievements. He had gathered around him on the YMMIA board prestigious educators who boasted graduate degrees from famous universities. Yet we see no indication this created a sense of inferiority because of his own limited education. He was not fearful he would be outshone or overpowered by them. Instead, he encouraged them to assert themselves, to speak their minds, to use their skills and educational attainments to the fullest, all to advance the work. And when one of them spoke out with fervor, in tones of academic thunder, he gently brought him into line with love and understanding in such a way that the person became his devoted disciple and frankly recognized the moral superiority of his leader.

This quality of Elder Smith's leadership shows the effects of the long, stressful process through which his years of illness had taken him. They seem to have refined from his character any pride, arrogance, or self-seeking. After he had faced the prospects of death and defeat for so long, after he had suffered anxiety about performing his apostolic duties or leading his family, merely being alive and well and able to work was reward and recognition enough. And in contemplating this aspect of George Albert Smith's character, one can hardly avoid comparing him with the Savior, whose servant he was. While one could not reasonably suggest that Elder Smith's sufferings even distantly approximated those endured by the Redeemer, yet there is a parallel. As the Savior's assumption of the sins of all assured that his judgments would be just (see Mosiah 3:10), so Elder Smith's long illness gave him vital insight into the frailties, infirmities, and fears of humanity, giving him compassion and understanding toward their faults and foibles.

Chapter Eleven

Growth in National Stature

Elder Smith's prominence in Scouting circles was only one element of his growth in national stature among those who were not members of the Church. His early political ties and his involvement in the executive work of the irrigation congresses had greatly expanded his circle of non-Mormon friends. Over the years, through voluminous correspondence and occasional personal contacts, he had kept in touch with these acquaintances. The effort to keep these relationships alive seems to have derived from two main sources. The first was George Albert's natural gregariousness and friendliness. He simply liked and enjoyed people. Therefore, once he had struck up a friendship, his natural impulse was to perpetuate it. The second had its roots in his apostolic responsibility and his orientation toward missionary work. In a sense, Elder Smith was never off duty. He felt keenly the need to plant and to nurture seeds of conversion or of friendship toward the Church. He knew that a friend in high places, though he were never baptized, could help create an atmosphere that would later smooth the way for the Church or its missionaries. And this effort was made easier when it involved people engaged in an activity that appealed to his native interests. Such was the case with Scouting, as it was with Elder Smith's activity in the Sons of the American Revolution.

An organization founded on patriotism and a reverence for ancestors was sure to have a magnetic attraction for George Albert Smith. He was a true patriot, and his love for his country was enhanced by a conviction that the foundations of the United States government were shaped by heavenly influences. He saw a divine pattern in the American Revolution and in the preparation and adoption of the United States Constitution. These convictions were strengthened by prophetic passages in the Book of Mormon and by modern revelations. His feelings about patriotism were expressed clearly when he became affiliated with the American Flag Association. In a letter to Louis A. Ames, the president of the association, Elder Smith acknowledged his appointment as a member of its board of directors, saying, "I appreciate very much being associated with you in this organization, and will be glad to assist in creating a sentiment of respect and reverence for our flag." In concluding the letter, he revealed the depth of his love for the United States of America. "Surely there is no nation under heaven that has greater need for gratitude," wrote he, "and no flag that I have ever seen is so beautiful to look upon as ours." (Letter of March 8, 1923, GASC, box 46, folder 1.)

Elder Smith entertained similar feelings about the Sons of the American Revolution, especially since one of its aims was to honor the patriots who were engaged in the fight for independence. Few people could equal George Albert Smith in the depth of his ancestral love. He had an almost worshipful attitude toward his forebears. And this characteristic, added to his convictions about the divine origins of the United States, shed a special light on those progenitors who fought in the Revolutionary war.

As already noted, he had been prominent in the Utah

Society of the SAR before his mission to England, serving successively as the chaplain, a member of the board of managers, and twice as its president. Soon after returning from England, he became involved on the national level. In May 1922, he headed the Utah delegation to the national SAR convention held in Springfield, Massachusetts. There he spearheaded an effort to designate Salt Lake City as the site of the next convention. This effort failed, but his prominence in promoting it and his stature in the Utah Society and in the Church resulted in his election as the vice-president general representing the Pacific Coast District, which included all of the Pacific Coast and Rocky Mountain States and Texas.

This commenced Elder Smith's involvement in the national councils of the SAR that would continue for over twenty-six years. He was elected to four consecutive terms as the vice-president general for the Pacific Coast District from 1922 to 1925. He likely would have been reelected again in 1926 had he not missed the national convention that year because of a conflict with the YMMIA June conference. He served two other terms as vice-president general in 1944 and 1946. Elder Smith might also have been elected president general of the SAR had it not been for time limitations imposed by his service in the Twelve and for a latent anti-Mormon sentiment among some members of the SAR. He frankly discussed this evidence of religious bigotry in a letter to Emily and her husband, Murray Stewart. "Perhaps I might be [elected president]," he wrote on March 21, 1923, "but for the fact that I am a Mormon, and there are many people in our organization who shy at a Mormon." Citing a specific incident, he added, "The president general told me of one man who was nearly horrified when he found that they had elected one of the authorities of the Mormon church as a vice president general." Typically, he brushed off this insult without rancor. "I have no doubt he will get over that." (Ibid., box 47, folder 16.)

It is apparent the SAR officials in high places did not share this biased view of Elder Smith. Indeed, they seemed

121

proud of his role as a General Authority of the Mormon Church. During a national tour with other SAR executives, he was repeatedly referred to as "the Mormon vice president," and often, as he conducted meetings, the president general introduced him as "a Mormon, the vice-president general George Albert Smith, the man we all love." (GAS journal, October 1925.)

Elder Smith's eloquence, honed through the years as a missionary and a General Authority, soon made him a vast favorite as a speaker among SAR chapters both within and outside his district. Audiences enjoyed his enthusiastic delivery, his apt use of anecdotes, his friendly personality, and his skillful treatment of historic and patriotic themes. And his earnestness and frankness carried conviction to his listeners. At a banquet in Oregon, he gently chided the local chapter for its failure to pray at its meetings. It pleased him that afterward several expressed approval of these remarks though they were considered to be quite unorthodox for an SAR gathering. (Ibid., January 13, 1923.)

At the national convention in Nashville, Tennessee, that year, Elder Smith's persuasiveness and his clout as a vice-president resulted in Salt Lake City being designated as the site of the 1924 SAR convention. Returning home from Nashville, Elder Smith immediately went to work with the officers of the Salt Lake chapter to plan for the event. During the ensuing months, a flood of letters flowed from George Albert's office to SAR officials all over the United States. In them, he promoted the coming convention with a chamber-of-commerce fervor. "We anticipate a big congress here in Salt Lake City," was a typical phrase used in his promotional correspondence.

In planning the convention, Elder Smith had two principal objectives in mind. The first was to showcase the Church and the community to prominent leaders from around the country. And the second was to introduce the visitors to some of the unique features of the western United States. His advertising flyers encouraged the delegates to include visits to some of the national parks in their plans—Yellowstone, Zion's, or Bryce. He played up the Great Salt Lake, where the visitors could bob like corks in its buoyant waters. And he extolled the marvels of Mount Timpanogos near Provo with its spectacular cave of stalactites and stalagmites.

A patriotic service kicked off the convention Sunday evening, July 20, 1924. It was held in a jam-packed tabernacle on Temple Square. A good attendance was assured when President Grant authorized announcements of the service to be made in sacrament meetings throughout the city, and these convened earlier than usual to encourage attendance at the Tabernacle. The agenda for the first general session the following day included talks by Utah's governor, Charles R. Mabey, and Salt Lake City's mayor, Clarence C. Neslen. Interspersed with the business session of the three-day conference were various social events, banquets, receptions, and tours designed to honor the visitors and to acquaint them with interesting features of the area. Buses took some of the delegates to see the sprawling open-pit copper mine at Bingham, across the valley from Salt Lake City, while others rode the funny little open-air train to Saltair, where the young at heart accepted Elder Smith's invitation to take a dip in the lake. And on the last evening, some delegates left left Salt Lake City on a special train to Yellowstone Park.

Every aspect of the convention functioned with assembly line efficiency. George Albert, with the help of an able committee from the Salt Lake chapter, planned and executed it with the same finesse and thoroughness he had shown in arranging the tour to Vermont in 1905. And the year following the SAR convention, Elder Smith again demonstrated his organizational skills when he directed the planning and staging of the giant Jubilee Celebration, commemorating the fiftieth anniversary of the MIA.

The flood of appreciative mail George Albert received after the convention attests to its success. Letters of thanks and congratulations poured in from all parts of the country. "I felt at home with 'you all,' " wrote a friend from his old mission field in Tennessee. One from Oregon appreciated the special treatment he had received in the Smith home: "You took me into the family and treated me as one of your own." Another from New York was confident that "every delegate and every guest . . . went home from Salt Lake City feeling that they had one of the real times of their lives." Still another from New Jersey felt Elder Smith was "the embodiment of an ideal host." And finally, a friend from Illinois who had attended Sons of the Utah Pioneers conventions for many years said he had "never known of one whose details were better arranged and where more attention and pleasure were extended to the attendants. The spirit of good fellowship appeared to me to be like one large family." (GASC, box 92, folder 7-8.) This was exactly the spirit Elder Smith wanted to convey, not only as representing the qualities of his own character but also the qualities inculcated by the Church and community.

When it was possible to do so, Elder Smith performed SAR duties in tandem with his Church and other assignments. We see this when he travelled to the SAR convention in Nashville in 1923. En route to Buffalo, New York, to confer with the secretary general of the SAR, he addressed a sacrament meeting and attended and spoke at a conference of the Reorganized Church at Omaha, Nebraska. He also conferred with prominent government and business leaders in Des Moines, including Iowa governor, Kendall; and he conferred with Northern States Mission president John H. Taylor and railroad officials in Chicago. At Buffalo, he addressed an SAR banquet, and later in New York City he conferred with bank and railroad officials, spending the night with the Eastern States Mission president in Brooklyn. In Washington, D.C., he renewed an acquaintance with Warren G. Harding and attended a service where the president spoke at the unveiling of a statue of Alexander Hamilton. He traveled from Washington to Nashville on a train that carried SAR delegates from New England and Eastern states. "It was a beautiful ride,"

Elder Smith reported to the First Presidency, "and the journey offered an opportunity to have several very interesting conversations." He felt he had been able "to allay considerable prejudice that had been in the minds of some." (Letter of May 2, 1923, ibid., box 46, folder 17.)

Elder Smith's visit with President Harding reflected a practice he had followed for many years of calling on the chief executive while he was in the nation's capital. Because of his early involvement in politics and his stature as a Church leader, George Albert usually found an open door when he visited the White House. He had called on President Harding the year before on the way home from Springfield, Massachusetts, where he had been elected a vice-president general of the SAR. Seeing that President Harding, who was a member, was not wearing his SAR button, Elder Smith gave him the one he was wearing. "When I called on the President of the United States," wrote Elder Smith, "I was his superior in the [SAR] and had a perfect right to decorate him for the good work he has been doing." (Ibid., box 43, folder 34.)

Warren G. Harding was only one of eight presidents of the United States with whom Elder Smith was personally acquainted. He met William McKinley during that president's tour of the United States. And, as noted, George Albert was at the Music Hall in Buffalo, New York, on September 6, 1901, and heard the shot that killed the president. McKinley's successor, Theodore Roosevelt, was the president with whom the apostle was best acquainted. They had been on the political hustings together before George Albert was called to the Twelve, and thereafter a strong bond of friendship had grown between them. Once when he called at the White House to see "Teddy," Elder Smith found a large crowd waiting. So he merely left his card with the clerk so the president would know he had called. Before he got out of the building, the clerk overtook him to say the president wanted to see him. "I am very glad to see you," said President Roosevelt, "and I never want you to come to Washington while I am president of the United States without coming to see me." (Ibid., box 124, pp. 11-12.) Years later, after his death, Elder Smith was invited to attend the dedication of a memorial to President Roosevelt. In expressing regrets at being unable to attend, he wrote in a letter to Walter M. Head: "Teddy Roosevelt was one of my dearest friends, and I would have been glad to be present to do honor to him." (Ibid., box 89, folder 10.)

Elder Smith was the chairman of the entertainment committee when President William Howard Taft visited Salt Lake City. Later he participated with President Taft in a meeting in Philadelphia to try to popularize the League of Nations. And after Mr. Taft became chief justice of the United States Supreme Court, Elder Smith spent an evening in his home with his fellow apostle, Senator Reed Smoot.

George Albert's easy access to the president of the United States traced to his own political connections and to the growing influence of Senator Smoot. Over the years, the senator's voice was heard and listened to more in the nation's capitol, especially during the administrations of Republican presidents. So, Elder Smith received a special invitation to attend the inauguration of Calvin Coolidge, and later he was granted a private interview when he presented the new president with a copy of the YMMIA Diamond Jubilee booklet. And he had similar special access to President Coolidge's successor, Herbert Hoover. "We have elected a wonderful man to be president," wrote Elder Smith after the 1928 election, "a God fearing, courageous, capable executive." Not forseeing the great depression and the tragic consequences it would have for the country and for the reputation of the president, he added, "Being personally acquainted with Herbert Hoover, I do not hesitate to say I believe he will be one of our greatest presidents." (Ibid., box 56, folder 2.) Shortly after the inauguration, George Albert called on President Hoover during an assignment in Washington. The apostle saw signs of worry and concern in the new chief executive, who had promised the country a "New Day," based upon the creative use of scientific and technological advances. While the devastating October stock market crash a few months later scuttled hopes for the "New Day," it laid the foundation for Franklin D. Roosevelt's cry for a "New Deal" during the 1932 campaign.

While George Albert was personally acquainted with Franklin D. Roosevelt, and, indeed, claimed a distant relationship, he did not have the same access to him as he had enjoyed with the president's predecessors. The same was true of President Roosevelt's successor, Harry S. Truman. The reason, of course, was rooted in politics. Both of these presidents were Democrats who saw no reason to give special recognition to a Republican of the stature of George Albert Smith. Moreover, with the defeat of Reed Smoot in the 1932 election, Elder Smith lost the special Washington contact who had opened so many doors for him in the past.

George Albert's correspondence reveals his political bias against President Roosevelt's administration. "I wish I had the assurance that you seem to have," he wrote to Senator W. H. King, "that President Roosevelt will be able to point the way for improvement in our country." (Ibid., box 60, folder 36.) And, politics aside, he took a dim view of Mr. Roosevelt's stand on liquor, which he considered to be a grave social issue. "The attitudes of the President of the United States and his wife toward the use of liquor," he wrote to his friend Roy Breg, "has acted like an invitation to many heretofore temperate people to become guzzlers of liquor." (Ibid., box 52, folder 3.)

Elder Smith's catalog of influential acquaintances included not only the presidential victors but the losers as well. Speaking of William Jennings Bryan, who was defeated by William McKinley and once by William Howard Taft, he wrote in a letter to John B. Larner, "While I did not agree politically with Mr. Bryan, he was a very dear friend of mine; in fact the last time I was in Florida I had a delightful visit in his home." But, political differences did not blind the writer to his friend's stature. "Surely Mr. Bryan was a great man and has left his impression on the civilization of our age." And Mr. Bryan's teetotaling habits won an accolade from Elder Smith: "The fact that he was a total abstainer impressed many good people and helped them to avoid wine and other liquors." (Ibid., box 52.) The list of George Albert's "dear friends" extended across the board of political, business, and professional leaders in all parts of the country. And he was assiduous in cultivating these friendships, never failing to write letters of thanks to those who had assisted him and never failing to pay a courtesy call when time would permit. But, in all this, he never acquired the reputation of the professional glad-hander who curries friendships only for personal gain or notoriety. The fact is that this quality reflected a deep-rooted attitude of love and respect toward people generally and was not limited to persons of prominence.

Chapter Twelve

The Measure of the Man

George Albert Smith was equally solicitous of ordinary people, especially those who were ill, discouraged, or down on their luck. He was often found in hospitals, nursing facilities, and the homes of the poor or the disheartened. Considering Elder Smith's character, undoubtedly most of his charities were unknown. Therefore, the evidence of those we see are but a shadow of the reality. "In the past week," wrote G. Homer Durham following President Smith's death, "I have come to realize that the body of the church and of the community have never really seen President George Albert Smith. . . . It is almost unbelievable, the quantity and magnitude of the acts of personal selfless service which he rendered to individual human beings." (GASC, box 150, folder 25.) The examples of such acts we know about are numerous and impressive. To mention a few provides a hint of the scope of Elder Smith's charitable nature. Once a stranger spoke to him in the Atlanta train depot about the stranger's brother, who was imprisoned in Utah for a homicide allegedly committed in self-defense. The man said his brother was basically a good person who had made a mistake and who ought not to be required to remain in prison longer. He asked for Elder Smith's help. Back in Utah, the apostle studied the case and, being convinced the man deserved help, immediately became involved. Elder Smith's prestige and perseverance soon won a parole for the prisoner, much to the joy of his family in Georgia.

Another family had similar cause to rejoice. Their teenage son had come to Salt Lake City to work. The boy's father, a friend of Elder Smith, told his son to call on the apostle to pay his respects and to seek counsel. The boy ignored these instructions until, through an association with bad company, he became involved as an accessory to robbery. Then he called. Elder Smith responded willingly. Soon, through the joint efforts of George Albert Smith and the father, the charges were dropped. This boy, who took to heart Elder Smith's oft-repeated counsel to "keep on the Lord's side of the line," later filled a mission and became respected and successful. When, in his maturity, he reflected on what his fate would have been had not Elder Smith intervened, he rejoiced because "one of God's Apostles cared enough to help his fellow man." (*Instructor*, November 1966, pp. 427-28.)

Elder Smith was always a soft touch for a loan. Members of the Church knew this and often used him as a financial resource when all other avenues of funding had closed down. A mother called once to seek money for her son's education. Although George Albert was hard pressed financially at the time, he borrowed $250 from the bank and gave it to the student on a non-interest-bearing note. Three years later, the young man, now a doctor, wrote a letter of thanks to Elder Smith, enclosing a check for $295, covering the loan with interest at 6 percent. "I wish there were some way to adequately express my appreciation," wrote he, "for your kindness in rendering me financial assistance at a time when my prospects were anything but encouraging." In answering, the apostle enclosed a dollar and nine cents representing an overpayment on the interest. "I will be fully paid," wrote he, "for any encouragement I may have been able to render to you . . . if . . . your life shall conform to the ideals of the Gospel and of good citizenship in the country." (GASC, box 53, folder 7.) Another debtor, who wrote apologetically, explaining why he couldn't pay on time, received an understanding letter from his benefactor. "When I let you have it, I had an idea that the time would be longer than you anticipated, so don't worry about my portion of the burden you are carrying." (GASC, box 49, folder 11.)

And it was not uncommon for nonmembers to put the touch on this kindly Saint. In 1914, when he lived just three blocks from the railroad depot, Elder Smith told a friend that his family fed one or two transients about every day. "We have made it a rule never to turn anybody away even though they . . . sometimes smell so strongly of liquor and tobacco that it is enough to knock you down." Occasionally he also gave money to some of these people who asked for it, but never when he felt they would use it for tobacco or alcohol because "there are so many who need it for the bare necessities of life." (GASC, box 36, folder 24.)

George Albert was a responsive friend, helping when asked, and a Good Samaritan, lending aid voluntarily. Once he read about a man he had known since childhood who had applied for parole from prison. Unasked, George Albert wrote the Utah State Board of Pardons, saying he was ignorant of the facts of the case but that he knew the man and had confidence he could be reclaimed. Showing insight into the factors that sway penal boards, Elder Smith concluded that the man's parole would be a blessing not only to the man and his family but also to his many friends. (GASC, box 55, folder 6.)

Even as man does not live by bread alone, George Albert Smith's charities were not restricted to giving temporal aid. He was anxious to lift people spiritually and to help them realize their potential. In 1935, G. Homer Durham, past Church historian and member of the presidency of the First Quorum of Seventy, was in New York City on the way home from his mission to Great Britain. As Elder Durham had helped organize Scout troops in the mission field, his mission president suggested that he pay a courtesy call at the national Scout office in New York City. There he asked to see a subordinate official but instead was ushered into the office of America's chief Scout executive, Dr. Fisher. After exchanging pleasantries, Dr. Fisher said a banquet honoring Lord Baden-Powell, the founder of Scouting, was being held in the Waldorf-Astoria, that George Albert Smith had reserved a table for ten, and that he was sure Elder Smith would want the young missionary to attend as his guest. Elder Durham's half-hearted protests lacked conviction as he accepted with alacrity. But at the hotel, intimidated by the grandeur of the banquet room and seeing no familiar face among the throng of distinguished guests, he had second thoughts. Why was he, a mere youth, so rash as to accept an invitation to be someone else's guest, especially someone as prominent as George Albert Smith? At that moment of doubt, however, Elder Smith entered the room and, walking directly to the grateful young man, extended his hand in welcome. Elder Durham's stammered effort to apologize for the imposition was interrupted by his gracious host. "Imposition? I should say not. I apologize to you for keeping you waiting. We have been busy in a meeting of the council. We became so involved that Dr. Fisher forgot to mention that you would join us until only a moment ago. Come right in, we're about ready to begin." And taking him by the arm, the apostle ushered Elder Durham to his table, where he was introduced to the other guests, prominent Latter-day Saint Scout leaders. To this young man who was struggling to find his niche in life, this was "a soul warming experience that [would] live forever." That a man of such prominence had gone out of his way to recognize a relatively unknown young elder convinced him "that the future can be friendly, not fear-filled nor insecure." And later in Salt Lake City, Elder Durham visited with the apostle at his invitation and received fatherly counsel that had a lasting impact on his life. Especially memorable were Elder Smith's parting words. Putting his arm around the young man's shoulders, he said, "Remember, we're living eternal lives." (*Improvement Era,* 54 [June 1951]: 478-79.)

Another young man, M. Russell Ballard, who later became a member of the Twelve, was also the recipient of similar loving treatment from Elder Smith. At a time when Elder Smith was the president of the Church, the Prophet had a vivid dream one night. In it his fellow apostle and former counselor in the YMMIA, Melvin J. Ballard, appeared to him. Some aspects of the dream implied there was a problem in the Ballard family. The next day, the president called Russell Ballard's father to ask if everything was all right in the family. He was told the only new thing was that his son, Russell, was leaving soon for a mission to Great Britain. On his own initiative, the Prophet attended the farewell and sat next to the young elder with his arm on his shoulder. Such a demonstration of love touched the young man deeply and made a lasting impression on him. While in the mission field, he wrote a letter of appreciation to the Prophet. In it he betrayed a youthful ignorance about the tenuous nature of life in suggesting that when President Smith met Melvin J. Ballard on the other side, he assure him that everything was all right in the Ballard family. The President's answer taught a gentle but pointed lesson. "If I get there first," he wrote, "I will be happy to do so." When he returned from his mission, Elder Ballard, whose maternal great-grandfather was President Joseph F. Smith, received an insight into George Albert Smith's deep-seated aversion to nepotism. Russell brought the Prophet a gift from Scotland and delivered it to his home, just a few months before his death. During the brief visit, the ailing Church president said, "You know your great grandfather made a mistake." Asked what it was, the Prophet answered, "He called too many of his relatives as general authorities." (As related to the author by MRB on October 25, 1987.)

To relate the numerous stories of Elder George Albert Smith's acts of kindness would be impossible in an abbreviated account of his life. Those included here are typical and illustrate the essential quality of his character. That quality, which we call charity, the pure love of Christ, is what sets him apart as one of the most conspicuous practitioners of Christian ethics known to the modern church. It would be easy but misleading to say, "He was just born that way." No doubt at birth he possessed inherent characteristics, legacies of his heavenly and earthly parents and of his own diligence in the premortal life, which portended the kind of man he would become. And these characteristics were influenced by the environment in which he was reared and by the trials to which he was subjected. But this hardly explains the Christ-like way he lived. There are many who are well born, who are reared in a moral environment, and who overcome great handicaps but whose lives do not approximate the charitable quality we see in that of George Albert Smith. As one searches for an explanation, two major factors appear to have had a profound influence in his development. The first grew out of his ordeal in St. George. The long months of convalescence provided an opportunity for deep introspection. During that time, he probed his interior world, weighing and analyzing his strengths and weaknesses, his responsibilities, and his motivations, searching for ruling principles to govern his life. From these musings and strugglings emerged what Elder Smith would call his "Creed," which was a self-imposed standard against which he measured his conduct. In a sense, the creed articulated an ethical goal toward which he would strive. In it can be seen the spiritual elements that were woven into his life:

> I would be a friend to the friendless and find joy in ministering to the needs of the poor.
> I would visit the sick and afflicted and inspire in them a desire for faith to be healed.

134

I would teach the truth to the understanding and blessing of all mankind.

I would seek out the erring one and try to win him back to a righteous and happy life.

I would not seek to force people to live up to my ideals, but rather love them into doing the thing that is right.

I would live with the masses and help to solve their problems that their earth life may be happy.

I would avoid the publicity of high position and discourage the flattery of thoughtless friends.

I would not knowingly wound the feelings of any, not even one who may have wronged me, but would seek to do good and make him my friend.

I would overcome the tendency to selfishness and jealousy and rejoice in the success of all the children of our Heavenly Father.

I would not be an enemy to any living soul.

Knowing that the Redeemer of mankind has offered to the world the only plan that will fully develop us and make us really happy here and hereafter, I feel it not only a duty but a blessed privilege to disseminate this truth. (*Improvement Era,* March 1932, p. 295.)

The other major factor that helps explain Elder Smith's character is the constancy with which he applied the tenets of his creed. And a powerful force that helped fuel this constancy appears to have arisen from his dedication to the principles of scouting. A "good deed a day" was more than a platitude to George Albert Smith. It was a compelling idea that motivated him to regularly and aggressively look for opportunities to serve and lift others. And through consistent application, the idea ultimately became a fixed habit. In whatever situation Elder Smith found himself, he also found a chance "to do a good turn," to help someone along the way. He was indiscriminate in selecting the objects of his bounty, recognizing no boundaries of age, sex, or economic status. And to him, a good deed was like a seed that would grow into a happy memory for both him and the one he had served. The young son of a Mormon bishop once a received an inscribed book from Elder Smith after the apostle's visit to his home in rural Utah. The event is still the subject of appreciative comment in the family of this boy, who is now over sixty years old and preparing for retirement. (Experience of Earl M. Bay.) A stake president in Arizona once received a letter of appreciation from Elder Smith, one of the hundreds he wrote during his lifetime. Touched by the thoughtfulness of the letter, which was personalized and not merely a perfunctory note, he answered to express thanks and to say that in all his years of service in the Church, he had never before received a letter of appreciation from a General Authority. (Letter of O. S. Stapley, September 21, 1939, GASC, box 57, folder 16.)

If we were to try to explain George Albert Smith's charity in biblical terms, we could do no better than to quote the Apostle Peter's appraisal of the Savior, who, he said, was one "who went about doing good." (Acts 10:38.) Owen Reichmen, who served as his stake president during the time he was president of the Church, said Elder Smith explained it in a typically self-deprecating way: "That he lacked the prowess of an athlete, that he was too homely to win popular favor, and that his weak eyes prevented him from becoming a scholar, but he could excel in human kindness. So, he made kindness his specialty." (As quoted in Pusey, *Builders of the Kingdom,* p. 301.)

Chapter Thirteen

Trails and Pageants

W e have already seen how Elder Smith's interest in the Church historical sites in and near Palmyra, New York, resulted in the acquisition of the Joseph Smith, Sr., farm and, later, the Hill Cumorah. He was aware of the value of these sites as a means of keeping alive the memory of the important events that happened nearby. These were the roots from which the Church had grown and from which its members could derive spiritual nourishment through the generations. But, to make this effectual, ownership of the sites was necessary so they could be properly maintained and made accessible to the members and to those interested in the Church. There visitors could reflect upon the miraculous events of the Restoration and be built up in faith and in dedication to the Church.

The single-mindedness with which Elder Smith pursued the purchase of these sites demonstrates an absorbing interest in history and the tenacity that characterized his life. When he first visited the Hill Cumorah in 1901, it was owned by George Sampson, "a sulky fellow who had no

use for Mormons" and would not even let George Albert
and his party climb to the top of the hill. (GAS letter to
Lucy Smith, GASC, box 135, folder 25.) As already seen,
he first met Mr. Sampson's successor, Pliny T. Sexton, in
1905. The apostle deliberately and consistently cultivated
the friendship of Mr. Sexton, who knew from the outset
of their acquaintance that his Mormon friend was eager to
purchase the hill for the Church. "In my conversations
with you in the past," wrote Elder Smith on March 8, 1909,
"I have not kept from you my interest in the hill Cumorah,
and my anxiety that it might be possessed by my people
who have a sacred interest in it." (Ibid., box 28, letterpress
book 2.) Not only did he maintain direct contact with Mr.
Sexton, but he also kept tabs on him through others. "I
hope you will keep in touch with him," wrote George
Albert to the caretaker of the Joseph Smith Farm on January
23, 1922, "and if anything develops that would afford an
opportunity for us to get possession of the Hill Cumorah,
do not fail to let us know at once." (Letter to Willard Bean,
Ibid., box 43, folder 5.) To make sure Brother Bean understood these instructions, the apostle repeated them in a
letter eighteen months later: "Don't forget to convey my
kindest regards to Mr. Sexton, and if it takes two or three
trips to do it, I hope you will find the time." (Ibid., box 4,
folder 5.) The astute Mr. Sexton, who was a former chan-
cellor of New York University, apparently assumed that
Elder Smith's anxiety to purchase the hill meant the Church
would be willing to pay an exorbitant price for it. In this
he was mistaken, as time and events proved. "Mr. Sexton
seems to think that we will pay a great big price for it,"
wrote George Albert, "but he may change his mind, and
if he should I would be willing to make a trip to Palmyra
in order to consummate the desire I have had for many
years, that is that the church should possess the Hill Cumorah." (Ibid.)

This desire was not fulfilled until February 1928,
twenty-seven years after Elder Smith first visited the hill,
when it was acquired from Pliny Sexton's estate.

Its acquisition, with the purchase of the Martin Harris home in Palmyra and the Joseph Smith, Peter Whitmer, and Inglis farms (all of which were purchased through the help and perseverance of George Albert Smith) provided the Church with an important showcase to portray its dramatic beginnings for all time. The Hill Cumorah, which was originally barren of trees, was reforested after the Church acquired it, providing a lush background for the annual pageants that are now staged there and that were promoted by Elder Smith.

His conception of the purpose and importance of monuments and historical markers was elaborated in a letter he wrote March 15, 1937. "It has been customary to build monuments to individuals that their memories might be retained," he wrote to Miss Leslie Loveridge. "Great events have also been more permanently established in the minds of people by building monuments. In this part of the world there are many points of interest that are being forgotten and the people have felt that it was desirable to mark them in a substantial way so that those who follow will have their attention called to important events." (Ibid., box 61, folder 1.)

The "people" referred to here consisted of a group of dedicated history buffs among whom George Albert Smith was a conspicuous member. These enthusiasts were convinced that history could best be taught to the masses by plaques and monuments erected at important historical sites. Even the illiterate could understand the meaning of a heroic monument showing, for instance, a man and woman standing, disconsolate, before an open grave, exposed to the weather. It does not seem accidental that one such as Elder Smith, whose genuine interest in people and events of the past was excelled by few, and whose weakened eyesight precluded him from engaging in extensive historical research and writing, became so industriously engaged in tracing and marking the trails of the pioneers.

For many years, Elder Smith pursued his historical interests alone, only occasionally working with others. Certainly this was true in his protracted negotiations to acquire historical sites around Palmyra. At length, he realized that his influence could be extended by channeling his efforts through an organization of like-minded people. Influenced by the Oregon Trail Memorial Association, which promoted the creation of trail associations in the West, George Albert called a group of friends who shared his historical interests to meet in his home in August 1930. Out of this came the organization of the Utah Pioneer Trails and Landmarks Association, which was organized the following month, September 1930. George Albert Smith was elected its first president. Organized as a nonprofit association, its stated purpose was to locate and mark historic trails and sites while honoring the pioneers who blazed them. By this means, the organizers hoped to promote the teaching and understanding of history in its "all American aspects," especially as it related to the growth and development of the western United States. To broaden its base of support, the association was expressly declared nonreligious and nonpolitical.

To provide seed money, contributions were solicited through the MIA organization. Local leaders were encouraged to hold what were called "plains dinners." Priced at only a dollar, these nevertheless proved to be a rich source of funds because the diners were asked to provide, prepare, and serve the food, and afterward to clean up and wash the dishes! At the same time, they were encouraged to purchase for a dollar or more Oregon Trail Memorial half dollars. By this means, augmented by several large corporate contributions and sizeable gifts from wealthy patrons, enough money was raised to carry on the work.

Ordinarily the association paid the cost of preparing and installing a monument but looked to local communities or groups to obtain, prepare, and maintain the site. Such joint participation reduced costs and helped protect against vandalism because of local self-interest and civic pride.

Significantly, the first project undertaken by Elder

Smith and his associates was a marker at Provo, Utah, commemorating the Catholic priests Escalante and Dominguez, who were the first Europeans to trek through the area. Like his father, John Henry, Elder Smith had a knack for bringing people of differing views and attitudes under a single umbrella and causing them to work together in unity. This gift, which was evident in his political activities and his work in the Sons of the American Revolution, was revealed again as he directed the trails association. Recognition of the two Catholic Fathers as its first project was a clear signal that relevance or importance to the Mormon Church would not be the ruling criterion in determining which persons or events would be memorialized; and such a signal galvanized the members of the association together regardless of their religious preference.

The Provo monument was the first of one hundred and twenty historical markers placed by the Utah Pioneer Trails and Landmarks Association. They extend from Nauvoo, Illinois, to San Diego, California, and will be found in most of the intervening states. What motorist traveling through the sparsely settled West has not welcomed the sight of one of these monuments along the highway? Reading the terse statement on the plaque, with its distinctive logo of an ox skull, in the place where it actually occurred, fixes a historical event in the mind in a way that reading about it in a book could never do. Reading about the ill-fated Donner Party, for instance, on a plaque in the barren desert west of Tooele, Utah, evokes a mental image of a harassed wagon train hurrying to cross the towering Sierra Nevadas before the snows fell. And reading a Jim Bridger plaque near the Bear River in Northern Utah brings up the scene of a grizzled mountain man tending his traps and curing and caching his pelts. It was just such an effect that George Albert Smith sought to create in organizing the Trails Association. And the substantial nature of the monuments, along with the watch care given to them by local communities and groups guaranteed that they would stand to teach and inspire many generations in the future.

To initiate such an organization, to give it form and substance and then direct it successfully toward a predetermined goal, required a rare combination of abilities. Creating the legal form, raising the necessary funds, and providing the proper context in which the people of varying backgrounds and motivations could work cooperatively was, in reality, the easiest part of the job. Next and more important came the staffing of the association. Seeing the simplicity of one of these monuments can mislead one to believe that only a skeleton organization was necessary to conceive and construct it. Quite the opposite was true. Behind the succinct narrative on the plaques stood a skilled research committee that had delved into the records to make sure that every statement was supported by solid historical facts. And because of the wide variety of individuals and subjects covered by the monuments, the research committee included many people with expertise in different phases of western history. Architectural help was needed to design the monuments, and legal assistance was needed to obtain the easements necessary to erect, maintain, and provide access to them. A government relations committee smoothed the way for contacts with local officials, and a publicity committee made sure that the activities were properly publicized.

George Albert Smith had all the instincts of a good publicist and showman. And he used his prestige and position to stimulate public support for the work of his association. A case in point was the dedication of a monument at Independence Rock, Wyoming, in June 1931, in honor of the Mormon Pioneers who had passed that way. News articles publicized the event long in advance, retelling stories about the Mormon exodus and about the sacrifices and privations of the pioneers. To dramatize what was to take place, Elder Smith organized an automobile caravan that left Salt Lake City on June 19. After stopping at Yellow Creek, where President Brigham Young became sick, and at Oil Spring, where the pioneers skimmed oil from the water to grease their wagons, the party camped

George Albert Smith, John Giles, and Rudger Clawson with Pioneer Trail marker

at Fort Bridger. Advance news of the caravan's itinerary attracted people from the surrounding area to the fort, where about a thousand people joined in a meeting around a huge bonfire that night. The next day the caravan drove to Independence Rock, where at night another bonfire meeting was held. The dedicatory services were held the following day, June 21. Elder Smith had persuaded President Heber J. Grant to attend; the Prophet arrived later in the day with his own party. Also in attendance were representatives of the governors of Utah and Wyoming. Local officials and hundreds of people from Casper and Rawlins, Wyoming, and other nearby communities joined in the services. In addition to the customary speeches, they included group singing led by Oscar A. Kirkham, who ten years later became a member of the First Council of the Seventy. John D. Giles played his violin, and Sister Manwaring played the accordian. The monument was unveiled by President Grant's daughter, Lucy Grant Cannon. Then the Prophet spoke and offered the dedicatory prayer.

143

Five years later, Elder Smith organized an even more impressive ceremony for the dedication of the heroic monument at the cemetery in Florence, Nebraska, honoring the hundreds of Latter-day Saints who died at Winter Quarters. Present were the governor of Nebraska, the mayor of Florence, many minor local officials and civic, professional, and business leaders. Elder Smith had persuaded the entire First Presidency to attend; they were accompanied from Salt Lake City by several hundred Latter-day Saints who traveled by train or automobile. The whole area, including neighboring Council Bluffs, Iowa, was caught up in the drama, which George Albert had skillfully stage managed, using the local press and radio to publicize the tragic events the monument memorialized. One of the side effects of the event that Elder Smith had deliberately sought was to improve the relations between the local population and the Church. The outpouring of public goodwill and the favorable publicity that attended the dedication opened many doors to the missionaries that had previously been closed.

George Albert returned home by automobile. He looked forward to the long drive in the crisp weather of late September. The Nebraska corn and wheat fields had ripened to a golden hue in the early autumn sun, and the vast grazing lands of western Nebraska and eastern Wyoming were turning sere and brown. It was an idyllic drive until the party reached Casper, Wyoming. There the weather changed. A cold front suddenly moved in from the northwest, bringing an unseasonable snowstorm not unlike the one that had caught the Willie and Martin handcart companies eighty years before. "We were right on the trail of the handcart companies," wrote Elder Smith on October 7, 1936, to his friend Harrold S. Alvord, "all the way from Casper to Three Forks and we had an idea of what they passed through when they met their disaster, one hundred and forty of them losing their lives from cold and starvation right along the same road that we were on." (GASC, box 89, folder 16.) But these modern-day travelers encountered a hazard unknown to the handcart pioneers. A car traveling east at a high rate of speed collided with Elder Smith's car, knocking it off the road. Fortunately, no one was injured seriously. But the damage to the car was such they had to hitch a ride to the nearest depot, where they caught a train to Salt Lake City.

During this period, Elder Smith commenced a project that took almost twenty years to complete. This was the monument at Whittingham, Vermont, commemorating the birthplace of President Brigham Young. Many aggravating problems delayed the project, mostly difficulties in obtaining clearances from government and civic agencies. Actually, this project had been conceived by Elder Smith many years before the trails association was organized. It gave him great pleasure to dedicate this monument on May 28, 1950, five years after he became president of the Church, honoring his distinguished predecessor. Two days later, President Smith participated in a ceremony in Washington, D.C., where a marble statue of Brigham Young was unveiled in the rotunda of the capitol. He offered the dedicatory prayer.

The most impressive project Elder Smith and his trails association conceived and completed was the This Is the Place Monument at the mouth of Emigration Canyon overlooking the Salt Lake Valley. The idea for the monument came to him in 1934. At the time, there was a small marker that had fallen into disrepair. Passing it one day, he felt it was wholly inadequate to commemorate one of the most significant events of the Mormon exodus. Soon after, George Albert commenced a letter-writing campaign to interest people of influence in the idea of a suitable memorial. He intended that it would commemorate not only the arrival of the Mormon pioneers in the valley but also the Indians, explorers, trappers, and Catholic fathers who had preceded them. Typical of the many letters he wrote was one to former Utah governor George H. Dern, a nonmember, who later became a high government official in Washington, D.C. In a letter dated December 29, 1934, he

shared with Governor Dern his concept of a large monument to be constructed on a knoll near the highway at the
mouth of Emigration Canyon and solicited his support.
(Ibid., box 58, folder 26.) Not long after, Elder Smith organized a committee to consider the feasibility of such a
memorial. Later he played a key role in persuading the
State of Utah to create an official Monument Commission,
which assured adequate funding and a broader base of
public support. President Heber J. Grant was appointed
as the first head of the commission with Elder Smith as
one of the vice-presidents and the executive in charge of
directing the work. Following the death of President Grant,
George Albert became its president.

From the beginning, the project bore the imprint of
Elder Smith's determination, persistence, dramatic flair,
and ecumenical spirit. Although it had official government
sanction and although George Albert was careful to involve
diverse elements in the community, there was opposition
to the monument, and many pitfalls were encountered
along the way. A chief obstacle was the acquisition of the
large site needed for a heroic memorial and the necessary
easements leading to it. This difficulty was compounded
by the fact that the site was near the border owned by the
United States government and was an integral part of the
choicest piece of undeveloped land in the valley. These
factors, added to the customary delays from government
red tape and inertia, made progress agonizingly slow and
uncertain. And there were questions about the design and
size of the monument. Elder Smith's original conception
was that it would be in the form of a large pyramid with
an appropriate plaque. But in considering the need to give
more recognition to nonmember influences, this gave way
to the form finally agreed on—a tower with people and
their mounts atop it, signifying the first Latter-day Saints
to see the valley, and on the wings of the tower a series
of figures representing the early explorers, trappers, and
missionaries. And this change in design greatly increased
the cost of the project. But Elder Smith patiently and cheer-

fully worked his way through these and a myriad of other problems. He was the personification of the Happy Warrior. He met obstacles and disappointments with a smile and a renewed effort to work around them. His position as a General Authority and as an officer of the government commission gave him enormous influence. And he was never reluctant to use this clout to achieve his objectives, although he was always careful not to arouse antagonism.

Thirteen years elapsed between the dream and its realization. The unveiling and dedication took place on July 24, 1947. Beforehand, the media was filled with stories about the monument and the people and events it memorialized. The commission, chaired by President Smith, had been busy feeding bits of historical data to the press and overseeing the many details connected with the event. One of these, so dramatic and unexpected, had all the earmarks of a George Albert Smith idea. For weeks in advance, near the hour of the dedication, seeds had been scattered around the base of the monument each morning to attract seagulls. By whatever means of communication birds use, word had spread throughout the seagull community that breakfast would be served each morning at the base of that interesting new structure near the mouth of Emigration Canyon. So on the day of the dedication, at the very moment when the monument was unveiled, the air was filled with dozens of seagulls, circling for the daily handout they had come to expect. And the agenda for the service also showed evidence of President Smith's handiwork. Among the speakers were a Catholic priest, a Protestant bishop, and a Jewish rabbi. Also, state, county, and city officials were prominently recognized. His terse diary entry about the event implies a deep satisfaction at the fulfillment of his dream. "A great day," he wrote. "Dedicated monument. Hillside covered with cars and people."

George Albert Smith was hardly a novice in staging dramatic events at the time the This Is the Place Monument was dedicated. Indeed, a flair for the dramatic seems to have been part of his makeup from the earliest years, as

147

shown by his childhood interest in staging theatricals in the barn behind the family home. And this tendency was reinforced when, as a young adult, he enjoyed dressing up in a garish outfit to sing funny songs. In his maturity, this characteristic revealed itself in an institutional way when in 1925 he spearheaded the plans for celebrating the fiftieth anniversary of the YMMIA. The highlight of this Jubilee Year was a mammoth parade on June 10, 1925, in Salt Lake City. Utah's capital had seldom seen anything to excel the pageantry in its streets on that occasion. The bands, banners, costumes, and floats typical of all parades were colorful and exciting. But the centerpiece of this parade, the thing that distinguished it from all others, was the mass participation of young people. An estimated ten thousand young men and women were included in the line of march. Rank upon rank of handsome and eager youths, the very flower of the Latter-day Saint community, passed in review before a large, appreciative audience, banked deep on both sides of the route of the parade. Such a sight against the background of martial music with its rhythmic drumbeat, bright uniforms, and colorful flags could hardly have failed to arouse a lump in the throat in even the most lethargic spectator. And the memory of such pageantry would never be erased from the mind of one who witnessed it, years later providing food for thought. Such is the hope of those engaged in the visual arts. And such, we can reasonably assume, was the hope of George Albert Smith in staging this parade.

Apart from the visual impact of the Jubilee parade is a symbolism that underscores one of the most significant aspects of Elder Smith's character and mission. While the main purpose of the Jubilee was to commemorate fifty years of an organization, George Albert, through his parade, converted it into a commemoration and celebration of people. The focus of his ministry was always on the individual. Unlike some who get caught up in organizational charts, statistics, and programs, he never failed to recognize that the Church is merely a vehicle designed to lift people here and to prepare them for a higher life hereafter.

Elder Smith's skill with people and pageantry and his intense interest in Church history presumably weighed heavily in his selection as the general chairman of the committee to direct the centennial celebration of the Church. His committee included two other future presidents of the Church, David O. McKay and Joseph Fielding Smith; his counselor in the YMMIA superintendency, Melvin J. Ballard; two members of the First Council of Seventy, B. H. Roberts and Rulon S. Wells; Presiding Bishop Sylvester Q. Cannon; and LeRoi C. Snow. The centerpiece of the celebration was a pageant titled "Message of the Ages," which was staged in the Salt Lake Tabernacle. A spacious platform was constructed in the west end of the building to accommodate the scenery and the large cast of players. The pageant depicted the influence of the gospel from the beginning. It was by far the most ambitious dramatic production of the Church to that time. The script, the music, and the staging were carefully monitored by Elder Smith and his committee throughout the long period of preparation and rehearsals. It was with understandable nervousness that they and the cast awaited the first performance. It was presented the evening of the last day of the April 1930 conference. During the preceding four days, the major addresses had focused on the unusual events surrounding the organization of the Church and its rapid growth in the century that followed. And the pageant was a fitting climax to the conference. It was received with critical praise and was enjoyed by capacity audiences during nightly performances for a month.

The last performance on May 5 brought a sense of relief and accomplishment to Elder Smith. Not only was the pageant a success, but it had been conceived, prepared, and promoted during a period when he had suffered a recurrence of the nervousness that had afflicted him years before. While the attack was not as severe or prolonged as those that had completely disabled him earlier, it was stressful and debilitating. Yet the exhilaration that accompanied the successful conclusion of the pageant produced a special aura of peace and well-being that the apostle savored.

Chapter Fourteen

The Final Testing

To hear George Albert Smith speak might have caused one to think his life consisted of an unbroken chain of happiness and good fortune. He was always positive and optimistic. He never complained, and he never mentioned in public his many adversities. Few people were aware of the variety and the complexity of the personal difficulties he endured. In the early years, most of his troubles related to health. And these continued throughout his life, although not to the same extent as before. Also, during the 1930s, Elder Smith and his family suffered from emotional trials that in some ways were more stressful than his physical illnesses. One of these concerned his daughter, Emily Stewart. Emily was called as a member of the Primary General Board in 1920 during the presidency of Louie B. Felt, who had served as head of the Primary for forty years. Because Emily Stewart was a registered nurse, Sister Felt appointed her to supervise the Primary Hospital for Crippled Children and sent her to Denver, Colorado, for a special hospital and medical training course. Following her return, she implemented many of the ideas she had learned in Denver, some of which were contrary to those held by May Anderson, then the secretary of the Primary, who had also studied convalescent hospitals.

When May Anderson succeeded Louie B. Felt in 1925 as president of the Primary, a conflict between her and Emily Stewart seemed unavoidable. Both women were able; both were strong willed; and both insisted that their views about hospital administration were correct. These differences, which lay dormant for six years, surfaced in late 1931. Emily, who was dissatisfied with the policies governing the Primary Children's Hospital, went to Presiding Bishop Sylvester Q. Cannon, who, with Elder David O. McKay, served as an advisor to the Primary organization. He advised that she discuss her concerns at a meeting of the general board, which she did on December 9, 1931. At that time, some members of the board who had shared Emily's views yielded to President May Anderson; but Emily and one other member refused to do so.

Unwilling to accept the decision of the Primary presidency and the majority of the board, Emily took her case to Elder McKay and Bishop Cannon on January 11, 1932. Their hands were tied. Since the controversy hinged on a difference of opinion, to side with Sister Stewart would have required the release of May Anderson or the rejection of her policies, which likely would have precipitated her resignation. Therefore, they turned Emily down and said her release would be necessary because she could not work harmoniously with the Primary president. Still unwilling to see that she had lost the argument and obviously not foreseeing the untenable position in which she would place her father, she went to him to tell her side of the story. Elder Smith was so upset that he wrote in his journal, "My nerves went to pieces and I didn't sleep at night." Indicating he had not understood the full implications of the controversy, he wrote the next day, "I am sorely grieved at the injustice to my daughter."

This, then, was the perspective from which Elder Smith

viewed the matter—that his daughter had suffered an injustice and was entitled to vindication. In his defense, it should be said that during the December meeting, the Primary presidency questioned Emily's veracity without apparent justification. On a personal level, therefore, there was seeming cause to take steps to remove any cloud from his daughter's reputation. But undoubtedly not understanding the full situation, he pursued the matter at an institutional level by seeking to have Emily reinstated on the Primary board. His first step was to meet with Elder McKay and Bishop Cannon on January 19, 1932. "We discussed Primary distress," he wrote on that day, "until my nerves were run down and I went home for the afternoon. Our meeting will I hope result in good." But, the differences were too deep seated to hope realistically that the matter could be patched up and Emily reinstated. This was borne out the next day when all the members of the board except two declined to rescind her release.

Attesting to his unswerving loyalty to Emily and his extraordinary persistence, eleven months later Elder Smith still hoped that his daughter would be vindicated by reinstatement on the board. "If Emily . . . could receive just treatment . . . I would be grateful," he wrote on Christmas Eve of 1932. Seven days later, following an unsuccessful meeting with Elder McKay and Bishop Cannon, he wrote regretfully of his "inability to make them feel further responsibility."

Having failed to gain his objective at the level of the Primary advisors, George Albert next took his case to a meeting of the Council of the First Presidency and Quorum of the Twelve on February 2, 1933. There he contended that a serious error had been made and that Emily should be vindicated. Elder Smith was "much distressed" at the negative reaction of the council to his plea. He next turned to a personal mediation between the aggrieved parties, arranging a meeting with the two advisors and the Primary presidency where Emily and her husband made a strong plea for Emily's reinstatement. Because of the protracted nature of the dispute and the feelings it had engendered, this was considered infeasible. However, Sister Anderson retracted her charge that there had been misrepresentation, and it was made plain that Emily Stewart was in no way under a cloud. Still dissatisfied, Elder Smith made one last approach. In a meeting with the First Presidency, he was told with finality by President Grant that he should let the matter rest. Obedient to this instruction, he never mentioned it again, nor did he harbor any resentment toward those who had opposed him on the issue. The mark of his character is shown by the fact that the one who had most consistently stood in the way of Emily's reinstatement, David O. McKay, was selected as a counselor when George Albert Smith became the president of the Church. And his characteristic of absolute family loyalty was shown clearly in this episode as he risked his personal reputation among the Brethren to try to satisfy the demands of a beloved, headstrong daughter.

In the midst of the misunderstandings over Emily's release from the Primary, illnesses in the family multiplied the pressures on Elder Smith. His own health, always fragile, was a constant concern. A stressful incident could suddenly drain his strength, making it necessary to retire to his home. "We discussed primary distress until my nerves were run down," he wrote on January 19, 1932, "and I went home for the afternoon. . . . Spent Wednesday at home trying to pull together." These intermittent sieges of illness ordinarily passed in a day or two, although a particularly powerful trauma could put him out of commission for weeks. But Elder Smith had lived so long with his physical disabilities that he had learned to cope with them and to gauge when it was necessary to withdraw, so as not to push himself into emotional exhaustion.

In many ways, he found it easier to endure his own physical problems than to watch his loved ones suffer. This was especially true of Lucy. It was during this period that Lucy entered the first phase of what proved to be six years of poor health, leading ultimately to her death. "Lucy very miserable," he wrote on January 2, 1932. "We took her to the hospital at night 7 p.m. I do hope she can pull together." Revealing the impact his dear wife's illness had on him, he concluded. "My nerves are nearly gone but am holding on the best I know how."

Lucy's illness was aggravated by attacks of neuralgia, diverting her attention from everything but the pain, which sometimes seemed unbearable. The effect of this, of course, was to upset the normal routine of the Smith household and to complicate George Albert's efforts to pull himself together during his occasional relapses.

Also during this period, Elder Smith's son-in-law George Elliot almost died of asphyxiation. An employee of the Utah–Idaho Sugar Company, the son-in-law was brought home from his office one day unconscious from the fumes of a defective stove. His condition was worsened by a mild case of multiple sclerosis that troubled him during most of his married life. The family, not knowing whether the incident would prove fatal, was greatly worried. And Elder Smith, who had genuine affection for both sons-in-law, was especially concerned, not only for the well-being of George Elliot but also for Edith, who was distraught over the accident. "Am trying to pull my nerves back to normal," he wrote soon after, "but am not strong." Fortunately, the victim recovered and was soon back at work.

In addition to his employment at the Utah–Idaho Sugar Company, George Elliot was also the secretary and bookkeeper of the Deseret Mortuary Company, work that he did in the evenings or on weekends to supplement the income from his regular job. Deseret, which was not as well known as other mortuaries in the area, had cut prices to attract business, a strategy that incurred the wrath of its competitors. Some of these, intent on eliminating this drain on their own business, had vigorously fought Deseret, attempting to persuade it to discontinue price cutting by whatever means. Learning that the principal owners of the company had sold so-called "burial certificates" to residents of Montana and had sent the certificates through the United States mail, these business competitors persuaded the U.S. district attorney in Billings, Montana, to bring an action for mail fraud, based upon the illegal mailing of the certificates. Indictments were handed down in Montana in April 1935 against the officers and directors of Deseret. Also caught in the toils of this legal net was George Albert's brother Winslow, who was a director of the company.

Word of the indictments reached Elder Smith while he was in New York City attending Boy Scout meetings. He was devastated by the news. Knowing little about the case and nothing about the abstruse workings of criminal justice, he was at first uncertain what to do. In this dilemma, he turned instinctively to Albert, who had completed graduate studies at Harvard University a few months before and who had already been appointed to the faculty of the Harvard graduate school of business. Father and son met the next day in Washington, D.C., where they hoped to confer with officials at the department of justice to unravel what had happened and decide what could be done to help. They made several appointments for the next day, none of which Elder Smith was able to keep. He was immobilized by the shock of what had happened and remained in bed at the home of Edgar and Laura Brossard while Albert kept the appointments alone. At the time, Edgar Brossard, whose wife was Matthew Cowley's sister, was a member of the U.S. Tariff Commission. His influence had opened many official doors for his friends in the past, but he was powerless to help solve the intricate legal problem in which Elder Smith's loved ones had become enmeshed. George Albert was once quoted as saying that "the mills of the Gods grind very slowly and exceedingly fine." If, indeed, the quote is accurate, it might well have been applied to the agonizingly slow movement of the wheels of justice as they ground out the fate of George Elliot and Winslow Smith.

For two years, the entire Smith family was kept in tension and uncertainty as the case in Billings moved with glacial slowness toward its conclusion. The defendants had to retain high-priced lawyers to represent them. Since George Elliot had limited resources, his father-in-law paid most of the legal fees he incurred. And because the venue of the case was in Montana, there were other heavy expenses for out-of-state travel and communications. Again, Elder Smith bore the brunt of these in aid of his embattled son-in-law. The apostle estimated that he spent nearly $6,000 during the course of this litigation. Such a sum, during the Great Depression, was a small fortune that George Albert could ill afford. But he doubtless would have spent twice that amount not only to protect the family reputation but also to remedy what he considered a gross miscarriage of justice. "These men are innocent of wrong doing," he wrote indignantly to his friend Gus Backman, "and it is a wicked act to jeopardize them as has been done." (Ibid., box 53, folder 32.) His outrage and family loyalty led him to exploit every available resource to help his kinsmen. Since he considered the charges against them to be contrived and vindictive, he was not reluctant to seek an extra-legal solution. So he used his vast influence to exert political and public pressure on the outcome. "[They] were not connected with the sale of the stock," wrote United States Senator William H. King, whom Elder Smith had interested in the case, "and had nothing whatever to do with the representations which were made by those who sold the stock in Montana." (Ibid., box 106, folder 34.) U.S. Senator Elbert Thomas was also called on for assistance, as were other political and community leaders. And George Albert rounded up an impressive cast of character witnesses who willingly paid their own way to Montana to help their friend and his family. Meanwhile, George Albert never lost an opportunity to speak out in defense of the accused and to drum up public support in their behalf.

The case finally came to trial in January 1937. Elder Smith and the family were shattered when all the defendants were convicted. The stress and excitement took its toll, especially on George Albert. He went to bed, where he remained for a month, suffering from nervous prostration and influenza. When the time came for sentencing, however, the family found cause for rejoicing. George Elliot was fined $1,000 but received no jail sentence. Winslow Smith was fined $2,000 but was also given a one-year suspended sentence. In writing to his son Albert about the outcome, Elder Smith told of the joy with which the family received the news that their loved ones would not be imprisoned. "When the word came I happened to be at Edith's and informed her of what had happened. Emily was there and Edith immediately said, 'Let's kneel down and thank the Lord for deliverance.' Her simple faith is always beautiful to me." (Ibid., box 62, folder 33.) Still later, through the combined efforts of Elder Smith and others, George Elliot and Winslow Smith received presidential pardons and their fines were refunded. This action brought the vindication the family sought and deserved. Winslow Smith and George Elliot were innocent victims, honest to the core, who had the incredible bad luck of being in the wrong place at the wrong time. As Senator King said in his letter to George Albert shortly after the indictments were handed down, "Their connection with the company was nominal and not active, and was not of such a character as to identify them with any acts or omissions which would come within the so-called mail fraud statutes." (Ibid., box 106, folder 34.)

During the month of the trial, Elder Smith and his family suffered what seemed to be a whole compendium of misfortune. He himself was not well. "My old time January John's Comforter is with me, 'lumbago,' " he confided to his journal on the seventh. Lucy was bedfast, as she had been for some time; and the nurse who attended her was injured in a fall in the home. Emily had been ill for several weeks, and Edith was expecting her second child. A grandson, Robert Stewart, was ill with a glandular infection. To top it off, George Albert was caught in a financial squeeze because of the heavy demands of his limited resources. "I have tried to be generous and helpful to others during the past year," he had written on the first day of 1936, "paying many hundreds of dollars to assist the needy in and out of my family." Of all these and other burdens, however, none was more stressful than to witness the gradual deterioration of Lucy's health. For several years, she had been in almost constant pain from arthritis and neuralgia. This crippled her so she could not perform her household duties. And by 1937, she required constant care. As early as 1933, however, her condition had seemed precarious. "Lucy quite distressed," George Albert wrote on May 9 of that year. "I am at a loss to know what more to do. We have had the advice and care of three physicians. Hospital treatment and observation for several days. A trained nurse has been with her day and night for four months but she does not appear to improve much, if any. She appears to derive temporary benefit from administration." To see the once vivacious sweetheart of his youth become a helpless invalid was devastating. Even by the standards of that day, she was still comparatively young. But, at a time in life when she could have traveled with her husband, enjoying his company, basking in the love and admiration showered on him as he visited stakes and missions, and making new friends and acquaintances throughout the Church, she was confined at home, and he was bereft of a traveling companion. But, they both endured these deprivations with stoic silence. Only seldom were they heard to complain. And then, invariably, they would counterbalance any mild protest with words of appreciation and praise. So, on the last day of 1936 when he had ticked off the long list of infirmities with which members of his family were then afflicted, he ended with the incongruous statement, "I am thankful to the Lord for my many blessings."

But the Smiths did enjoy many blessings, and they savored each one. The choicest of these was connected with their family. Each anniversary or other significant event was the cause for a celebration. One of these occurred

Lucy Woodruff Smith

on July 6, 1935, when Albert was sealed in the Salt Lake Temple to Ruth Nowell by Elder Smith. Every adult member of the family was present to witness the nuptials and to share the joy of the occasion with the newlyweds. Yet, even that special event was alloyed with the spectre of Lucy's advancing illness; she had to be carried up the stairs to the sealing room in a chair. Every wrenching movement of the chair sent throbs of pain through her arthritic body. "Lucy stood the ordeal very well," wrote her husband, "but is nervous."

Because of the difficulty of moving Lucy about, and to spare her the intense pain she invariably suffered when she ventured out, family celebrations were ordinarily held in the parents' home. Sunday, April 4, 1937, George Al-

160

bert's sixty-seventh birthday, was such an occasion. The whole clan, except Albert and his wife, who were in the East, gathered at the Smith home. It was a double-barreled affair. In addition to honoring the family patriarch, its purpose was to confer a name and a blessing on Edith's new baby girl. It was a special day. The recent conclusion of George Elliot's legal nightmare had brought an aura of peace and contentment to the entire family. This was enhanced by the miracle of the new infant, whose arrival coincided with the stirrings of spring on Yale Avenue and in the canyon behind the Smith home. The name selected for the baby, Nancy Lucy, honored the ailing grandmother. And the family patriarch was honored when he was asked to name and bless the child. After light refreshments and visiting, the members of the family departed early to avoid tiring Lucy. Soon after, they received the shocking new that she had suffered a major heart attack. For ten days, Lucy lingered near death. Albert was summoned from Boston on the assumption that her passing was imminent. But the crisis soon passed, and by April 24, George Albert was able to record hopefully, "She is much stronger today." And on their wedding anniversary, May 25, he wrote pensively, "We were married 45 years ago today."

Lucy Smith battled death for several more months. It was an uneven contest, for the odds were heavily against her. The long years of illness, her advancing age, and an increasing sense of frustration had sapped her strength and weakened her will to live. Discouraging entries in George Albert's journal and correspondence trace her steady decline. "Lucy not improving," he wrote on June 7. A month later, he reported that his wife "suffered all day with neuralgia." On July 12, he wrote to his friend German Ellsworth, describing Lucy's condition. "This morning when I left, Sister Smith was so weak that she could hardly speak loud enough for me to hear." He shared the sense of futility her long illness had created and his resignation to the inevitability of her death. "Long ago I told our Heavenly Father that if He is not going to heal her, I wish He would relieve her from her pains and distress and let her go home." (Ibid., box 60, folder 19.) Three days later, another infirmity was identified when the frail patient was diagnosed as having glaucoma in her right eye. "Lucy sleeping most of the last 48 hours," wrote Elder Smith on August 17. "Doctor says she may remain that way indefinitely." However, she threw off this comatose condition several weeks later and seemed to rally. "Lucy is doing her best to get well," he wrote on September 27. But this signaled only a meaningless pause in the inexorable journey toward death. "Lucy weaker again," wrote the diarist eleven days later. "Her heart flutters and throbs more today." And on October 14, this: "Lucy had a sinking spell and I was excused from council meeting."

In the midst of Lucy's travails, George Albert continued to suffer intermittent sieges of the old illness. "Awoke at 4 a.m.," he wrote on August 7, "my heart being very irregular. I could feel the pulse in my head. Am not at all well." Notwithstanding his infirmities and Lucy's frailty, Elder Smith continued to perform his church duties. Shortly before Pioneer Day in 1937, he reorganized the Pioneer stake presidency, releasing President Harold B. Lee, a promising young leader who four years later would join George Albert in the apostleship and thirty-five years later would follow him into the Prophetic office. And on September 27, he conferred with Utah's governor, Henry Blood, to consider the "appointment of a committee to prepare plans etc. for a monument at This Is The Place."

Away from the death struggle he watched each day at home, he attended work as usual, concealing his anxieties about Lucy and trying to ignore his own recurring illnesses. To the casual acquaintance or those who knew him only by reputation, he projected the same image of poised self-confidence as before, seemingly immune from the trials and tribulations that afflicted others.

But those who knew him well, those associated with him in the inner circle of Church leadership, were aware of the struggle and sought to buoy him up. Expressions of love and support from such as these touched him deeply and sometimes evoked a response that revealed his feelings. Such was the effect of a thoughtful note from President J. Reuben Clark commiserating about Elder Smith's misfortunes. "When a man has had distress in his home as long as I have," wrote George Albert in answer, "I feel that people generally take it as a matter of course; and occasionally when a man or woman who is very dear to me expresses sympathy as you have done and as your dear wife has done repeatedly, it is more than appreciated and you must know that it helps over the rough road that one is travelling." (Letter of October 29, 1937, ibid., box 60, folder 13.)

The journey over the rough road ended for Lucy just a week later. On November 5, 1937, Elder Smith went to the Yale Ward, a few blocks from home, to speak at the funeral of his friend James B. Wallis. When he awakened that morning, he found that Lucy was "just recovering from a nervous attack." The ever-present nurse was there to help the fragile little patient, readjusting the bed clothing, smoothing her hair, and generally bringing order out of another chaotic night of a seemingly endless illness. The odor of Lucy's assorted medications hung heavy in the sick chamber as George Albert entered to kiss her good-bye and to whisper words of endearment. It was a repetition of what had occurred hundreds of times in the past few years. The only thing different about it was that it was the last time. As the husband stepped into the brisk air of a Salt Lake autumn, thanksgiving weather, he was unaware that he would return to the home a widower.

Elder Smith was the last speaker at the Wallis funeral. As he sat down after eulogizing his friend and speaking words of comfort to the family, he was handed a note saying he was needed at home immediately. "I left the chapel at once," he wrote later, "but my darling wife had breathed her last before I arrived home. She was passing away while I was talking at the funeral."

Although Lucy's death came as no surprise, it still created shock and sadness in the family. "I am bereft of a devoted helpmeet and will be lonely without her," wrote Elder Smith. "While my family are greatly distressed, we are comforted by the assurance of a reunion with mother if we remain faithful." And the assurance that the separation was merely temporary was a great solace. "The Lord is most kind," wrote the apostle, "and has taken away every feeling of death for which I am exceedingly grateful."

Albert, the only child living out of state, was immediately informed about his mother's death. He arrived in time for the funeral four days later. The Yale Ward chapel overflowed with relatives and friends who assembled to honor Lucy Woodruff Smith and her family. The president of the Church, Heber J. Grant, was there, as were all the other General Authorities in the city. The two brethren selected to speak, Melvin J. Ballard and J. Golden Kimball, had been especially close to the deceased. Lucy had served on the general board of the YWMIA during all the years Elder Ballard served as a counselor to Elder Smith in the YMMIA superintendency. Because these two boards had worked almost as a single unit, Lucy had looked on Elder Ballard as one of her file leaders and as a special friend because of the relationship between him and her husband. And ever since the days early in her marriage when she had worked in the mission field under his leadership, Lucy had looked on J. Golden Kimball as a surrogate father.

The eulogies given at the funeral, or the expressions of condolence made later, revealed aspects of her life that were generally unknown. The concentrated attention focused on her husband as a member of Twelve had tended to obscure her achievements and talents. Not only had she served on the YWMIA board during the entire period of her husband's tenure as YMMIA superintendent, but she had also served in that position since 1908 and was still serving at the time of her death twenty-nine years later. Before that, she had served as the president of the Seventeenth Ward and Salt Lake Stake YWMIA. She directed this auxiliary in all of Great Britain and Europe during the time Elder Smith served as European Mission president; and, as already noted, while there she represented the YWMIA at the International Council of Women Congress in Oslo, Norway. She was also a charter member of the Daughters of the American Revolution. Lucy Smith had a native eloquence and was deeply spiritual. A friend once said to her, "You need only to open your mouth and the words seem to flow without effort." Perhaps the most succinct appraisal of her character was made by a long-time associate in the work of the YWMIA. "She was our friend," wrote Clarissa Beasley, "our loyal understanding friend. Simple and modest in dress and in conduct, one felt instinctively that any form of sham or insincerity was out of place in her presence. She was thoroughly genuine." (*Improvement Era,* 41 [January 1938]: 44.)

Undoubtedly Lucy's most significant work was that performed in the home, away from the spotlight of public attention and acclaim. There she managed the Smith household with calm efficiency and directed the training and discipline of the children. Because of the frequent illness of her husband and his frequent absences from home on Church and civic assignments, these domestic responsibilities fell chiefly on her. A slender household budget, the result of her husband's modest living allowance from the Church, dictated that she become a jack of all trades around the home, making minor repairs and solving unexpected mechanical problems on an emergency basis. "Lucy was . . . wise and able and ambitious," wrote Richard R. Lyman on learning of her death. "She did the work of a man as map maker and office woman when in her youth. She had a clear mathematical mind. She always exhibited a great interest in anything of an engineering nature. And thus experienced and well trained, she came into your life and home to be your fond and devoted wife, the mother of your children." (GASC, box 61, folder 3.)

Despite this practical bent and the menial household tasks thrust upon her during her husband's illness or absence, Lucy was the epitome of charm and femininity. Her

165

home was always tastefully decorated. Her love of beautiful flowers fueled an interest in gardening, and in time she became an amateur horticulturist, avidly interested in her flower garden and other plantings around the home. If one believes that personality traits and work habits are rooted in heredity, it would be easy to trace these qualities in Lucy Smith's makeup to her maternal grandfather, Wilford Woodruff. Throughout a long life, he showed a keen interest in husbandry, working industriously in his garden when his busy schedule allowed. And since Lucy had been reared in his home, she had watched him over the years, tending his plants and fruit trees, pruning, weeding, and fertilizing.

Whatever the source, George Albert's wife possessed a wide variety of skills that made his home life enjoyable and relieved him of many domestic burdens he otherwise would have had to carry. But, of greater importance to him was her loving concern for his welfare, her solicitous attention to his every need, and her devoted interest in his ministry. Lucy Woodruff Smith was her husband's most avid supporter. She understood the importance of his ecclesiastical calling. And having been reared in the home of an apostle who later became the president of the Church, she had special insight into the needs of one who occupied the position held by her husband. So to George Albert, Lucy was much more than a wife and homemaker; she was a companion, confidant, and counselor. Within the limits of his duty of confidentiality, he could share with her things of a sensitive or troubling nature, knowing that she would not divulge them to others and that the counsel she gave would be wise and reliable.

As Lucy's physical ailments multiplied, she was less able to perform the duties she had routinely done in the early years of her marriage. This had interrupted the peaceful routine of the household and imposed heavier burdens on George Albert, which taxed his frail constitution to the limit. And toward the end, Lucy's life seems to have become an unwanted burden to herself. Apparently recognizing that her age and accumulated infirmities made it unlikely she could be restored to health, Lucy seems to have yearned for death during her last days. To the extent this is true, her passing came as a blessed release. But for George Albert, it came as a profound shock, even though it was not unexpected. "It is a lonesome house I am in tonight," he wrote on the day following the funeral. "But my family are here to minimize, as far as possible, the sorrow of parting."

Chapter Fifteen

A Time of Healing

To suddenly sever a bond that had endured for over forty-five years was devastating. Elder Smith tried to put the best possible face on the situation and adjust to a life of celibacy. Though he was only sixty-seven years old and would have been an attractive suitor to many single women, George Albert seems to have decided at the time of Lucy's death never to remarry. And so he began to live alone, with his daughters and employed domestic help taking care of the home and his needs. He reflected with pleasure on his long, happy marriage with Lucy and confidently expected that their relationship would be resumed when he finished his work and passed to the other side. He took comfort in the knowledge that theirs had been a union of love and respect. As his friend Richard R. Lyman had said in his letter of condolence at the time of Lucy's death, "I don't know that there ever was a more perfectly mated couple than Lucy and yourself." (GASC, box 61, folder 3.)

What remained for Elder Smith were happy memories with no regrets, confidence in a joyful reunion in the fu-

168

ture, and much work. The greatest therapy to help him over the difficult transition was his apostolic calling. Soon after the funeral, he attended a stake conference in Ephraim, Utah, and then traveled to the Eastern States, holding a stake conference in Chicago en route. In New York City, he attended a meeting of the National Executive Board of the Boy Scouts of America and then traveled to Boston for a visit with Albert and Ruth, who presented him with a new grandchild.

While in New York, George Albert visited the famous Mormon pugilist, Jack Dempsey. During his reign as the heavyweight champion of the world, Dempsey had been known as the "Manassa Mauler" because he was born in the small Mormon town of Manassa, Colorado. Elder Smith and his brothers had taken an interest in the fighter because of his Mormon roots and periodically contacted him to express their friendship and support. And as if to demonstrate his cosmopolitan interests, while he was in Boston, Elder Smith paid a courtesy call on James B. Conant, the president of Harvard University, where Albert was a member of the faculty.

On returning home, he found the same lonely house he had left. During all the years of his service as a General Authority, he had always found Lucy or one or more of the children there to greet him and to welcome him to the comfort of his home after a long trip. It was there he could relax, away from the glare of public attention he always received while on the road. But an empty house gave him no comfort. These considerations and the problems of the security and maintenance of the home during Elder Smith's absence from the city led to the decision that Emily and her family would move in with him. This arrangement also provided him with someone who could serve as a hostess when he entertained. Emily, who was an excellent manager and who had a good sense of protocol, was well suited for this role. And her husband, who by now was an established attorney and who had always maintained the attitude of a natural son, wholeheartedly approved of the arrangement.

Yet, even after the Stewarts moved into his home, George Albert was still lonely and restless. Perhaps sensing this, President Grant gave him an assignment to help ease the traumatic transition through which he was passing: he was assigned to tour the missions of the South Pacific. Before George Albert left in January 1938, the Prophet gave him a blessing. In it, he expressed thanks that Elder Smith's life had been preserved, even though many doubted he would live. He promised him health and protection during his long journey and urged him to rely on his traveling companion, Rufus K. Hardy, to conserve his strength. Elder Hardy, a member of the First Council of Seventy, was waiting for him in Hawaii.

Elder Smith was in a festive mood as he left Salt Lake City by train on what would be a six-month tour. With him were several Church members who were also traveling to the Pacific. Two of these, Matthew Cowley and George Q. Morris, would later become members of the Twelve. Elder Cowley, whose wife and daughter were with him, was traveling to New Zealand, where he would become the president of the New Zealand Mission. Elder Morris, superintendent of the YMMIA, was going to Hawaii with his wife to participate in Church meetings.

The travelers boarded their ship at San Francisco, which even then was feverishly preparing for the World Fair to be held there the following year. A giant landfill was being completed in the bay to hold most of the exhibition buildings and entertainment facilities. As the huge line maneuvered through the crowded bay and the Golden Gate to the open sea, Elder Smith began his long voyage in the Pacific.

The name of this ocean implies the main difference between it and the often turbulent Atlantic. But though comparatively pacific, it is rough enough occasionally to give a landlubber a tinge of seasickness. So, as the huge ship breasted the waves and groundswells off the coast,

Elder Smith and most of his friends suddenly lost their appetites. And some lost more than that. But the discomfort was short lived, and after a day at sea, they settled into a relaxed, comfortable routine. This included turns on the deck for exercise, reading, visiting, and watching the gliding, swooping albatross that followed the ship for several days.

The long periods of uninterrupted leisure were like a soothing balm to George Albert, whose nerves had been taut for so many months during Lucy's final illness. To have no duties whatsoever, no appointments, no schedules, and no trains to catch put him in a reflective mood that eased the tension he had suffered for so long.

Although he was free from official duties, Elder Smith was not idle during the voyage to Hawaii. There was much to occupy his mind. The presence aboard of George Q. Morris, newly called as the superintendent of the YMMIA, afforded the opportunity to counsel about this organization. Because of his long association with the YMMIA, Elder Smith had a somewhat proprietary attitude toward it. He therefore welcomed the opportunity to discuss it and to impart information and counsel to the one who now had the principal responsibility to chart its course. He also was pleased to spend unhurried time with Matthew Cowley, whom he had known from his youth. Matthew's father, Matthias, had lived in the Seventeenth Ward where George Albert had lived for so many years. And for two years, Elder Smith and Matthias had served together as members of the Quorum of the Twelve. Moreover, Elder Smith had set Matthew apart as a missionary to New Zealand in 1914 and had performed his sealing to Elva Cowley in the Salt Lake Temple several years later. There was, therefore, a special bond between these two, a bond that would be strengthened even more when, eight years later, George Albert Smith called Matthew Cowley to fill the vacancy in the Twelve created when Elder Smith became the president of the Church.

At Honolulu, the travelers were given the customary

Hawaiian reception replete with leis, loving greetings, and warm alohas. Elder Smith was not a stranger to the outgoing and charming ways of the Polynesian people. He had visited the Hawaiian Islands in November 1936 on an assignment to attend a conference of the Oahu Stake. Then he had first become acquainted with stake president Ralph E. Woolley, the first president of this the 113th stake in the Church—the first outside the North American continent—which was organized June 30, 1935. During that visit, he had endeared himself to the Woolley family when he gave President Woolley's wife, Romania, a special health blessing shortly before she underwent surgery. Her illness had prevented Elder Smith from enjoying the hospitality for which Romania Hyde Woolley had become famous, earning her the title "queen of hostesses," conferred by President David O. McKay when he was in the islands. During his visit in 1938, however, George Albert was treated to the gracious ministrations of this granddaughter of Orson Hyde; she was not only a hostess without peer but also a noted violinist who once served as the concertmaster of the Honolulu symphony orchestra.

While in Honolulu, Elder Smith presided at a conference of the Oahu Stake. Later, he crossed the island to visit the beautiful temple at Laie and then flew to Kauai to see the Saints there and hold a special meeting with them. Everywhere he went during the ten days he was in the Hawaiian Islands, the apostle was greeted with the warmth and enthusiasm for which the Hawaiian Saints are noted. In his case, the treatment he received was extraordinary because of the lingering fame of his kinsman, Joseph F. Smith, fondly remembered as "Ioseppa," who had first come to the islands as a boy missionary and who later came there in exile as a member of the First Presidency during the dark days of the underground.

Elder Smith's traveling companion, Rufus K. Hardy, whom he met at Honolulu, was well known to members of the Church throughout the South Pacific. He had served there as a missionary for many years and in 1934 had been inducted into the First Council of the Seventy. Like George Albert Smith, this dignified man wore a mustache and a well-trimmed goatee. Quiet, competent, and dreamy eyed, he would be the apostle's guide, interpreter, and confidant during the next six months.

This distinguished-looking pair, accompanied by Matthew Cowley and his family, boarded the *Mariposa* in early February 1938 at Pearl Harbor. Since a Polynesian farewell is hard to distinguish from a Polynesian welcome, an onlooker would have been hard put to know whether the travelers were coming or going, except for the direction of the ship. It maneuvered through the harbor, densely crowded with naval and commercial craft, across the wide belt of white coral that gives this famous port its name and out into the open sea.

The *Mariposa's* skipper first aimed her toward Tutuila, a small speck of an island in the Pacific southwest of Hawaii. By now, George Albert had gained his sea legs and was fully adjusted to the alternate pitching and rolling of the ship. He settled comfortably into the customary shipboard routine, sleeping, reading, visiting, and walking the deck. Although sumptuous meals were served to the passengers, the apostle ate sparingly, supplementing what little he took from the ship's fare with a special concoction of cereal he carried with him in his bags. Through long years of illness, he had learned what foods were congenial to his delicate system, so he always ate with discriminating care.

This pleasant routine was interrupted a few days out of Honolulu when a radiogram advised Elder Smith that his sister, his mother's namesake, Sarah Pond, had passed away. Because he had acted as a surrogate father to all the children after John Henry's death, George Albert mourned doubly at the news, regretting that he was unable to be present at the funeral to offer comfort to Sarah's family. But, his mourning was not of the conventional kind. It was intermixed with a sort of fatalistic stoicism and with a realistic understanding of the nature and purpose of physical death as taught by the Church. Sarah was all right; she had safely passed through the portal everyone must enter someday. Any mourning, therefore, was reserved for those left behind who would have to negotiate the remainder of the mortal journey without her comforting presence.

Looming up out of the sea to a height of two thousand feet, the mountains of Tutuila were visible long before the *Mariposa* eased into the harbor at Pago Pago, the largest city on the island and the capital of American Samoa. Although not the highest of Tutuila's volcanic peaks, Mt. Pioa attracts more attention from visitors than the others because of the cloud cover that usually hovers over it like a halo. Nicknamed "the rainmaker" because of the seemingly constant presence of clouds brooding around its crest, Mt. Pioa symbolizes the most striking aspect of Tutuila discovered by George Albert and members of his party— rain. To one like Elder Smith, accustomed to Utah's arid climate, it was almost inconceivable that Pago Pago was drenched with an annual rainfall averaging more than half an inch a day!

Ashore, Elder Smith and his companions found the results of Tutuila's abundant rainfall. The island was heavily laden with lush vegetation, tall ferns and tropical trees; and in the cultivated areas, coconuts, bananas, pineapples, papayas, and breadfruits grew in profusion. The constant rains seemed to have banished dust from the island, and mud was in short supply because of the porous volcanic mass of which the island is composed. And this feature of Tutuila, at its lower levels at least, had essentially eliminated rivers from its topography. While in the highlands gushing streams could be found, their waters practically disappeared before reaching the sea as they percolated into the permeable soil.

This was a new world to Elder Smith. And the culture he found was equally new and intriguing. He became acutely aware of the cultural differences between his home and the islands when he attended the forty-ninth annual

Samoa conference, or Huitau, in Pago Pago. The members of the Church from around the island and the neighboring islands gathered for an event unlike anything the apostle had witnessed before. While there was conventional singing and preaching of the kind to which he had become accustomed over the years, these seemed overshadowed by the extravagant native dances, chants, and songfests with which the usual worship services were interspersed. This was made more dramatic by the colorful costumes of the worshipers and their outgoing and sometimes boisterous mannerisms and gestures. With all this, he found these friendly Saints among the most genuine and lovable of any he had met.

Elder Smith paid the usual courtesy call on the governor of the island, who received the distinguished visitor with appropriate pomp and pageantry. He also visited the homes of some of the Saints who lived in grass huts in a beautiful setting near the sea. Here he was received with less ceremony but with more affection as they sat in an elongated circle to feast and to fraternize.

Leaving Tutuila, the *Mariposa* now steered toward Auckland, New Zealand. En route there, it made an intermediate stop at Fiji, where the Mormon apostle was welcomed warmly.

At Aucklund, Elder Smith installed Matthew Cowley as the president of the New Zealand Mission. Here the Mormon Maoris greeted the apostle and their new Tumuaki with a display of native enthusiasm and pageantry even more extravagant than the one demonstrated at Tutuila. What made it so was the presence of their old Tumuaki, Elder Rufus K. Hardy, who had become like a father to them during the years he had served in the Pacific. That the old Tumuaki had become a member of the First Council of Seventy was a matter of intense pride among the Maoris, who assumed a proprietary attitude toward "their own" General Authority. That pride was wounded seven years later when Elder Hardy passed away at the comparatively young age of sixty-six. A memorial service was held for him in Auckland shortly after his death on March 7, 1945. While one of the speakers was bemoaning the death of Elder Hardy and their loss of a "representative" among the General Authorities, he stopped and, turning to Tumuaki Cowley, said, "Wait a minute. There's nothing to worry about. When President Cowley gets home, he'll fill the first vacancy in the Council of the Twelve Apostles, and we'll still have a representative among the authorities of the church." (As quoted in Smith, *Matthew Cowley, Man of Faith*, p. 162.) Because of his long acquaintance with the Maori people and their spiritual sensitivity, Matthew Cowley knew this was not a chance remark. He said of them, "These natives live close to God. They have some kind of power. I guess it's because they accept miracles as a matter of course. They never doubt anything." (Ibid.) It therefore came as no surprise to him when, only a few days after returning from New Zealand, he was called to the Twelve by President George Albert Smith to fill the vacancy created when he became the president of the Church.

All this lay in the distant future as Elder Smith held meetings in Auckland with the two Tumuakis and the Maori Saints at the time Matthew Cowley was installed as the president of the New Zealand Mission. Soon after, he and Elder Hardy boarded their ship for the thousand-mile voyage to the northwest, through the Tasman Sea, to Sydney, Australia, that country's oldest and largest city. At sea, the ship's captain asked the two distinguished-looking elders to conduct a religious service on Sunday. They did so obligingly in true ecumenical spirit. The music was provided by a string trio of professional musicians who were on board; the congregation sang Episcopalian hymns; and Elder Smith delivered a lively sermon laden with good Mormon doctrine. Among the worshipers were members of a circus family on their way to performances in Australia. The most extraordinary of these were a woman who was reported to tip the scales at 740 pounds and a man with a face that was half black and half white.

Sydney, named in 1788 after Lord Thomas Townsend

Sydney, England's home secretary at the time, began as a scruffy convict colony, the home of many of England's felons who had been victimized by Britain's rigid criminal code. Now, a hundred and fifty years later, Elder Smith and his companions found it a modern metropolis of striking beauty. Built on low-lying hills surrounding the harbor, the city seemed to sparkle under Sydney's brilliant sunlight and blue skies. Had they known about it, the two Mormon elders doubtless would have concurred in Captain Arthur Phillip's appraisal of this huge harbor, with its innumerable bays and inlets. On seeing it for the first time in 1788, the famed explorer fired off a dispatch to the home secretary, declaring it "the finest harbor in the world, in which a thousand sail of the line may ride in the most perfect security." Showing as much savvy in diplomacy as in seamanship, he then named the little colony he established "Sydney Cove," which still remains the heart of the modern city that grew up around it.

The travelers' arrival in Sydney on February 21, 1938, marked the beginning of a six-week stay in Australia. During that time, they traveled 8,800 miles by train and automobile. They visited all the major cities on the east and south coasts, as well as Perth on the west, called by some the most isolated city in the world. Their guides were Elder and Sister Thomas D. Rees, who presided over the Australian mission.

At Sydney, Elder Smith commenced a routine that, with few variations, was followed in all the cities he visited in Australia. Meetings were held with the missionaries, who were hungry to hear of news from home and to be built up in their spirits and resolve. Then came preaching services with the small clusters of Saints found in these cities, most of whom had never before met a General Authority, not to mention two at once. These meetings were always held in rented facilities, as the Church then owned no chapels in the entire country. At Sydney, George Albert laid the foundation to change this as he discussed plans for a chapel with President Rees and the local leaders. After meetings with missionaries and members, the next priority was to visit local government, religious, and community leaders. Interspersed with these activities were occasional jaunts to inspect things of historic or current interest. So, while at Sydney, the two brethren visited a nearby animal preserve where they enjoyed the antics of Australia's two most famous indigenous animals, the kangaroo and the koala bear.

Traveling north to Brisbane, the main port and capital of Queensland, the visitors found another vibrant, modern city that also began its life as a dreary penal colony. Here the two General Authorities paid a courtesy call on Archbishop James Duhig of the Church of England, who received them with restrained cordiality. Any coolness in the archbishop's demeanor would not have derived from concern about inroads on the membership of his church by Mormon proselyting, as the Latter-day Saints had only a tenuous foothold there at the time. Instead, it likely would have come from the condescension often shown by those in positions of entrenched power or privilege toward an unknown newcomer.

In Brisbane, Elder Smith repeated a practice that had become habitual with him since his emergence as a dominant leader of Scouting in the United States. He called on chief Scout executives there to exchange pleasantries and share information about the status of Scouting in their respective countries. And in the process, of course, he found opportunity to cultivate friendliness and tolerance toward the Church. Such was his impact on the chief Scouters in Brisbane that they arranged for him to speak on Scouting over the radio, an experience that was repeated in other Australian cities during his tour.

And in Brisbane, Elder Smith performed another habitual ritual when he called on a relative to strengthen family ties. In this case, the relative was a member of the Reorganized Church, Ina Inez Smith Wright, the daughter of Alexander Smith, who was one of the sons of the Prophet Joseph Smith. At first, this mother of ten children was

178

extremely shy, not quite knowing what this official of the "Utah Church" had in mind. Elder Smith's friendly, disarming manner soon dissolved her reticence, however, as the pair enjoyed tracing relationships and sharing Smith family lore.

Traveling south of Sydney through the coastal city of Wollongong, Elder Smith's party went inland in a southwesterly direction to Canberra, the federal capital of the commonwealth of Australia. Here they were witnesses to the emergence of a new metropolis. It was only eleven years before that Canberra had been officially designated as the nation's capital, robbing Melbourne of that distinction. Slowed by the debilitating effect of the world-wide depression, the development of Canberra had lagged during the early 1930s. But at the time of George Albert's visit, the tempo of construction had quickened, although the city was still in an embryonic state. He wrote that it had "a few attractive buildings and a few residences and business places," but that it was almost entirely "devoid of population."

Traveling on to Melbourne, recently spurned by Australia's legislature, Elder Smith discovered a thriving city that, unlike the origins of Sydney and Brisbane, was founded upon the restless energies of two private citizens, John Batman and John P. Fawkner. These shrewd entrepreneurs had negotiated with the indigenous tribes for the purchase of large tracts of land on the northern shore of Port Phillip Bay. The city that grew on these acquired lands reflected the spirit of enterprise and daring of its founders, giving it a character different from most of Australia's other coastal cities. Here the apostle and Elder Hardy held the usual meetings with the missionaries and with a small knot of Latter-day Saints who were awed by the presence of two General Authorities.

Leaving Melbourne, the travelers moved on to Adelaide, the first Australian city formally organized according to law. Legally incorporated ninety-eight years before Elder Smith's arrival, Adelaide was named in honor of Queen

Adelaide, consort of the British King William IV. Arriving there in late February at the height of its summer season, the apostle enjoyed the city's balmy temperature, which hovered near seventy degrees, reminiscent of the Mediterranean climate of pleasant Italy.

Crossing the Mt. Lofty and Flinders ranges, the tourists headed toward Perth on the west coast. Along their path lay the famous Nullarbor Plain, whose descriptive Latin name meaning "no tree" suggests the character of the terrain through which they traveled. The absence of trees on the plain and the scattered presence of saltbrush and bluebrush reminded George Albert of the western United States and aroused nostalgic feelings. These feelings were heightened when groups of Australian aborigines were encountered; these, like some American Indians, were trying to eke out an existence on barren, unproductive land. And like San Francisco on the west coast of the United States, Elder Smith found that Perth owed much of its early growth to the discovery of gold in the interior of the state. On learning that a former member of the Seventeenth Ward was working as an engineer in the mines, George Albert sent a telegram inviting his friend to meet him in Perth, which he did. While this old acquaintance was flattered to think the apostle would single him out this way, he probably knew him well enough to realize that this was how George Albert Smith treated all his friends, regardless of their station in life.

On leaving Australia during the first week in April, the apostle wrote that "kindness and courtesy" had been offered everywhere. Arriving in Auckland on April 4, 1938, his sixty-eighth birthday, he found a similar outpouring of love awaiting him. He also found more than fifty congratulatory cablegrams and letters. Deeply touched by this demonstration of love, he confided to his journal, "Surely I am a favored man. . . . I am grateful for friends who help me on my way by saying kind things of and to me. I desire to be worthy of such blessings."

As President Matthew Cowley had had six weeks to

become acquainted with his new duties, he was now prepared to conduct the visitors on a tour of the New Zealand Mission. Soon after the Brethren arrived from Australia, the party left Auckland by automobile on a four-week tour. Their destination was Wellington, on the southern shore of the north island. The procedure was similar to that followed in Australia, with missionary and member meetings being held all along the way. The main difference here was the composition of the Church membership. While in Australia most of the members traced their ancestry to Europe or North America, in New Zealand most of the members were of Maori descent. Therefore, the meetings with the New Zealand Saints were far different from those in Australia. The Maoris, outgoing and demonstrative, brought a verve and enthusiasm to their gatherings that were unknown to the more reserved Australians.

This difference was never more glaring than at a four-day Hui Tau at Ngaruawahiu, the estate of the Maori Princess Te Puea Herangi. Elder Smith must have known something unusual was in store when, at the entrance to the estate, "the sentry began shouting and jumping up and down." Inside the gate, the visitors were greeted by a company of native warriors dressed in "full regalia." Behind them stood a large group of beautiful native women, attired in colorful dresses that accentuated their smooth brown skin and luxuriant black hair. Soon a way opened through the crowd to the porch of a carved temple called the "House of Ancestors." There they were greeted by the princess and other dignitaries who had assembled for the opening ceremonies of the four-day celebration. Being seated in comfortable chairs that had been reserved for them, Elder Smith and his party were treated to a symbolic pageantry that was not difficult to understand but was much harder to describe.

First came the landing of a crew of burly Maori oarsmen from a war canoe, intended, apparently, to represent the arrival in New Zealand of the first Polynesian invaders. Then followed a series of vigorous, almost frenetic, dances performed by bareheaded and barefooted Maori warriors, who were naked to the waist and below the knees. These portrayed the struggle through which the newcomers had passed as they established themselves in their new land and protected it from attack. These militant dances were accompanied by the most extraordinary contortions, grimaces, grunts, and shouts. "The Hakae," wrote Elder Smith of one the most energetic of these, "was presented with great vigor and might make a timid person uneasy." The fearful impact of these warrior routines was muted by the graceful, seductive dances of the Maori women, which portrayed the romantic aspects of Maori life. Once the "Princess's program" was over, "the LDS Maoris gave an exhibition that was fully as fine as the others."

Two speeches then capped these inaugural ceremonies, one delivered by a native Methodist minister and the other by Elder Smith, who responded in behalf of the guests, expressing thanks for such an extravagant display of hospitality. This was the signal for the large crowd to come forward to shake hands and to hungi (rub noses) with the guests. Afterward, the princess conducted George Albert on a tour of the House of Ancestors, which contained elaborate carvings that representing the genealogies of her ancestors. From there, she guided him through the "king's house" where he also found "some very fine carvings, paintings and furnishings."

This was the beginning of the four-day Hui Tau, which was attended by several thousand people. Since it was the annual conference of the Church in New Zealand, it was marked by a wide variety of meetings, interspersed with enthusastic dancing, singing, and socializing. It was unlike anything the Mormon apostle had seen before. Nor would any conference he attended in the future quite measure up to this one in pageantry, variety, and excitement.

The final event was a marathon eleven-hour testimony meeting with the missionaries. Each was allowed to speak unhurriedly, declaring faith, elaborating gospel themes, or sharing sacred experiences. It was a time of spiritual refreshment for Elder Smith, carrying him back to his own service as a missionary and mission president and arousing pleasant memories of the beloved woman who had served as his companion on both occasions.

During the Hui Tau, Princess Te Puea became ill and called for the apostle, who gave her a priesthood blessing. In gratitude, she presented him with a prized kakahu tarriko, or ceremonial rug, as a memento of his visit. This distinctive gift would always remind him of the love and friendship he had received from the Maoris and their gracious princess.

At Wellington, Elder Smith made courtesy calls on government leaders, who received him cordially but hardly with the enthusiasm shown by his Polynesian friends. These officials appreciated the positive influence of the Church on the Maoris, whom some erroneously believed were the only objects of Mormon proselyting in New Zealand. It remained for later missionaries to change this misconception by working more aggressively and successfully among the Europeans.

The travelers reached Tonga in early May. Their reception in Nukualofa demonstrated why Captain Cook named these the Friendly Islands. The Polynesian cousins found there, dressed in their valas and wreathed in friendly smiles, welcomed the visitors with warm enthusiasm. Also present in the welcoming party was Emile C. Dunn, president of the mission, who would be their host and guide during their stay in Tonga.

President Dunn had arranged the most ambitious meeting schedule of any the two General Authorities had encountered on their tour. No less than fifty-six Church meetings were held during their month's stay, including several baptismal services. The first of these was held at Nukualofa, where they saw twenty-five converts baptized in the sea. One member, taking advantage of the presence of Elder Smith, requested and received an apostolic blessing. Suddenly, thirty-six others were lined up for the same favor. None of them was turned away.

Most memorable of the baptismals were two held on the islands of Naifu and Haabai. Here Elder Smith found in reality the kind of South Seas setting most of us carry in our imagination—the natives living in grass huts amid a paradise of waving coconut palms, tropical fruit trees, and white beaches bathed by the surf. Such a setting at Haabai put Elder Smith in a reflective, poetic mood as he described a baptismal service held on the beach at sunrise. "The trek through the woods in the dim light," wrote he, "passing native homes and under cocoanut palms, bread-fruit trees and banana trees was weird and interesting. The moon shone bright from mid sky, and all was still except ourselves as we walked and chatted." As they approached the beach, they could hear the roar of the sea. And drawing near, they saw the tide pounding on the coral reef, sending salt spray shooting high into the air, then cascading down into a sheltered lagoon where the baptisms were to be performed,

Almost two hundred people were found sitting quietly on the sandy beach facing the lagoon, "with a beautiful forest of trees behind them, with cocoanut palms pushing high in the sky from the depths of the woods." It was now daylight, "and the rays of the approaching sun tinted a few fleecy clouds on the horizon with a golden glow, and soon the glory of the sunrise [appeared]; and it was beautiful." The idyllic scene became perfect when "at a signal all arose and sang 'The Day Dawn is Breaking.' " There was more singing sandwiched between the baptisms. And, at the end, Elder Smith addressed the assembled Saints, conferring on them an apostolic blessing none would ever forget.

Nor would the apostle ever forget the enchantment of that scene and the expressions of love and joy on the faces of the Tongan Saints as they sat before him on the beach. The setting, time, and circumstances seemed to generate a feeling of renewal in Elder Smith and to release the pent-up loneliness and frustration from Lucy's death. Evidence of such a transformation appeared on the return trek to the village. A young Tongan offered his bicycle to Elder Smith, who, to the surprise of all, accepted the offer, and, mounting the wheel, rode off with carefree abandon.

The crowded agenda of Church meetings planned by President Dunn was augmented by an equally ambitious schedule of civic and governmental appointments. The visitors found here a constitutional monarchy. The ruling monarch of Tonga at the time of Elder Smith's visit was Queen Salote Tupou III, a descendant of a sacred line of monarchs who had ruled Tonga and other Pacific islands for nine centuries. Indeed, at one time the Tongan monarchs had exercised sovereign jurisdiction over islands as far away as Hawaii. By 1938, however, that regal authority had shrunk to a cluster of 170 islands known as the Tongan group, only 36 of which were permanently inhabited. And the queen's sovereign sway was further restricted by a 1905 treaty with Great Britain that made Tonga a British protectorate and gave the British consul veto power over Tongan decisions in foreign affairs.

Still, Queen Salote had enormous authority and prestige, especially in domestic matters, and prominent visitors to the islands always sought an audience with her. Desiring to meet the queen, Elder Smith purchased a new white suit for the occasion and, accompanied by Elder Hardy and President Dunn, called on the prime minister Villiame Tugi, through whom such appointments were made. George Albert was interested to learn that the queen did not share his repugnance toward nepotism, since the prime minister was her husband.

During the royal interview, which the prime minister willingly arranged, Elder Smith was able to outline for her majesty the structure, doctrine, and aims of the Church. He also explained how the Church had helped improve the health and happiness of the Tongan members and strengthen their allegiance to her reign. In turn, Queen Salote expressed thanks for all the Church was doing for her people and wished the visitors well during their stay. Elder Smith and his party also visited the governors of some of the islands, as well as the lord mayors and other officials of various cities and villages.

Everywhere they went, it seemed, the hospitable Tongans wanted to fete and feed them. And a Tongan feast was something to behold. Seated cross-legged on the grassy ground, the diners consumed with ease what seemed to be mountains of fish, chickens, roast pork, bread, vegetables, fruits, and cake. Between the numerous courses of a meal, the diners were entertained by the singing and dancing of beautiful Tongan women and athletic and very vocal Tongan men. Dominating every aspect of these occasions was a carefree gaiety and friendliness that seemed to wash away every woe and worry.

From the standpoint of his health, the visit to Tonga was the high point of Elder Smith's Pacific tour. And these feelings were heightened when, on May 25, he received a welcome cablegram from Albert commemorating the forty-sixth anniversary of his parents' marriage. This reminder evoked Elder Smith's love and gratitude for the many years he and his wife had spent together and for the children and grandchildren who had sprung from their union. All the sadness and gloom that attended Lucy's death had disappeared. The visit to the islands had achieved its purpose.

But, one stop still remained before the apostle would return home. This was a visit to Western Samoa, where the Saints had geared up for a Jubilee celebration. The visitors' ship, which anchored offshore at Apia, was met by a seventy-foot war canoe that carried them to the beach. Manned by twenty-six muscular Samoan oarsmen, the canoe was festively decorated with a variety of colorful flowers which grew in abundance on the island. Awaiting them on the dock was a crowd of Latter-day Saints, estimated at two thousand, four brass bands, and a host of government leaders who extended an official welcome. Accompanied by mission president Gilbert R. Tingey and his wife, the visitors were driven to the mission home in a car that, like the war canoe, was festooned with flowers.

The parade to the mission home was led by two hundred Relief Society sisters dressed in white. Most of those who had welcomed the General Authorities at the dock followed in the line of march, along with the four brass bands, which blared out their martial airs with vigor and enthusiasm. Seldom, if ever, had Apia seen such a festive greeting extended to visitors. Certainly, Elder Smith had never experienced anything like it before.

Nor was he quite prepared for the elaborate reception that followed at the mission home. There throngs of happy Samoans, some dressed in white and others in colorful prints, came to shake hands or merely to gaze in awe at the two General Authorities, especially Elder Smith. It was such a rarity then for an apostle to visit the remote islands of the Pacific, almost a once-in-a-lifetime event, that these Saints savored every minute of the occasion, doubtless recording in memory every move and comment of the frail, bearded traveler, to be told and retold to family and friends over the years. And later when this same man became the president of the Church, his visit took on a new meaning and significance for them, even conferring on them a reflected distinction, especially on those who had spoken to him personally or shaken his hand. And later a hundred and forty-eight of the Samoan Saints could boast, perhaps with a little unsaintly pride, that they had received an apostolic blessing under his hand.

The leaders and members of the Church in Apia had prepared long and well for their Jubilee celebration, marking fifty years of the Mormon presence in Western Samoa. The elaborate welcoming ceremonies had been planned carefully to the last detail. And the actual celebration, which commenced on June 16 and lasted for several days, was a model of precision and organization. Aside from the usual preaching services there were training sessions, interviews, talent shows, and, of course, the entertainment and cultural events. Here were repeated the colorful song and dance routines the travelers had seen in other Polynesian communities, with special variations peculiar to Western Samoa.

As at Tonga, Elder Smith and his party paid courtesy calls on government officials during his stay in Apia. High on the list was the British governor, D. A. Turnbull, who had thoughtfully attended the reception at the mission home on the day the travelers arrived. They later visited the governor in his official residence, the Mansion House, which had been built by famed Scottish author Robert Louis Stevenson, who adopted Samoa as his home in his later years and died there in 1894.

Unfortunately, Elder Smith did not enjoy good health in Apia. His heartbeat was erratic much of the time, producing fatigue and listlessness. Nonetheless, he followed the ambitious schedule arranged by President Tingey without complaint, participating in all the meetings and festivities of the Samoan Jubilee.

By now, the Apostle was ready to go home. Because of his heavy schedule of preaching, interviewing, and counseling, this six-month, twenty-seven-thousand-mile trip through the South Pacific could hardly be called a vacation. Yet, it served the same purpose for Elder Smith. The change in scene and routine; the sights, sounds, and smells of new places and things; and a whole host of new friends and co-workers had broadened his vision and provided him with new themes for reflection and action. It seemed to have the same effect upon him as a conventional vacation might have upon a harassed father who takes his family on a hectic camping trip to get away from it all. It was a change but not a rest.

He did, of course, rest on the voyage to the West Coast. On the way there, the ship made port at Pearl Harbor to refuel. The travelers found it crowded and busy as usual. But it gave no hint of the chaos and carnage to be inflicted on it by the surprise attack three and half years later.

George Albert's ship docked in Los Angeles on July 11, 1938. Waiting for him on the pier were Emily and Edith and their children, who had traveled from Salt Lake City to greet him. The sight of them ignited again the deep love for family that lay at the root of his very being. He would later confide these sentiments to his journal, which reflects the devotion he had toward his family and his own feelings of self-worth. "I can't think of anybody in the world that has ever lived that I would change places with," he wrote, "and I hope to adjust myself from now on that I will be worthy to have my own loved ones as my companions in the Celestial Kingdom forever."

Chapter Sixteen

The Friend on Yale Avenue

The traveler needed several days to unwind from his long trip. Never had the home on Yale Avenue looked more inviting. He enjoyed strolling around, examining the yard and the flower beds, and inspecting the canyon behind the house. Everything reminded him of Lucy, whose presence had made this house a home. But the memories were no longer poignant. They had mellowed into pleasant reflection that shed a genial ray of contentment on his life.

In 1938, General Authorities discontinued stake conference assignments during July and August. This so-called recess enabled them to spend time with their families and take care of any personal matters. Since Elder Smith arrived home during the recess, he had several weeks of relative inactivity at Church headquarters when the temple and other regular meetings were not held. This enabled him to tie up the loose ends of his trip and spend some time puttering around the house. He dictated numerous thank-you letters to those who had helped him during the Pacific tour, sending little gifts to some of them. He also dispatched copies of the Book of Mormon and other Church literature to nonmembers he had met. But this took comparatively little time, affording ample opportunity to enjoy the comforts of his home and to renew acquaintances in the neighborhood.

Most of the homes were then occupied by members of the Church. It was as if Elder Smith dwelt in a large and loving family with his siblings living nearby in their separate homes. Indeed, this was the reality of George Albert's life on Yale Avenue, and those who lived nearby who were not members of the Church were still regarded as brothers and sisters. And he treated them as such. He may even have given them special treatment because of the proselyting instincts that always burned brightly within him.

Such was his influence and reputation in the neighborhood that a large photograph of the apostle was placed in the Yale Ward Chapel. The picture hung there for many years until a Church policy dictated that all pictures be removed. And his influence extended far beyond the confines of the Yale Ward into other neighboring wards of the Bonneville Stake.

Elder Smith was happy in this sheltered environment. Adding special contentment was the presence in his ward and stake of fellow General Authorities and other special friends, whether members of the Church or not.

George Albert Smith lived and worked in this pleasant setting during the remaining years of his life. Though a high leader of the Church, he participated in the activities of his ward and stake like any other member. When his travel and speaking schedule permitted, and when he was not ill, Sundays always found Elder Smith in his place on the stand at the Yale Ward chapel. And occasionally he bore his testimony there at fast meetings, as he did on September 2, 1945, just a few weeks before the Solemn Assembly when he was sustained as the eighth president of the Church. On this occasion, he seemed to feel the need to share with his most intimate friends and associates the feelings of his heart as he faced the awesome task of leading the Church.

Ordinarily Brother Smith attended only the sacrament meeting in his ward. Occasionally, however, if his schedule and energy permitted, he also attended priesthood meeting or Sunday School, or both. But only rarely did he participate to the extent he did on Sunday, August 22, 1948. On that significant day, the president of the Church not only attended both the Yale Ward priesthood meeting and Sunday School in the morning, but he also visited and spoke to every Aaronic Priesthood quorum and every class in the Junior Sunday School. In the evening, he returned to the chapel for sacrament meeting where a farewell testimonial was held for a departing missionary. During the afternoon, he made unannounced visits to the homes of some of his relatives and savored the beauty and restfulness of his home. "Enjoyed walking around the house and in the canyon," he wrote at the end of the day. "Flowers are delightful and everything is beautiful. I have everything to be grateful for."

Whenever his family was affected, and within the limits of crowded schedule, Elder Smith became involved in ward activities. So on August 11, 1945, only seven weeks before the Solemn Assembly, he accompanied his grandson Tom Elliott and the Yale Ward Scout troop on an outing at Camp Steiner, high in the Wasatch Mountains east of Salt Lake City. The seventy-five-year-old apostle wrote, "10,500 feet made my heart flutter," a condition that caused him to cut short his stay in camp.

About that same time, the surrender of Japan had been announced to the delirious joy of all America. "Am grateful Japan is done," Elder Smith wrote succinctly; "populace excited." And thoughts of the impending Solemn Assembly, only six weeks away, doubtless produced recurrent feelings of anticipation. It seems appropriately symbolic that the administration of this man of love and peace would be ushered in as the curtain fell at the end of a long and bloody world war.

*George Albert Smith
relaxing at home*

When George Albert Smith wrote in his journal that he had arisen early, he was talking about 7:00 A.M. In his later years, he was not an early riser within the usual meaning of that term. His frail physique and long years of illness had sapped his strength and weakened his recuperative powers. So his body required more rest than is normal to snap back from the rigors of his daily routine. Ordinarily he slept from nine and a half to ten hours a night. And when he logged less than this, his system rebelled. "Short night," he wrote complainingly on July 2, 1945, because an event at Provo had kept him up until midnight and an urgent meeting made it necessary to arise at 7:45 the next morning.

Usually Elder Smith was in his office by 9:00 A.M. In his later years, he gave up driving and depended on rides from others, or on public transportation. Sometimes he

193

walked, although he seldom walked far, as neighbors driving to town would pick him up. While he was alive, Samuel O. Bennion of the First Council of Seventy often gave Elder Smith a ride to town. Eight days after Elder Bennion's death on March 8, 1945, George Albert was back walking when he "was picked up by Mr. Allen." If their schedules jibed, which was not often, Murray Stewart gave his father-in-law a ride to town. And sometimes his nephew, Robert Farr Smith, or neighbors like Elder Ezra Taft Benson, performed this service. After he became the president of the Church, someone from the office usually picked him up in the Church car, either Cannon Lund, Preston Nibley, or, after he came aboard, D. Arthur Haycock. Whenever Brother Smith could control the driver, anyone seen walking to town was invariably given a ride. And sometimes it became a bit crowded in the car, as it did on November 28, 1945, when he picked up five pedestrians. Only a few weeks later, the Prophet and his passengers were delayed getting to work because the Church car broke down. A parade of Good Samaritan neighbors, George R. Hill, Wallace Bennett, Harry Jones, "and others [stopped and] tried to make it go but failed." This incident may explain why, soon after, the Church purchased a new Lincoln Zephyr for the Prophet's use. Since Brother Smith's personal car at the time was a well-worn 1936 Ford, one gets the feeling he was uncomfortable riding in this rather ostentatious limousine. Any objection he had to the purchase apparently was overcome by his counselors, who, presumably, were embarrassed that the president of the Church had to stand in the cold, peering into the Ford's motor, while, seemingly, the whole world stopped to try to fix the broken-down church car. Whether to upgrade the quality of his private transportation so as to reduce the contrast between the Zephyr and the Ford, or whether his jalopy just stopped running, we know not; but, whatever the reason, he turned in his old car soon after. "Sold [my] 36 Ford for $450," wrote he on July 25, 1946, and "bought [a] new Ford for $1450.64."

The sight of the bearded apostle walking toward town, accepting or offering rides to town, or sauntering around to visit, arrange projects, or perform acts of mercy endeared him to the neighbors and, seemingly, gave them a feeling of proprietorship toward him. He was "their" General Authority in much the way the Maoris claimed a vested interest in Rufus K. Hardy and, later, in Matthew Cowley. And the presence of the large picture of Elder Smith in the Yale Ward chapel seemed to symbolize that relationship.

After Elder Ezra Taft Benson and his family moved to Harvard Avenue, a special bond developed between him and Elder Smith. Although rooted chiefly in their mutual apostolic duties, the relationship transcended this ecclesiastical tie. Living in the same ward, they saw each other at sacrament meetings during the recess and on other occasions when there was a break in their travel schedules. On these occasions, they sat side by side on the stand. The times when Elder Benson drove his neighbor to the office afforded opportunities for conversations at a more personal level than was possible during working hours at Church headquarters. Beyond these ties was their shared descent from prominent church leaders who held the Apostleship and whose names they bore. From July 16, 1846 when the first Ezra Taft Benson — who was called Ezra T. — was ordained to the Apostleship, until October 6, 1868 when the first George Albert Smith — who was called George A. — was called to the First Presidency, their ancestors and namesakes had served together as member of the Quorum of the Twelve. To avoid being confused with his ancestor, George Albert commenced to use the full name early in his Apostolic career. Only a few months after Elder Benson's call to the Twelve, President Smith gave him similar counsel which he followed obediently. Thereafter he always used the full name, Ezra Taft Benson. In the same letter which contained this counsel, Elder Smith, as President of the Twelve, also gave his new associate valuable counsel about Apostolic demeanor and objectives. He was to befriend prominent non-members as a means of extending the influence of the church and of opening doors to future proselyting. He also was reminded that the solution to the world's ills lay in the principle of repentance which was the keystone of his Apostolic message.

These neighbors also shared a common interest in scouting. Shortly after his call to the Twelve, Elder Benson was appointed to the National Boy Scout Committee where he joined the President of his quorum who had served with the same body for many years. And this pair held similar views about politics and about the status and role of the constitution in the American scheme of government. In a 1948 general conference address, President George Albert Smith spoke out about the constitution, expressing views which his neighbor, Elder Ezra Taft Benson, heartily endorsed. "To me the constitution of the United States of America is just as much from my Heavenly Father as the Ten Commandments" said President Smith. "When that is my feeling, I am not going to go very far away from the Constitution, and I am going to try to keep it where the Lord started it." (*Conference Report*, April 1948, p. 182.)

Only seven months after he became the head of the Church, President George Albert Smith called his neighbor, Ezra Taft Benson, to preside over the European Mission. He would there follow in the footsteps of President Smith who had occupied that position twenty-five years before. But though the position was the same, the duties were far different. Not only would Elder Benson have the customary duties of a mission president, he was given the charge to direct relief and rehabilitation efforts to help the European Saints recover from the devastating effects of World War II. President Smith attended and spoke at the farewell for Elder Benson held in the Yale Ward in mid January, 1946; and two weeks later, set him apart, promising, "There is not anything desirable that you will not be able to do with the aid and help of the Lord . . . if you do your full part." And the day of Elder Benson's departure, January 29, 1946, President Smith stopped at the Benson's Harvard Avenue home to bid farewell. There seemed to be almost a filial relationship between the two of them as the aging Prophet embraced his young associate and gave him a good-bye kiss.

During Elder Benson's absence, President Smith maintained a neighborly watch care over the Benson family. And when the baby, Beth, became ill, he visited the home to give her a blessing.

After Elder Benson's return from Europe, the Prophet continued to show a special interest in the family, attending and speaking at the son Reed's missionary farewell held in the Yale Ward on June 22, 1947; and on October 6 that same year, President Smith left a General Authority dinner served in the Lincoln Ward in order to attend a Benson family reunion being held in the Yale Ward.

The interest shown in the Benson family by Elder Smith was typical, not exceptional. Many others in his ward and stake received similar treatment. The prominence of this family, however, helps to underscore the genuine interest he had in his neighbors and friends.

Chapter Seventeen

The Apostle at Work

U pon returning from the South Sea tour, Elder Smith settled back into the routine he had followed for thirty-five years: meetings, travel, speaking, and counseling. Aside from the regular stake conference assignments he continued to fill, he was in constant demand as a speaker at funerals, graduations, missionary farewells, and civic events. He found it hard to say no when he was asked to speak. Indeed, there is no evidence that he ever said no, except when he was ill or had a conflicting appointment. The apostolic charge he had accepted seemed to color, even to dominate, every aspect of his life.

A funeral he attended a few months after returning from the South Pacific almost resulted in his death. The services were held in Provo in memory of his aunt, Grace Smith Cheever. Driving near Lehi, Utah, Elder Smith sounded his horn to pass an automobile going in the same direction. Unaccountably, the other driver suddenly swerved, colliding with the apostle's car and forcing both vehicles off the road. The lead car crashed into a telephone pole, toppling it onto the Smith car. One of Elder Smith's passengers, Mrs. Martin Larson, the wife of a Salt Lake District judge, suffered several broken ribs and deep cuts from flying glass. Daughter Edith and the other passengers were shocked and bruised. A grateful George Albert Smith was not injured. "But for the special blessing of our Heavenly Father," he wrote, "we would have been much more seriously injured or killed."

Until automobiles came into general use with the development of the highway system, Elder Smith traveled by train or horse-drawn vehicles in fulfilling his appointments. Then as flying emerged from the novelty stage, he took to the air. Once the trauma of his maiden flight with Albert from the continent to London had subsided, he began to seriously consider flight as an alternate means of transportation. In August 1927, a year after Western Airlines inaugurated passenger flights out of Salt Lake City to and from the West Coast, George Albert flew to Los Angeles and back again to fill an assignment. At that early day, the flight was made in two hops, four hours from Salt Lake City to Las Vegas, where he stayed overnight, and from there to Los Angeles in two hours. Thereafter, he flew intermittently and soon became a flying enthusiast, promoting the development of the aviation industry.

To some, Elder Smith's penchant for flying represented a death wish or a lack of good judgment. The more extreme critics reasoned that if God had intended for peope to fly, they would have been born with wings. Some of the Brethren were stubbornly opposed to flying, most notably J. Reuben Clark, who used his considerable influence as a member of the First Presidency to keep the General Authorities out of the air. His opposition was rooted in concern for the safety of his associates. Another critic, using that argument, admonished Elder Smith to stop flying because it was dangerous. "What do you mean dangerous," he asked. "Well, so many people are killed," came the answer. "Listen to me, my friend," the apostle answered jokingly; "there are more people die in bed than any place else. Can't I go to bed either?" (GASC, box 96, folder 1.)

Elder Smith was hard put to sustain that argument when, in the late twenties and early thirties, the nation was shocked by a rash of plane crashes. This generated wide publicity and a powerful backlash against flying. The opponents of flying, many of whom were encouraged or supported by automobile or railroad interests, dwelt on the finality of airplane accidents, from which a survivor rarely emerges. Undeterred by these criticisms, and having no motive other than to encourage what he envisioned as the transportation giant of the future, Elder Smith sprang to the defense of the aviation industry. He took up his pen and used his powers of persuasion whenever possible to blunt criticism and publicize the positive aspects of air travel. At the time, he encouraged leaders in the industry to orchestrate an advertising campaign to counter the adverse publicity caused by these crashes. And in private correspondence, he extolled the virtues of flying and downplayed the dangers. (See letter to Glen Perrins, January 6, 1930, ibid., box 58, folder 1.)

Beginning in the 1930s, when flying was still an oddity, George Albert Smith would fly to Los Angeles in the morning, transact his business, and return to Salt Lake City the same day. This enabled him to do in one day what would otherwise have taken four to five days to accomplish. He was pleased when, in 1936, a Salt Lake City newspaper publicized one of his jaunts to and from Los Angeles. Afterward, he wrote a jubilant letter to Alvin P. Adams, president of the Western Air Express Corporation, reporting on the article and implying that he had struck another mighty blow for aviation. He reported how people telephoned him after reading the article, or stopped him on the street, to discuss it. (Letter of June 7, 1936, ibid., box 59, folder 3.)

Only a few days later, Elder Smith wrote Mr. Adams again, offering suggestions about how Western Air could increase passenger interest and enjoyment during the

George Albert Smith (center) with airplane

flights between Salt Lake City and Los Angeles. He described several landmarks along the flight pattern and suggested that the stewardesses be briefed about them so they could inform the passengers. (Ibid., folder 4.)

So interested was Elder Smith in the terrain and landmarks over which he flew that he often described them in his journal. One desert scene looked to him like an ocean with huge waves of sand. Another stretch was so smooth it reminded him of plain linoleum. And the Great Salt Lake looked "like a mirror of smoothness." During some of his early flights, when passengers were scarce, the pilots would fly low enough to give him a close-up look at of interesting sights. In this way, he obtained a birds-eye view of Zion's and Bryce Canyons and other famous landmarks and enjoyed sharing his insights with others. "From his own thorough knowledge of the country," wrote an acquaintance, "he compiled historical data which is a standard guide for all passengers as they travel over this region." Elder Smith also surfaced another matter about air travel that he felt needed the attention of airline executives.

On a particular flight, he became nauseated because of the cigarette smoke of some of the passengers. During much of the flight, he sat with his face near the window to breathe some of the fresh air blowing in through a crack. But it did not ease his discomfort. He later wrote a letter to the vice-president of the company, James G. Woolley, expressing the hope that smoking could be controlled on airplanes as it had been on trains and street cars. (GASC, box 57, folder 23.)

Although Elder Smith did most of his flying on Western Air, he occasionally flew on other lines as he did on September 17, 1935, when he flew from Bozeman, Montana, to Salt Lake City on the National Park Airways. And a few days after the Centennial celebration when the This Is the Place Monument was dedicated, he accompanied his friend Harold Fabian on a charter flight to Jackson Hole, Wyoming. The seventy-seven-year-old Prophet seemed as excited as a teenager to report that he rode in the pilot's seat part of the way and that he was able to identify old Fort Hall as the plane flew over it. While at Jackson Hole, he further demonstrated his youthful spirit when he went for a speed-boat ride on the lake.

Elder Smith's interest in aviation was not limited to passenger comfort and enjoyment. It also extended to passenger safety. He recognized that wide public acceptance of flying as an alternate means of transportation would require government-supervised standards of safety. So in the mid-thirties when Congress began to consider legislation to regulate the infant airline industry, George Albert became involved. In 1937, he learned about two bills pending in the United States Congress, Senate Bill No. 2, sponsored by Senator McCarran and House Bill No. 7273, sponsored by representative Lea. Wanting to be heard on these proposals as one who had been a citizen pioneer in flying, Elder Smith wrote to William H. King, United States senator from Utah, about them. George Albert endorsed legislation that would increase safety in flying, thereby broadening its acceptance by the public. He explained that he had no financial interest in aviation but only an interest in fostering an industry that would save the time and increase the convenience to those who had to travel. (Ibid., box 60, folder 3.)

In 1942, Elder Smith accepted an invitation to become a member of the board of directors of Western Airlines. Unlike many corporate appointments, this one was not made merely to add an illustrious name to the company's letterhead. The Western executives recognized in Elder Smith a man of sound judgment and creative outlook whose views would be helpful in formulating company policy. Thereafter, the apostle regularly attended board meetings held in Los Angeles, usually flying down and back the same day to save time.

Time was a priceless commodity to this busy man. But, he was never too busy to extend a helping hand to one who was in need. Over the years he engaged in numerous charitable activities, most of which were personal and private. One, however, was institutional and highly publicized. This was Elder Smith's involvement in work to help the blind. His interest in those with impaired sight seems to have been kindled by his own visual problems. His inability to read for any length of time and the pain he suffered because of his eyes made him very conscious of those who had similar problems. When the Society for Aid of the Sightless in Utah was incorporated in 1904, George Albert Smith became its vice-president. He worked to promote the objectives of this organization during the remainder of his life.

Elder Smith originally became involved in the Society for the Sightless at the invitation of James E. Talmage, whose brother was blind. When Elder Talmage, who later became a member of the Twelve, died on July 27, 1933, George Albert succeeded him as the president and served in that capacity for sixteen years. Thereafter, to the end of his life, President Smith retained an active interest in the organization, advancing its objectives through contributions of time or money, or through the prestige of his office as president of the Church.

The society published a monthly magazine, *Messenger for the Sightless,* intended to publicize the plight of the blind and enlist the support of those who could see. Then, in 1912, when it also began to be published in Braille, it became an organ for communication among the sightless. The society also provided audiotapes and records for the use of the blind, furnished counseling, and helped the sightless obtain public funding. Classes were conducted at the blind center in a variety of academic or arts and crafts subjects. Later, through Elder Smith's leadership, the society employed a sightless person, Irene Jones, who went into the homes of the blind who could not participate in the activities at the center to teach them handicrafts or how to read braille.

In September 1935, Elder Smith and his brother Nicholas called on the President of the Braille Institute of America to discuss printing the Book of Mormon in braille. Following this discussion, the Smith brothers, with the society, took steps to make this possibility a reality. Within months, the project was completed. Elder Smith was jubilant when the braille publisher of Louisville, Kentucky, delivered the finished product, "a very attractive set" consisting of seven cloth-bound volumes embossed in gold.

George Albert was instrumental in persuading the Church to donate property to the State of Utah for the construction of a facility for the blind. And when a new center was completed at 138 South Second East in Salt Lake City, it was Elder Smith who offered the dedicatory prayer in his role as the president of the Society for the Sightless. This took place on November 4, 1937, the day before Lucy passed away.

Never content merely to go with the flow of events, the apostle was an activist in promoting the cause of the sightless in Utah. During 1941, for instance, he visited the facilities for the blind in other states to glean ideas for use by the Utah society. And during March of the same year,

George Albert Smith greeting Helen Keller in the Hotel Utah, 1941

he arranged for Helen Keller to visit Salt Lake City. The appearance of this world-famous woman in the Salt Lake Tabernacle was a media event that focused the attention of Utahns on the plight of the blind as nothing else could have. But the event also focused attention on the potential of the blind. To learn how this woman had struggled successfully against the handicaps of blindness and deafness to carve out a life of productivity and achievement was an inspiration. And Elder Smith orchestrated her appearance and the resulting publicity so as to augment his continuing effort to advance the work for the blind in Utah.

Such indefatigable dedication to the cause endeared George Albert Smith to the hearts of the sightless in Utah. To demonstrate their appreciation, members of the society hosted a celebration in his honor on his seventieth birthday. It was held in the Lion House in Salt Lake City. At a reception preceding the dinner and program, the apostle was able to greet everyone in attendance personally. Following the banquet, there were laudatory remarks by the hosts and a response by Elder Smith. Perhaps most significant to him were the remarks of the blind caseworker, Irene Jones, whom Elder Smith had hired to help the blind shut-ins. "The blind of this community," she said, "have not had to seek far for someone to lead them spiritually out of their mist and darkness. They are being gently guided by Apostle George Albert Smith. . . . So sweet has been his influence and so complete his understanding that it is impossible to express the gratitude of the blind toward him." The speaker then read a poem she had composed for the occasion. The opening verses seem to capture the love and appreciation his co-workers and the recipients of his services had for him:

When life beats hard with stormy hands
And bitter teardrops fall
When friendless winter chills my soul,
And empty echoes call
Tis then I turn with eager hope
My steps though spent and lame
To find an understanding heart
Where burns a friendly flame
A heart where gentle Wisdom dwells,
Compassionate and kind
Whose faith in God and man has taught
A like faith to the Blind

I lay my troubles at his feet
Each trial, each bitter loss
And burden of a hundred more
He helps me bear the cross
Consecrated by our Lord
With Apostolic light
Consecrated in his soul,
He makes our darkness bright
A loving radiance he sheds
That comes from God to man
And we who walk in life-long night
Can see as others can
(Ibid., scrapbook 1, box 124.)

The members of Elder Smith's family were so pleased with this poem that they requested that it be read in its entirety at his funeral.

The apostolic light to which the poem refers burned with intensity to the end of Elder Smith's life. Each day offered a new opportunity and challenge to use it in a different way under different circumstances. He saw his role as a messenger of the Good News, or the gospel. And whenever he was in public, he was on duty, delivering the message in one way or another. Preston Nibley, who traveled with him occasionally, was amazed that during short trips Elder Smith seldom settled down to rest or read like most passengers. "Each time I observed that as soon as the journey was well underway, he would take a few gospel tracts from his bag, put them into his pocket, and then move about among the passengers." He would strike up a conversation with one, then another, gauging his approach as he perceived the personality or interests of the individual. Ultimately, however, he would work around to a gospel subject, discussing a principle or telling a story or personal experience that illustrated a gospel principle. "Conversation after conversation would follow with one passenger after another until the journey was ended." (*Improvement Era,* 53 [April 1950]: 270.)

Many would be intimidated to do even once what George Albert Smith did repeatedly as a matter of habit. In this way he met literally thousands of people as he traveled through the years, leaving with them a gospel message or a thought, or at least the perception that they had been exposed to a person of Christ-like character. "I never met one for whom I developed so much admiration in so short a time as I did for you," wrote a doctor whom Elder Smith met on a trip to Hawaii. "If there were more people so unselfishly interested in the welfare of their fellowmen as I found you to be, there would be no excuse for changing this existence in the hope of finding a better one." (Letter of J. E. Strode, January 4, 1937, GASC, box 62, folder 1.)

If Elder Smith found himself in a strange city with no appointments to keep, he would usually stir around to meet someone new whom he could expose to the Church. A notable example occurred in Little Rock, Arkansas. Having a few spare hours between train connections, he went to the state capitol building, where, without prior appointments, he met, among others, the secretary of state, the attorney general, several members of the supreme court, and the commissioner of agriculture. To each new acquaintance, he gave one of his calling cards, on the back of which were printed the Articles of Faith. Perhaps to demonstrate how missionaries could maximize the use of their time, he later told of the experience in a letter to mission president Charles A. Callis. (Letter of December 13, 1923, Ibid., box 46, folder 7.)

While Elder Smith ordinarily gave out Church literature to people he met, he occasionally gave copies of small booklets by nonmembers that extolled Christian virtues. These he purchased in large numbers for distribution to friends and new acquaintances. A recipient of one of these was former Colorado governor Ralph Carr, whom George Albert met at a luncheon at the Alta Club in Salt Lake City on February 23, 1945. It is conceivable the governor mentally reviewed his conduct at the luncheon when he later received from Elder Smith the booklet "Beauty Is as Beauty Does."

The *Improvement Era* was also a favorite gift Elder Smith distributed as he traveled about or later mailed to someone whom he had met and thought would be favorably influenced by it. He once wrote to Richard L. Evans, who was then affiliated with the *Improvement Era*, that he often carried two or three copies with him to distribute while he was on the road and that they were excellent door openers to gospel conversations. (Letter of July 31, 1936, Church Archives.)

The arsenal of Church literature he carried around in his bags also included assorted tracts. *The Vitality of Mormonism*, by James E. Talmage, and *Mr. Durrant of Salt Lake*

City, by Ben E. Rich, were special favorites. (GASC, box 103, folder 1.)

To think of Elder Smith preparing for a trip, stuffing various books, pamphlets, and magazines, among his gear, arouses the analogy of Johnny Appleseed, who always carried appleseeds in his saddle bags to be planted where there were no trees. Like Johnny Appleseed, George Albert Smith planted his seeds of ideas persistently, profusely, and purposefully. Everywhere he went, he left in his wake a trail of new friends whose minds had been turned, temporarily at least, from the routine existence of a pointless life to the themes of eternity. He never knew how many of his seeds took root. But, that did not deter him from planting them because of his confidence that some would fall on fertile soil and in time produce a hundred-fold.

The Christmas season offered a good excuse for Elder Smith to send literature to some of his nonmember friends, or even to prominent people whom he did not know personally. The Book of Mormon was a favorite and logical gift under these circumstances because of its purpose as another testament of Jesus Christ. "In a few days the Christian world will celebrate the birth of the Savior," wrote Elder Smith to a Mr. Wernicke shortly before Christmas in 1925, "and it is customary at that time to remember our friends." He said he was sending a copy of the Book of Mormon, sometimes called the "Mormon Bible," under separate cover as a Christmas present. The letter expressed the confident belief "that you will be glad to have this in your library." An answering letter confirmed this belief when Mr. Wernicke assured the giver, "The book will have place on our shelves and will be read 'from kiver to kiver' with open-minded thoroughness." Elder Smith had in mind an objective for the book far beyond that foreseen by Mr. Wernicke, who wrote, "It cannot fail to broaden the views and increase the spirit of tolerance of all who read it thoughtfully." (Ibid., box 47, folder 33.) It was, of course, the apostle's unabashed hope that his friend would not only read the book thoughtfully but also that he would pray about it earnestly, be convinced of its truthfulness, and join the Church promptly. Nothing less than the conversion and baptism of the whole human race was the objective of this whole-souled man. He had taken as a personal responsibility the charge Jesus gave to the early apostles to "preach the gospel to every creature." (Mark 16:15.)

For Elder Smith, this goal far transcended the bounds of duty; for him it was a labor of love. It entailed not merely preaching the gospel and baptizing but the responsibility he and others had in the actual redemption of those who were precious to him. Those who had not yet joined the Church were not merely "non-members" or "gentiles" in his eyes. They were literally brothers and sisters, the children of a common Father.

The major sermon Elder Smith delivered at the Solemn Assembly where he was sustained as the president of the Church focused on this theme. "I realize the great responsibility that is upon my shoulders," he told the audience in the Tabernacle that autumn day. "As I stand here, I realize that in this city, in the Catholic church, the Presbyterian church, the Methodist, the Baptist, the Episcopalian, and the other churches, I have brothers and sisters [whom] I love. They are all my Father's children. He loves them and he expects me and he expects you to let our light so shine that these other sons and daughters of his, seeing our good works, will be constrained to accept all the truth, not a little part of it, but accept all the truth of the gospel of Jesus Christ our Lord." After pointing to the opportunities and blessings of those who teach and influence others, he offered a word of counsel: "Let us not complain at our friends and our neighbors, because they do not do what we want them to do. Rather let us love them into doing the things that our Heavenly Father would have them do. We can do that, and we cannot win their confidence or their love in any other way." (*Conference Report*, October 1945, pp. 173-74.)

Elder Smith's approach to his apostolic duties was

never one-dimensional. While planting the seed was essential, preparing and cultivating the ground was equally important. A friendship created today could clear the way for someone else to plant or teach tomorrow. Therefore, he was sedulous in his efforts to create friendships. A classic example of his friendshipping produced a quite unexpected result. It occurred during Elder Smith's visit to the Century of Progress Exposition in Chicago. Impressed with the skillful way the exhibits had been arranged, he asked at the Church booth who was in charge of the exposition. Told that the man's name was Dawes, Elder Smith assumed it was Henry Dawes, an acquaintance who was the brother of Charles G. Dawes, a former vice-president of the United States and ambassador to Great Britain. The apostle promptly called Mr. Dawes's secretary to request an appointment. She informed him there were already a hundred people waiting to see the director, all wanting jobs. "Well that may be true," said George Albert, "but I am probably the one man he would like to see, because I already have a job." He then identified himself, saying that he was an acquaintance of Mr. Dawes and merely wanted to pay his respects. With that, the secretary invited him to the office, and when he arrived took him to a side entrance, bypassing the crowd of job applicants. When the door opened to the director's office, there stood a complete stranger who introduced himself as Mr. Dawes. "He was very pleasant," Elder Smith reported later, "but you can imagine how embarrassed I was. He was Mr. Dawes, and he was Ambassador Dawes brother, but he was Rufus Dawes. I did not know there was a Rufus Dawes in the world." (*Improvement Era,* August 1946.)

George Albert stammered out an apology, explained that he merely wanted to congratulate him on the organization of the exposition, and started to beat a hasty retreat. But Mr. Dawes insisted that he come in. "No," answered the apostle, "there are a hundred people waiting to see you." Assured by his host that none of them would say anything as nice as he had said, Elder Smith went in, although he was at a loss as to what else to say. Groping for words, he said after sitting down, "By the way, Mr. Dawes, where do your people come from?" Asking whether the question implied an interest in genealogy, and being told about the Church's extensive genealogical library in Salt Lake City, Mr. Dawes excused himself and returned carrying a small box. "He took his knife," Elder Smith wrote later, "opened the carton and took out a package wrapped in white tissue paper. He took the tissue paper off and put on the table one of the most beautiful bound books I have ever seen. It was well printed and profusely illustrated, and the cover was elegantly embossed with gold."

During the ensuing conversation, George Albert commented on the exquisite beauty of the record. "It ought to be," responded Mr. Dawes. "It cost me twenty five thousand dollars." When Elder Smith said that it was well worth the price, his host asked, "Is it worth anything to you?" Assured that it would be of great worth if he had it, Mr. Dawes answered, "All right, you may have it."

The apostle wrote later with a sense of disbelief, "Twenty five thousand dollars worth of genealogy placed in my hands by a man whom I had met only five minutes before! . . . I was amazed. Our visit continued but a short while longer. I told him how delighted I was to have it and that I would place it in the genealogical library in Salt Lake City." (Ibid.)

There was an interesting sequel to this unusual story. Before Elder Smith left the office, Mr. Dawes explained that the book he had given contained his mother's genealogy, the Gates family, that a similar record was being prepared of the Dawes family, and that when it was finished, he would also give a copy of it to Elder Smith. "Fifty thousand dollars worth of genealogy!" exulted the apostle, "and just because I tried to be polite to someone." (Ibid.) Rufus Dawes passed away before the second volume was completed. Concerned that this might prevent the Church from obtaining a copy of it, Elder Smith mentioned the incident to Charles G. Dawes, the elder brother of Rufus Dawes, who said, "I know all about it, and we will have another of my father's line for you as soon as it is completed." (Ibid.) This volume was later added to the one already in the Church's genealogy library.

Elder Smith felt that his acquisition of these valuable records was not accidental but resulted from spiritual influences triggered when he acted on the impulse to contact the director of the Chicago Exposition. Throughout his ministry, he acknowledged the source and the importance of these spiritual impressions and often urged members of the Church to rely upon them in performing their duties. These admonitions came to be sloganized in the phrase "Give the Lord a chance." He used it often, but especially while he served as president of the European Mission. He once told an elder, who had been assigned to a town where the missionaries had been repeatedly denied permission to hold street meetings, "Now remember, give the Lord a chance. You are going to ask a favor. Give the Lord a chance. Ask him to open the way." (*Improvement Era,* July 1946.) Following this instruction, the elder went directly to the mayor's office but found he was not there. Outside the mayor's office, the missionary saw a sign, "Chief Constable's Office," down the hall. Without planning an approach he, Nephi-like, walked in, and, after introducing himself, said he and his companion would like permission to hold street meetings in town. "Well, what street corner would you like?" came the response. Quickly regaining his composure, the elder said with feigned nonchalance, "I don't know this city as well as you do. I would not ask for a corner that would be undesirable, or where we would block traffic. Would you mind going with me to select a corner?" Apparently impressed by the young man's sincerity and self-confidence, the constable said, "Surely I will go with you." Elder Smith was pleased with the result of the elder having followed his counsel. "Just think of a missionary asking the chief constable to pick a corner on which to preach the gospel," he wrote later. "In fifteen minutes they had one of the best corners in town, with permission to preach the gospel of Jesus Christ where it had not been preached on the streets since before the war." In retelling the story, Elder Smith emphasized, "The Lord has a way of accomplishing things that we are unable to do, and never asks us to do anything without preparing the way." (Ibid.)

In telling this story, Elder Smith was reminded of another one involving John A. Widtsoe. Finding himself in a strange Scandinavian city, Elder Widtsoe felt impressed to visit an inconspicuous bookstore on a side street. There he found a large collection of genealogical records, which he was able to purchase at a nominal price. Wrote Elder Smith of the incident: "If he had not been praying about it, and if he had not been looking for them, and if he had not obeyed the promptings of the Spirit, he might not have found them. And these particular records could not have been duplicated nor otherwise obtained in any manner known to us." (Ibid.)

These and many other similar experiences Elder Smith enjoyed or learned about over the years confirmed his faith that God would give sure guidance to anyone who fervently sought it. "If you have something that the Lord asks or expects you to do," he said, "and you don't know just how to proceed, do your best. Move in the direction that you ought to go; trust the Lord, give him a chance, and he will never fail you." (Ibid.)

Words such as these, repeated frequently, tend to lose their significance unless one reflects deeply upon them. To George Albert Smith, they were a way of life. Called and ordained as an apostle, a special witness, he had committed himself to a lifetime of preaching the gospel and testifying of the truthfulness of the Church and the divinity of its head, Jesus Christ. It was in his role as a witness that he performed his most important work. His skills in administration, public relations, molding opinion, organization, and charitable ministering were all important. But these were all subordinate to the one preeminent element that qualified him as an apostle. This man *knew*. His testimony was not based on hearsay or reasoning and analysis; it was based on personal knowledge acquired by spiritual means. He was one of those to whom it is given "by the Holy Ghost to know that Jesus Christ is the Son of God, and that he was crucified for the sins of the world." (D&C 46:13.) Repeatedly throughout his ministry, he bore powerful testimony of this fact, as he did upon returning from his European mission. "I stand here today profoundly grateful for the knowledge that has come to me," he said during a general conference address. "I am thankful that I am not dependent upon any individual for the testimony that I possess. Of course, I am grateful for the encouragement I received from others who possess light and truth, and who give encouragement by lives of righteousness, but I do not depend upon any of them for a knowledge that God lives, that Jesus is the Redeemer of mankind and Joseph Smith is a Prophet of the Lord. These things I know of myself." (*Conference Report,* October 1921, p. 42.)

Elder Smith did not always have a testimony of such certainty and power. He once described for the *Liahona* the process by which he obtained it. It began when he was a child and "was taught to pray and read the scriptures and lead a righteous life." Next was the example of his father and mother: "My parents lived as they desired me to live and I soon learned that they believed and practiced what they taught." In such an environment, "secret and family prayers were attended to by each member of the household." Then came a testimony of what he had learned by precept and example. "I learned quite early in life," he wrote, "that the Lord would answer prayer, for he answered mine and in many ways He gave me evidence of His watchful care." Once he had acquired a conviction that God lives, he began to assess the claims of different churches that purported to be the earthly instrument through which God promulgated his gospel and executed his will. "As I grew older," he wrote, "I compared the faith I had espoused, with the beliefs of others, and found

215

that the gospel of Jesus Christ embraced all that the other churches taught that was good, and many other beautiful truths that the scriptures contained that were apparently overlooked by the Christian world." Such conviction was bolstered by reading the Holy Scriptures and by serving in the mission field, where he "witnessed the power of the Lord in softening the hearts of men and providing for my necessities and preserving my life." (*Liahona*, 12:501.)

Out of this process, and through a spiritual communication that he never sought to explain or describe, came the powerful testimony he bore repeatedly throughout his life and shared with the readers of the *Liahona* on the occasion already noted. "I know that this is the work of the Lord," he wrote, "that Jesus [is] a prophet of the Lord. I know those who have succeeded him [are] men of God, who have honored the calling placed upon them." (Ibid.)

In bearing such a testimony, Elder George Albert Smith performed the most significant work carved out for him as a special witness of the Lord Jesus Christ. And when it was inappropriate to bear his testimony formally, he resorted to other ways of communicating his message. He subscribed to Paul's formula for conversion: "I have planted, Apollos watered; but God gave the increase." (1 Corinthians 3:6.)

A favorite device for planting new seeds or cultivating seeds already planted was his correspondence. Over the years, this burgeoned into a veritable mountain of paper. "My correspondence is doubled," he wrote to Rufus K. Hardy on January 6, 1931, "as a result of writing letters to people, not members of the church, many of whom I have met under varying conditions and I have kept up a correspondence with them hoping to interest them in the gospel." (Copy in Church Archives.) What he did not mention to Elder Hardy was that he often wrote to people he had not met. Following his trip to Hawaii in 1936, for instance, he wrote a long letter to Mr. Barry Baldwin, a major developer in the islands, whom Elder Smith had never met. After introducing himself and explaining that his relatives were among the first missionaries for the Church in Hawaii, he wrote: "I have always had an interest in the island people and during my visit this time, I was delighted with what is being accomplished by you and your associates in improving conditions for the natives in providing them employment so that they can take care of themselves." After commenting on how Mr. Baldwin had helped the Hawaiians build homes and chapels, he interjected this comment, which, presumably, he hoped would open the door to a future gospel discussion: "Not many people can know of the advantage that you have been to the people of Hawaii; but our Heavenly Father knows and those that you have helped will know and I am sure you are laying up treasures in heaven." (GASC, box 60, folder 3.)

Earlier, George Albert had written a letter to Edsel Ford, expressing great satisfaction with the Ford automobile he had driven, commending the Ford family for an enlightened attitude toward labor relations, and indicating a desire to meet him or his father, Henry Ford. This brought a warm response and an invitation to contact Mr. Ford in the future when Elder Smith was in Detroit. Repeatedly he wrote to various officials of railroad companies, commenting favorably on their service or their comfortable accommodations. This not only won friends for the Church but often secured special services or considerations for himself by people grateful, or perhaps starved, for recognition.

No person was too high or too low to receive a letter of commendation from George Albert Smith. He once found an opportunity to write to the Honorable Bonar Law, the prime minister of Great Britain, passing on complimentary remarks Senator Reed Smoot had made about the British government during a talk he had delivered in Salt Lake City. To make sure that the Church also got its due, Elder Smith added this telling postscript: "I forgot to mention the fact that Senator Smoot is a prominent member of The Church of Jesus Christ of Latter-day Saints, commonly known as the Mormon Church, which church has thousands of adherents in Great Britain." (Ibid., box 46, folder 29.)

When someone responded to one of his random letters, such as the one to the prime minister, the apostle always followed up with another one and so on indefinitely as long as the person to whom he had written continued to answer. So, he never ended a correspondence. Perhaps the most extensive of these interchanges was one he carried on for at least sixteen years with a noted English lecturer, George Hancock. (See ibid., boxes 48, 50, 52.) The correspondence began while Elder Smith was the European mission president. The apostle was especially anxious to retain contact with him because Mr. Hancock often talked about Utah or the Mormons as he lectured in different parts of England. Such was the relationship Elder Smith created through his letters that Mr. Hancock became a stout defender of the Church. "I have some arguments here over your religion," he wrote on March 19, 1924, "and I always beat them and find that they know nothing at all about you, only lies they have read." He then described some of the ammunition he used to "beat them." Wrote he, "I point them to the fact that wherever the Mormons have gone, the land has brought forth abundantly. God has blessed you as he did the children of Israel and that beats them proper."

In a letter dated December 19, 1925, Mr. Hancock told of a confrontation he had had with an English cleric. "At one lecture, I had a chat with one of the leaders of the Church of England about Salt Lake City," wrote he. "He was bitter against you good people and so I had a good gruelling with him. At the finish, I found out that he had got his knowledge from some ignoramous editor of a newspaper who scarcely knew where Salt Lake was." What followed resembled the kind of comment one might expect from an agent of the Church. "You can depend upon me always supporting your church, state and people. I told the big audience, if our English folk were half as energetic, kind and good as the Utah people, things would be different here."

While Elder Smith appreciated Mr. Hancock as a friend and supporter of the Church, he had more than friendship in mind for him. He aimed for brotherhood. "I am also satisfied," he wrote on May 11, 1926, "that if you were to understand the Gospel as it is taught by the Latter-day Saints, you would find in it all the beautiful things that you have learned in any other Christian organization, and in addition many other wonderful teachings that would enrich your life." He then held out to his pen pal the prospect he considered of prime importance. "It would offer to you the opportunity some day to hold the Priesthood," he wrote.

Elder Smith never succeeded in bringing Mr. Hancock into the Church. But that did not deter him from trying to do so as he tried with countless others over the years. He was indefatigable in his efforts. And if priesthood brotherhood proved to be infeasible, he was content with friendship. His most notable friendshipping effort took place with his Smith cousins in the Reorganized Church. Through the years of his apostolic ministry, he never lost the hope of seeing all the progeny of Asael Smith joined under the banner of one church—The Church of Jesus Christ of Latter-day Saints. As a representative of the John Smith branch of Asael's family, he repeatedly held out the olive branch to the descendants of the Prophet Joseph Smith, whose father was John Smith's brother.

When George Albert Smith became a member of the Twelve, the president of the Reorganized Church was Joseph Smith III, who was the elder of the two by more than thirty years. This son and namesake of the Prophet Joseph Smith was only a boy when his father was murdered at Carthage. Within three years after the martyrdom, the exodus was at flood tide, leaving in the backwater in Illinois the Prophet's widow, Emma, and her brood of children. At odds with Brigham Young and other leaders of the Church, Emma later married a man who had little apparent knowledge of the Prophet and his teachings, or of the Smith family. Reared in such an environment, Joseph Smith III was essentially cut off in childhood from all contact with the members of his father's family who had joined in the exodus. This included the descendants of Hyrum Smith, the Prophet's brother, and John Smith, the Prophet's uncle. That Joseph Smith III and his family missed this association and yearned for a resumption of it is suggested in a letter. Frederick M. Smith wrote to George Albert on October 4, 1912: "I have frequently thought," he wrote, "that the various branches of the Smith family see too little of each other socially. But fate seems to so have ordered." (Ibid., box 33, folder 16.) And this was a yearning shared by George Albert and his father, both of whom had a compelling sense of family. John Henry Smith had repeatedly made overtures to the Prophet's descendants, trying to mend the bonds severed after the martyrdom. That he succeeded in part is implied in a letter Joseph Smith III wrote to George Albert Smith November 8, 1913. Referring to John Henry Smith, the letter read: "[He] met me on one of my visits to Utah with such frankness and kindly exhibition of manly friendship, notwithstanding our differences of belief, in such courtliness of manner as won my confidence and esteem." The letter also mentioned that the writer was always pleased to exchange "courtesies" with John Henry Smith. (Ibid., box 35, folder 29.)

After the death of his father, George Albert Smith continued with the effort John Henry had undertaken to build bridges of understanding between these branches of the Smith family. It was not an easy task. Deep-seated animosities existed toward the church headquartered in Salt Lake City by certain members of the Reorganized Church, though not necessarily by the Smith cousins. So when George Albert wanted to place markers on the graves of Mary Duty Smith, Joseph Smith, Sr.'s, mother, and Jerusha Barden Smith, in the cemetery adjacent to the Kirtland Temple, permission was denied. An appeal to Frederick Smith and Israel Smith brought only an interview with a member of the First Presidency of the Reorganized Church, who merely sustained the decision of the Kirtland cemetery officials.

Elder Smith did not allow a rebuff such as this to interfere with his efforts to solidify relations with these Smith cousins. These included both correspondence and personal contacts. "I believe absolutely that your grandfather [Joseph Smith Jr.] was a Prophet of the Lord," he wrote to Israel Smith, "and it is a pleasure for me on all occasions to so testify. During my short experience in life I have done everything possible to bring honor to his name and to further the interests that the Lord entrusted to his care." (Ibid., box 40, folder 17.) And when he traveled east from Salt Lake City through Missouri or other states where Smith relatives lived, he tried, if possible, to stop and visit. On a trip east in the spring of 1923, he stopped in Omaha, Nebraska, to visit some cousins who were members of the Reorganized Church. It was a Sunday morning, and they invited him to attend church services. There he accepted an invitation to speak. Afterward an old man approached him timorously and pressed a dollar bill into his hand while whispering, "I received a witness that you hold the Priesthood." (Ibid., box 46, folder 17.)

How many others in the Reorganized Church, if any, received a similar witness will never be known. It is unlikely, however, that the presence or absence of such a witness in any of them would have altered in the least George Albert's persistent efforts to bring harmony into the Smith family. He seemed to take as a personal responsibility, owed to Asael Smith, their common ancestor, the task of resolving the differences that separated the various branches of the clan. It was Father Asael who had predicted that a great prophet would appear among his progeny, a prophecy fulfilled in his grandson, Joseph Smith, Jr. And as he did in the letter to Israel Smith already mentioned, George Albert often alluded to the life and ministry of the Prophet as the rallying point around which the entire family could gather in complete accord. But it was a tricky approach. While all accepted the Prophetic role of Joseph Smith, Jr., they had vast differences about the meaning of some of his teachings and sayings. Most notable among these were succession in the presidency and the plurality of wives.

An opportunity to put these differences in the background arose as plans were formulated to celebrate the centennial of the founding of Nauvoo, Illinois. Elder Smith was assigned to represent the Church in coordinating these plans with representatives of the Reorganized Church. A few months after returning from the South Seas, he traveled to Illinois to meet with representatives of the Reorganized Church to finalize the arrangements. He was accompanied by Albert E. Bowen, a new member of the Twelve. After the work there was completed, George Albert accepted the invitation of his cousin Frederick M. Smith to drive with him from Nauvoo to Independence, Missouri, where George Albert wanted to confer with the Church's mission president who resided there. During the long drive in early December 1938, these two descendants of Asael Smith spent many unhurried hours discussing the relationship between the different branches of Asael's family.

A lengthy journal entry Elder Smith made of this conversation reveals a frankness and urgency never reached before nor afterward in the relationship with his cousins in the Reorganized Church. "We are nearing the end of our mortal lives," he told Frederick Smith, "and we are responsible to the Lord for the use of our brief time here on earth." He admonished his cousin that animosity and bitterness should have no place in the Smith family and reminded him of the sacrifice made by Joseph and Hyrum as martyrs for the cause. Wrote he, "They would expect us as members of the Smith family to do everything possible to disseminate the truth as presented by the Prophet in his lifetime." He also expressed the opinion that an inheritance in the celestial kingdom depended on their faithful dissemination of these truths and suggested that the contention that had existed between the branches of the family was inconsistent with the spirit that should actuate those professing to be disciples of Christ and of his prophet.

Such straight talk apparently did not alienate the good feelings Frederick M. Smith had toward his cousin. On reaching Independence, they enjoyed a pleasant meal at the home of Frederick's daughter, and later Frederick personally drove George Albert to the mission home. And at the Centennial celebration in June 1939, the two cousins shared the pulpit at special meetings at the Nauvoo temple site and at the Carthage Jail. Moreover, the relationship between them remained cordial throughout their lives. Yet, such personal accord was insufficient to bridge the wide gulf of doctrinal interpretations between the two institutions they represented. Therefore, George Albert's dream of the entire Smith family being joined under the banner of a single church was never realized. Still, his efforts helped mute the angry exchanges that had sometimes occurred between the two groups and to create a better climate of understanding and respect.

While Elder Smith's main effort in working with dissident groups was with the members of the Reorganized Church, he also made similar overtures to those affiliated with other splinter groups. His correspondence reveals a consistent pattern of reaching out to those connected with the Church of Christ, the Bickertonites, the Cutlerites, the Hedrikites, and the Strangites. Although none of the Smith cousins appear to have found their way into these sects, George Albert was almost, though not quite, as diligent in trying to coax them back into the fold. Emulating the example of the Good Shepherd, he did this with his habitual love, persistence, and buoyant optimism.

Chapter Eighteen

One of the Twelve

D uring his years of service in the Twelve, Elder Smith demonstrated unqualified loyalty toward his quorum and its members. At the time of his return from the South Pacific in 1938, he had been affiliated with it for thirty-five years. He found among his brethren in the quorum bonds of fraternity and mutual responsibility that in many ways transcended even the bonds of the family to which he was so deeply committed. The oath he had taken on being inducted into this select group committed him to an earthly service from which he would never be released except by death, transgression, or elevation to the First Presidency.

Since he was only thirty-three years old when he was set apart as a member of the Twelve, George Albert went through a long apprenticeship as he watched and learned from the older members. The first quorum president under whom he served was his cousin, Francis M. Lyman, who became president of the Twelve only two days before George Albert was inducted on October 8, 1903. The son of Amasa Lyman, who had been a member of the Twelve, and the father of Richard R. Lyman, who would become a member of the Twelve two years after his father's death, Francis M. Lyman served as president of the quorum for over thirteen years. Because of the family relationship, President Lyman took a special interest in George Albert, shepherding him along and providing helpful insights into his apostolic role. This relationship became even more significant following the death of John Henry Smith in 1911, when Francis M. Lyman almost assumed the role of father to George Albert. This was so not only because of the blood relationship but also because President Lyman and John Henry were called to the Twelve at the same time, were ordained on the same day, and for thirty years sat side by side in the meetings of the Twelve. Both of them, therefore, had a protective attitude toward George Albert from the time of his induction into the quorum.

At the death of Francis M. Lyman in November 1916, Heber J. Grant became president of the Quorum of the Twelve, serving for only two years when he succeeded Joseph F. Smith as president of the Church. The relationship between President Grant and Elder Smith was cordial and cooperative, notwithstanding basic differences in their personalities and perceptions. These seemed to trace in large part to their early years and upbringing. President Grant's father, Jedediah M. Grant, died only nine days after Heber was born. An only child, he was reared by his widowed mother and lived at the edge of poverty during his formative years. Even as a boy, he was imbued with the desire to earn the means to care for his mother. Therefore, the acquisition of wealth became almost an obsession with Heber J. Grant, who channeled most of his youthful energies toward that goal. Without a powerful father to counsel him and smooth the way, he developed an independence and self-confidence that colored his relationships with others and his perceptions of individual responsibility.

Elder Smith, on the other hand, was reared in the heart of a close-knit, nuclear family headed by an influential father and grandfather, with numerous siblings and assorted aunts, uncles, and cousins always nearby to lend support and encouragement. In such an environment, it was only natural that George Albert would develop more of a paternalistic and protective attitude toward others than would a person like President Grant, who had battled and competed alone to carve out a niche for himself and his widowed mother.

Such differences in background and temperament brought about occasional conflicts between this pair. But these were always salved over and forgotten in the overriding apostolic unity that dominated their relationship. The nearest thing to a rift between them occurred during the depression over the question of the entitlement of ZCMI retirees to pensions as to which they had no legal rights. President Grant, as chairman of the board, reluctantly concluded that the pension payments would have to be suspended in the interest of assuring the continued life of the company. Elder Smith, a board member, dissented, asserting that the company should continue the payments, regardless of the consequences, fulfilling what he considered to be a moral though not a legal obligation. His resignation from the board a few months later is believed to have been prompted by this difference of opinion. But, it was without rancor on the part of either man and had no lasting impact on their generally amicable relationship.

When Heber J. Grant became the seventh president of the Church, he selected Anthon Henrik Lund as his first counselor. At the same time, President Lund, who then ranked second in apostolic seniority to President Grant, also became the president of the Twelve. However, because of President Lund's heavy duties in the First Presidency, the administrative work of the quorum fell chiefly on Rudger Clawson, who officially became its president on March 17, 1921, following the death of President Lund.

President Clawson was the last quorum president under whom George Albert served. And following the death of Reed Smoot on February 9, 1941, Elder Smith was second in seniority. Because at that time President Clawson was eighty-four-years old and in frail health, Elder Smith then began to assume many of the administrative duties of the Twelve, as directed by President Clawson.

While serving in this unofficial capacity, George Albert made another of his numerous trips to the East. He left Salt Lake City on February 13, 1942, amid the tensions created by the bombing of Pearl Harbor two months before. Such was the shock on the American mentality created by this incident that an almost paranoid fear of bombing attacks gripped most of the western United States. That fear had extended even to the remote fastness of Salt Lake City, where the street lights were turned off at night and windows were shrouded. And trains travelling to Salt Lake City from the West Coast at night routinely curtained all of their windows to prevent the lights from serving as a beacon to the ubiquitous oriental airmen whose supreme skill, it was assumed, would enable them to bomb a fast-moving night train.

As he entered Salt Lake City's Union Depot, Elder Smith found military personnel waiting for transportation to training bases or military units. Most of them were in uniform, although some raw recruits were still in civilian clothing. The apostle was cordially greeted by the railroad personnel from the ticket agent to the porters, all of whom recognized the man with the neatly trimmed beard and mustache who was now bundled in a heavy coat to protect against frigid winter weather. So often had Elder Smith been in and out of this depot that he knew most of these employees by name; and because of his interest in others, he probably also knew something about their background and families. Waving good-bye to members of his own family who had come to see him off, Elder Smith entered the warmth and comfort of his Pullman sleeper and settled down for the long trip, which, like numerous others in the past, would provide the opportunity for reflection and study, work on the papers he carried in his valise, and, as always, conversation with his fellow travelers.

After having shuttled back and forth across the American continent for thirty-seven years, the apostle probably paid little attention to the familiar scenery that flashed by his window as the train wound through the canyons of the Wasatch up to the wind-swept plateau of Wyoming, blanketed now with a mantle of snow. It is also safe to assume that the war news that had dominated the press and radio since December 7, 1941, and the riveting sight of military personnel in the depot and on the train, evoked serious reflection about the terrible conflict into which his country had been drawn and the consequences it held for the Church and the members of his family. He had already lived through one world war and understood the physical and economic devastation warfare brings.

Whatever were Elder Smith's ruminations as his train crossed lonely Wyoming and Nebraska, they were swallowed up in reality when he arrived at his first stop in Des Moines, Iowa. There he was met by the mission president, Leo J. Muir, who took him to his hotel, where he held meetings with the missionaries and the Saints. The lack of adequate church facilities there was one reason for Elder Smith's visit to Des Moines. During his stay, he and President Muir inspected potential building sites for church facilities. As always, the apostle was interested not only in the size of the site but also in its location. Here the major considerations were convenience to the majority of the Saints living in the area, zoning restrictions, and the quality of the neighborhood and the nearby buildings. George Albert and his brethren were always conscious of the image of the church projected by the location and appearance of its chapels. And this is why, whenever possible, one of the General Authorities, and preferably a member of the Twelve, personally inspected proposed building sites, not leaving the final decision to local leaders whose knowledge about the overall strategy of the Church was limited. The local leaders usually identified alternate sites for the inspection of the visiting General Authority, as President Muir did at Des Moines.

The same procedure was followed by the mission president in Illinois, who had identified proposed building sites for Elder Smith's inspection when he visited Springfield. In places like this, another element entered the formula for selection — the proximity of the proposed site to historic buildings like Abraham Lincoln's family home, which attracted many visitors. Ever aware of the need for the identification of the Church in the public mind, Elder Smith and his Brethren often would opt for a location with higher visibility to a larger number of people, all other factors being equal.

The biting winter winds that blew off Lake Michigan onto Chicago's Lake Shore Drive were a freezing reminder that cold though it might be, Salt Lake City's February weather was mild by comparison. Here the apostle attended to his customary duties, building the Saints and motivating the missionaries. The young elders were already beginning to feel the pressure from some who wondered, occasionally aloud, why healthy physical specimens such as they were not in uniform. These pressures and the burgeoning demand of the military for more recruits would soon diminish the Church's missionary corps to a miniscule pool of elders, most of whom had physical disabilities, and to a few sister missionaries to work in the mission offices. The dwindling number of missionaries would be an aggravating problem with which Elder Smith would grapple during most of the time he served as the president of the Twelve, the quorum that serves as the general missionary committee of the Church.

In New York City, to which the apostle traveled after leaving Illinois, he repeated the procedure followed in Chicago. But in addition, he transacted some personal and Church business, consulted with national Boy Scout officials, and, as time allowed, kept alive his contacts with influential friends. Constraints on his time and pressing demands at home prevented him from detouring to Cambridge to visit Albert and his family, as he often did, or from stopping at Palmyra to check on the development of his pet projects there. Elder Smith derived immense satisfaction from the fact that by this time there was an attractive visitors' center at the Hill Cumorah, directed by his longtime associate in the promotion of trails and monuments, John D. Giles. Also, the hill, which had been barren of any vegetation but grass when George Albert first began to negotiate with Pliny T. Sexton for its purchase, now boasted a healthy stand of trees. It has been said that to see a dream come to fruition is one of the richest rewards of life. To the extent this saying has validity, George Albert Smith was made rich indeed by the acquisition and development of the Hill Cumorah.

The apostle returned home in time to help commemorate the 135th anniversary of the birth of Lucy's grandfather, President Wilford Woodruff, who was born on March 1, 1807. Elder Smith was asked to be the main speaker at the family gathering, which was held the day after the Prophet's birthday. George Albert had special qualifications for the assignment. He was well acquainted with President Woodruff, having been brought up in the neighborhood where he had lived for many years. And because Lucy was reared in her grandfather's home, the relationship between her grandfather and her husband was almost that of father-in-law and son-in-law. Another tie that bound Elder Smith to Lucy's grandfather was that Wilford Woodruff and George A. Smith, Elder Smith's grandfather and namesake, were ordained to the apostleship and set apart as members of the Twelve on the same day, April 26, 1839. The ordinations took place on the temple site at Far West, Missouri. In a revelation given to the Prophet Joseph Smith on July 8, 1838 (D&C 118), the Twelve were directed to leave from the temple site at Far West on April 26, 1839, for their mission "over the great waters." The Saints were driven from Missouri before this date, which had prompted enemies of the Church to boast that the revelation would never be fulfilled. But Brigham

Young and other members of the Twelve returned to Far West from Illinois on the appointed day and held a meeting on the temple site during which the cornerstone of the temple was laid and the ordinations were performed. This, then, was the starting point from which the missionary work abroad was launched. And the involvement of Wilford Woodruff and George A. Smith in that historic work and the fact that they were ordained the same day under such unusual circumstances had created a special bond between their families. The best evidence of this is seen in the experience of George A. Smith's son. When John Henry Smith was called to the Twelve in 1880, John Taylor was the president of the Church. He thought it likely, therefore, that President Taylor would ordain and set him apart. But because of the special relationship his father had enjoyed with Wilford Woodruff, he was anxious that Elder Woodruff ordain him. However, he was reluctant to express this desire openly for fear it would be misunderstood. So he prayed fervently in silence that his desire would be granted. It was. At the ordination ceremony, President Taylor first ordained Francis M. Lyman. Then, after hesitating, the Prophet, instead of doing it himself or calling on one of his counselors to do it as is customary, he asked Wilford Woodruff, then the President of the Twelve, to ordain John Henry Smith.

George Albert was well aware of this incident and of the special relationship between his grandfather and Wilford Woodruff. Therefore, when he eulogized President Woodruff on his 135th birthday, he spoke with the knowledge and authority of a friend and neighbor, an admirer, a surrogate son, and a brother in the holy apostleship.

The weekend after the Woodruff family reunion found Elder Smith in his home stake for its quarterly conference. The Bonneville Stake then held its quarterly gatherings in the Assembly Hall on Temple Square. Here, just across the street from where he had been born and reared and received news of his call to the Twelve, George Albert occupied the pulpit from which his father had spoken often during his ministry. The general session on Sunday, March 8, 1942, was conducted by stake president Owen G. Reichman, a young Salt Lake City lawyer, who, the year before, had succeeded Marion G. Romney, another Salt Lake lawyer, when he was called as the first assistant to the Twelve. At this session, Alma J. Larkin, a Salt Lake mortician, was sustained as a patriarch.

In a sense, this gathering was as somber as meetings held in Alma Larkin's mortuary, located several blocks east of the Assembly Hall on South Temple Street. The machinery was then in place for the forced movement of Japanese Americans from their homes on the West Coast to inland camps. One of these, named Topaz, had been built at a dreary site near Salt Lake City; and within three weeks after the Bonneville Stake Conference, loyal Americans, guilty of no offense other than their Japanese descent, began to be herded into the Topaz "relocation center," which could hardly be distinguished in appearance from a prisoner of war compound. The frenzy of fear and foreboding into which the United States had been driven by the war now overshadowed every aspect of American life.

The exigencies of the war prompted the First Presidency to close the April general conference to the general Church membership and restrict attendance to several hundred priesthood leaders who convened in the Assembly Hall. Thus, a month after the Bonneville stake conference, Elder Smith was once again at the Assembly Hall pulpit, this time instructing priesthood leaders as a senior member of the Twelve.

In the interim, however, he filled three other stake conference assignments. The first took him to Morgan, Utah, the rural community where, thirty-seven years before, Daniel and Moroni Heiner had attested to Elder Smith's angling prowess when he caught "the big fish." This time, the apostle and his companion, Charles A. Callis, were angling for a new stake president and found him in the person of George Sylvester Heiner, a kinsman of

the two fish witnesses. Only the most rabid members of
the Isaac Walton Society will see a significant relationship
between the two events.

The second conference was at Tucson, deep in the
Arizona desert. Returning by train, he stopped in Phoenix,
Arizona's capital, another desert community that was just
beginning to show signs of the giant metropolis it would
become. The apostle was met at the Phoenix depot by a
tall, genial, athletic man named Delbert L. Stapley, a counselor in the Phoenix stake presidency and the son of the
founder of a thriving hardware and farm implement business. Elder Smith and Delbert Stapley were kindred spirits,
sharing a love for Scouting and for the Southern States
Mission, where both had served as young elders; and both
men reflected in their demeanors the charitable qualities
of the true Latter-day Saint. Within eight years, this pair
would also share the apostleship when Delbert L. Stapley
would become the last of three men called to the Twelve
by President George Albert Smith.

Elder Smith spent four days in Phoenix with Elder
Stapley as his guide and host. They drove to nearby Mesa
to visit and bless Orley S. Stapley, the family patriarch,
who was in poor health. This prominent man, whose business empire bore his name, The O. S. Stapley Company,
had struggled out of obscurity to establish an enviable
reputation in Arizona's commercial community. There the
name Stapley stood for character and dependability, qualities that were reflected in the lives of the family, especially
in Delbert.

Taking full advantage of the presence of a member of
the Twelve, the presidency of the Phoenix Stake, then one
of only two stakes in the entire Salt River Valley, had
arranged a full schedule of events for the apostle. Elder
Smith spoke to a large gathering of the MIA, addressed
the workers at the Mesa Temple, dedicated a new chapel,
and paid a courtesy call on Arizona's governor. Meanwhile, he complied with the request of the stake president,
J. R. Price, to ordain his son Reed an elder. This young

man later became the president of one of the many stakes in the Phoenix area.

Elder Smith entrained for Los Angeles on March 27, noting in his journal, a pocket-sized book he carried around with him, "Have been most kindly treated by [the] Stapley family." Some of these little journals, which were written in his own hand and often reflected in their wavy script the fact that the entries had been made aboard a moving train or airplane, contained a note such as this on the inside cover: "If mislaid, the finder will confer a great favor by sending to 1302 Yale Avenue, Salt Lake City, Utah." Also at the top of most entries were recorded vital weather data, cryptically indicating whether it was hot, cold, rainy, snowing, or "a lovely day."

On arriving in Los Angeles, Elder Smith received a surprise message from Salt Lake City asking him to go to Thatcher, Arizona, with Elder Joseph F. Merrill to reorganize the presidency of the St. Joseph Stake. The incumbent stake president, Jesse Udall, who had been called to replace the ailing Henry H. Blood as president of the California Mission, was then in Los Angeles. So, Elder Smith, accompanied by Elder Merrill and President Udall, boarded a train the next day, returned to Phoenix, and then traveled to Thatcher, Arizona, in the southeastern part of the state. This little community, named after Moses Thatcher, a former member of the Twelve, had once served as a way-station for members of the Church who practiced plural marriage and were migrating to the refuge of Old Mexico. Here, on March 29, 1942, Elders Smith and Merrill installed J. M. Smith, the offspring of a Mormon polygamous family, as the new stake president.

Weary from travel and the pressures of his ministry, Elder Smith arrived in Salt Lake City in time for the truncated general conference. And when he had finished his duties there, the apostle, exhausted, went to bed for several days with a heavy cold.

One may wonder at the vitality that enabled a seventy-two-year-old man, weakened by debilitating illness much of his life, to maintain the frenetic schedule George Albert Smith continued to follow. And the constant travel and the pressure of his duties were aggravated by the ever-changing quality of his sleeping arrangements and diet. He usually stayed in the homes of members, who went out of their way to accommodate him. But it was difficult to enter a strange home and sleep in a strange bed. And, naturally, the wives in these homes often outdid themselves in loading their tables with delectable dishes and desserts. Elder Smith usually had to decline the rich fare that had been so lovingly prepared, or to pick and choose miniscule portions from among the rich variety offered. He feared that this would be an affront to his hosts. But to do otherwise was an affront to Elder Smith's delicate digestive system. So, he diplomatically explained his dietary limitations so his hosts would not be offended were he to decline certain foods or eat the grain concoctions he carried with him. Sometimes he would ask for one of his favorite foods, bread and milk. And he would not decline a piece of cheese to flavor it. Often, leaders served for so long in their callings that they knew of Elder Smith's limitations without being reminded of them. Indeed, for many of these leaders, having George Albert come to stay was like welcoming home a family member.

This was certainly true of Elder Smith's first assignment following the April 1942 general conference. This was the one on May 1 at the St. Johns, Arizona, stake. There, a member of the Udall family had served as the president of the stake from the time of its organization in 1887. The first president in St. Johns was David King Udall, who had served for more than thirty years when he was replaced by a son who was serving in 1942 at the time of Elder Smith's visit. The apostle's host was President Levi S. Udall, whose sons Stewart and Morris would later give the Udall name national recognition, the first as a member of the cabinet of President John F. Kennedy and the second as a prominent United States congressman who would be touted as a presidential candidate thirty-four years later.

235

The conference, which included Saturday meetings and two general sessions on Sunday, attracted members who lived in small satellite communities within fifty miles of St. Johns. Following a pattern set by the Prophet Joseph Smith, the Saints in this and other similar areas seldom lived on isolated farms or ranches but clustered together in small communities, commuting to and from their labors. The distances involved and the absence of sufficient hotel facilities required that most conference visitors be accommodated in the homes of the Saints at the center of the stake. This tended to solidify the relationships among the members of the Church in a widely scattered area.

At St. Johns, Elder Smith was pleased to renew acquaintances with his kinsman Willard Farr, who was the stake patriarch. And he was also pleased to have as his traveling companion Elder Alma Sonne, who, the previous year, had been called as one of the five new assistants to the Twelve. This quintet of new General Authorities, which included George Albert's brother Nicholas G. Smith, was at this time being trained in their duties by members of the Twelve. Since Elder Smith was the senior active member of the quorum at the time, he assumed much of the responsibility for training these new brethren. So the week following the St. Johns conference found Elder Smith in Park City, Utah, with Elder Marion G. Romney, another new assistant to the Twelve who was Elder Smith's stake president in the Bonneville Stake at the time of his call.

Because of the short distance involved, Elder Smith was able to drive home Sunday night after the conference in Park City. There, he capped the day with a big bowl of bread and milk. A few months later, he enjoyed a similar repast, noting on January 31, 1943: "Enjoyed a bowl of bread and milk. Am thinking of buying a cow." Within a week he acted on his impulse and had found a farmer, Hans Grillenberger, who agreed not only to care for and milk the cow Elder Smith purchased but also to regularly deliver the milk to the Yale Avenue home. Thereafter, the apostle was able to indulge his taste for bread and milk at will, confident in the source and with the satisfaction of ownership.

During several weeks following the Park City conference, Elder Smith made three trips to the East in the interests of the Boy Scouts and the Sons of the American Revolution. The first was to St. Paul, Minnesota, where, for three days in mid-May, he participated in Boy Scout meetings and workshops. As usual, he interspersed these meetings with attendance at Church gatherings. On the evening of May 13, for instance, he drove to nearby Minneapolis to meet with the missionaries in the area. He shared with his audience some of his insights about how to cultivate friendships and about the value to the Church and the satisfaction to be derived from being friendly to others. This was a subject about which the apostle spoke with authority and conviction. And it was a subject that lay at the root of the two organizations whose interests he served while in the Twin Cities — the Church and the Boy Scouts.

A month later Elder Smith traveled to Chicago to attend meetings of the National Executive Board of the B.S.A. And between these two jaunts, he traveled to Virginia for a convention of the Sons of the American Revolution. Here, in the heartland of Colonial America, George Albert's heredity and patriotic interests were renewed as he visited historic Jamestown and Yorktown, reflecting on the struggle of the British colonists to establish plantations in the New World. And at Williamsburg, he was excited by the efforts of the Rockefeller Foundation to restore the old village to its original colonial appearance. Seeing this extraordinary restoration, Elder Smith may have been struck with the idea of a similar development at Nauvoo, Illinois. He passed away before such a dream became a reality. However, his nonmember friend Harold Fabian, who had ties with the Rockefeller family and shared Elder Smith's interest in monuments and markers, became involved with Nauvoo Restoration, Inc., serving on its board of directors.

Before leaving the charming ambiance of Virginia,

Elder Smith paid a courtesy call on its governor, Colgate W. Darden, and on the president of William and Mary College, John Stewart Bryan. The apostle doubtless left with these distinguished men some Church literature and a lasting impression of his unusual quality of friendliness. As for Elder Smith, he gained two more names for his ever-growing list of friends and correspondents.

The flow of life—and of death—continued as George Albert returned to Salt Lake City in late June. Death came to former Utah governor, Henry H. Blood, who had been released from his California mission because of illness. Elder Smith attended the funeral with his cousin and fellow apostle, Richard R. Lyman. And George Albert was reminded of the continuing flow of life when, two days after the funeral, he attended a party at Liberty Park honoring Salt Lake City's senior citizens. "Lovely Old Folks Day," he wrote approvingly of the event. The following weekend found him in Los Angeles again, this time for his final stake conference assignment before the annual summer break.

Although stake conferences were suspended for six weeks during the summer of 1942, Elder Smith and the other General Authorities were not off duty. The special conditions created by the war imposed urgent demands of continuous leadership. It was during this period that the Brethren took aggressive steps to instruct members of the Church to plant gardens, bottle fruit and vegetables, and store coal. These measures, with previous instructions to discontinue institutes, conventions, and auxiliary stake meetings; to postpone the celebration of the Relief Society centennial; and to limit recommendations for full-time male missionaries to seventies and high priests indicate the mantle of austerity that had descended upon the Church because of the war.

But, these and other steps taken to economize and simplify did not extend to holding quarterly stake conferences. These periodic meetings were considered indispensable to preserving doctrinal purity and ensuring uniform-

ity of procedure throughout the Church. To this end, one
and often two General Authorities were assigned to these
conferences. Since at this time there were a hundred and
forty-four stakes and only twenty-seven General Authorities available to attend stake conference, (excluding the
First Presidency and Elder Rudger Clawson), the Brethren
were spread very thin and therefore were almost constantly
on the move. So, beginning in mid-August following the
recess, Elder Smith was on the road again, attending stake
conferences at Monroe, Utah; Malad, Idaho; and Oakley,
Idaho, on successive weekends.

In these and other rural communities, the apostle found
the descendants of early converts to the Church, the fruits
of countless, nameless missionaries who had reaped the
fields in Great Britain and Europe, harvesting those ripe
for conversion and gathering them to the hundreds of
Latter-day Saint communities along the the Rocky Mountains from Canada to Mexico. And often, as was true with
Malad, Idaho, whose pioneer stock came chiefly from
Wales, those converts congregated in communities
peopled with those who shared their national origins, enabling them to preserve customs and traditions and often
to compensate for the severance of family ties caused by
their acceptance of Mormonism. The strength these members received from the visit of the apostle was reciprocated
in the encouragement he received to continue on the course
his calling dictated.

That course soon took him east again; in mid-Septem-
ber, he presided at the quarterly conference of the Chicago
Stake. Here he found the leadership of this six-year-old
stake to be comprised chiefly of men and women whose
roots extended back to rural Mormon towns like Monroe,
Malad, and Oakley. Educational and business opportunities had drawn these expatriates from their western moor-
ings, a magnetic process that in the future would draw
others like David B. Haight, an Oakley native, and David
M. Kennedy, who was born in tiny Randolph, Utah. In
burly, brawling Chicago, this future apostle, and this fu-

239

ture U. S. Cabinet member and special representative of the First Presidency would become associated in Church leadership with John K. Edmunds, the Chicago stake president, who was a native of another Mormon town in the West and whose wife, Jasmine Romney Edmunds, was a classmate of David Haight's in Oakley, Idaho. Such were the patterns of Mormon migration Elder Smith and his brethren found repeatedly as new centers of Latter-day Saints strength were established in the cities of the eastern United States.

Finishing at Chicago, Elder Smith went on to New York City for special Boy Scout meetings. While there, he squeezed out two days for a side trip to Boston to visit Albert and his family. The apostle could not conceal his pride in this son. And the son, who reflected in his character the best qualities of the Smith and Woodruff families—a concerned interest in others and a penchant for hard work—admired and loved his famous father. Albert was pleased to show the apostle around the campus and to introduce him to his colleague, Dean Donald Kirk David.

While in Boston, Elder Smith counseled with President Reeder of the New England Mission; and back in New York City, he conferred with President Iversen of the Eastern States Mission, whose mission secretary, Stewart L. Udall, was the future cabinet member and the eldest of St. Johns stake president Levi Udall's two sons.

Since Elder Smith had no other stake conference assignments before the October general conference, he decided to take the long way home. Predictably, his first stop on the detour was Palmyra, where he greeted his old friend John D. Giles. The apostle held a meeting with a small group at the Hill Cumorah visitors' center, and, during the two days that followed, he and his friend, perhaps envisioning still other monuments and markers, visited the Joseph Smith and Martin Harris homes and the grave of Alvin Smith.

An arctic air mass moved into the area while Elder Smith was at Palmyra, turning the weather icy cold. He became so chilled that he donned extra underwear and at night curled up with a hot water bottle to keep warm. It was a losing battle. For once, Elder Smith was glad to leave this favored spot, if only to find a place where it was warm.

From Palmyra, he traveled to Carthage, Illinois, via Chicago. There he visited the old jail where his deceased kinsmen, Joseph and Hyrum Smith, had been murdered, martyrs for the cause that now dominated his life. Restricted in his reading because of poor eyesight, George Albert learned more history by visiting places like Carthage and hearing narrations of significant events, spoken in the surroundings where they had occurred, than he learned from history books. To see the upper room at the jail where his cousins had been shot, and to see dim stains on the floor, reputed to have been made by their blood, etched in memory an understanding that no amount of reading could impart. Through his avid promotion of trail marking and monument building, Elder Smith has become a historian of sorts to unnumbered thousands who have visited the sites that his energies identified and memorialized.

From Illinois, he traveled to Missouri. There he visited Richmond and Liberty, where his martyr cousins had been jailed. And at Far West, he stood on the cornerstone at the temple site, where, a hundred and three years before, his grandfather and namesake, George A. Smith, and his grandfather-in-law, Wilford Woodruff, had been ordained to the apostleship. Filled with the sights of these historic places and the impressions they had aroused, Elder Smith held several important meetings in Independence with missionaries and members before traveling home on September 29 in time for the semiannual general conference.

The second day after his arrival in Salt Lake City, George Albert remained in bed to recuperate from his long trip and the chilling experience at Palmyra. On that day, President Heber J. Grant called at the Yale Avenue home to consult with him about filling the office of patriarch to the Church. At the conference, Joseph F. Smith, a grandson of President Joseph F. Smith through Hyrum M. Smith, was called.

"Am rushed and somewhat nervous," Elder Smith wrote two days after the conference. The pressure this diary entry reflects was caused not only by the stresses of the conference but also by the arrival of Albert from Boston and the apostle's preparations to leave the next day on a month-long mission tour. During this tour, he stayed overnight in twenty different cities, holding meetings and conducting interviews in each one. And he spent several nights in the cramped discomfort of a lurching, rocking Pullman sleeper. Indeed, the apostle commenced his tour in this way when, on October 7, he took the night train on the D&RG from Salt Lake City to Denver. Perhaps no other stretch of railroad in the entire United States is more enjoyable in daylight and more miserable at night than this one. In daylight, one enjoys the magnificent scenery of the Royal Gorge of the Rockies with its towering peaks, majestic pines, and roaring streams. But the tortuous road bed, with its sharp turns and cutbacks, is hardly conducive to comfortable sleep.

The well-traveled septuagenarian, smiling and bright despite a fitful night on the D&RG Prospector, was met at Denver's railroad depot by the Western States mission president, Elbert R. Curtis. Within six years, this able and personable young leader would be called as the ninth general superintendent of the Young Men's Mutual Improvement Association. One who sees special significance in associations and relationships will be interested to learn that Elbert G. Curtis, who was a direct descendant of President Brigham Young, the founder of the YMMIA, was called to head that organization by President George Albert Smith, who was its sixth general superintendent.

After spending a day and night with President Curtis, meeting with missionaries and members in Denver, Elder Smith traveled to Louisville, Kentucky, via St. Louis, Missouri. There he joined the president of the East Central States Mission to tour a vast area, part of which was orig-

inally in the Eastern States Mission and part in Elder
Smith's old mission, the Southern States. The traveling
party left Louisville by automobile on October 12 with
Nashville, Tennessee, as the first destination. En route they
encountered an unusual sight and obstacle that would become a commonplace to American tourists during the next
few years—an army convoy. The mission president pulled
off the road to allow a long line of military vehicles to
pass—jeeps, trucks, weapon carriers, and touring cars, all
painted in camouflage to match the drab fatigue gear worn
by the armed troops crowded aboard them. Here were
fighting men, presumably on their way to a port of embarkation for duty overseas or to field maneuvers to prepare for combat. And at the side of the road were the two
missionaries, men of peace, who sought to end war using
only the weapon of ideas. And the many young soldiers
aboard these vehicles were in contrast to the ever-dwin-
dling number of young elders in the mission field who
were being siphoned off to make war, not peace. It was a
sobering sight and thought, indeed.

The next day, Elder Smith was reminded that honor
and courage are not restricted to the battlefield. That day,
he visited a small monument, not far from Nashville,
erected to the memory of John H. Gibbs and William S.
Berry, two Mormon elders who were gunned down by a
mob in 1884. The two elders were preparing to hold a
preaching service in the home of James Condor when a
mob of masked gunmen appeared and shot the elders dead
without warning or provocation. Killed also were two
young men, nonmembers who tried to defend the elders.
James Condor's wife was seriously injured. B. H. Roberts,
Elder Smith's long-time associate among the General Authorities, was in charge of the Southern States Mission at
the time, headquartered in Chattanooga. Using a disguise,
he entered the area, which seethed with anti-Mormon
hatred, obtained the bodies, and shipped them to Utah
for burial in their hometowns.

The contrast between the public hatred toward the

Church at that time and the warm reception Elder Smith received in Nashville fifty-eight years later was striking. He was received with respect and held peaceful, well-publicized meetings attended by both members and non-members.

Of special concern to him was the well-being of the missionaries. By listening to their testimonies and holding personal interviews, he was able to gauge their worthiness and dedication and to give encouragement or admonition as required.

The pattern set during the meetings at Louisville and Nashville was followed during the remainder of the mission tour. Since there were no stakes in the area at the time, the mission president had jurisdiction over both the missionaries and the district and branch leaders as well as the members residing there. So in these cities and the others he visited, Elder Smith divided his time with the missionaries, the local leaders and the general membership, usually in that order of priority.

From Nashville, the party traveled to Chattanooga, where, for Elder Smith, the meetings were doubtless marked by nostalgia. It was here he and Lucy had lived together both as newlyweds and as missionaries, serving under their good friend J. Golden Kimball, who had been killed in a terrible auto accident near Reno, Nevada, the year after Lucy's death. Left alone, George Albert Smith, the survivor, had continued on the course he and Lucy and their friend had followed, now with new companions and new friends. But regardless of how kind and thoughtful the new friends and companions were, they could never replace the ones who had shared the struggling years of his early ministry. Following a practice from which he seldom deviated, Elder Smith probably did not share with his audience in Chattanooga any intimate reflections about his past experiences there.

Leaving Chattanooga, the party traveled to Knoxville, Tennessee, and then back into Kentucky for meetings at Lexington. Moving into West Virginia, they held meetings during four days in Huntington (where a new chapel was dedicated), Charleston, Wheeling, and Fairmont. Then, for eight days, the travelers held the usual meetings in seven different cities, four in North Carolina and three in Virginia. The tour ended at Richmond, Virginia, on November 2, 1942. There remained a wearing three-day trip home on the train before Elder Smith could again enjoy the comfort of his own bed.

He completed his stake conference assignments for the year with short trips to Cedar City and Ogden, Utah. Then he spent the holiday break at home, where, on Christmas day, he "enjoyed a grate fire." He closed out the year with his friends at the Blind Center, where he enjoyed a banquet and spoke to them. Returning home, he wrote appreciatively, "Am grateful for my blessings of 1942 and hope to live worthy of a continuance, Amen."

This simple sentence masks a profound philosophy that governed the life of George Albert Smith. Even in the most dire circumstances, he could always find something to be grateful for. His persistent search for the good and the positive in life is reminiscent of the man who, when treed by a bear, congratulated himself on the magnificent view from the treetop. Elder Smith found positive things even in adversity. And his expression of the "hope" he would "live worthy of a continuance" implied an understanding that the way he lived determined whether he would be happy or unhappy. Elder Smith was not given to philosophizing. His strength as a teacher lay principally in his example and in the buoyant, motivational feelings his words and actions inspired. He seemed not so much interested in explaining principles as in demonstrating their importance by the way he lived.

The year 1943 would bring significant changes in the life of George Albert Smith, but at first it seemed essentially a routine replay of 1942. He was back on the stake conference circuit in mid-January, going first to Burbank, California, and then to American Fork, Utah. At month's end, he was back home where, after attending meetings in Salt

Lake City the last day of January, he "enjoyed a bowl of bread and milk."

Following a conference of the Garland stake in Bear River, Utah, in mid-February, Elder Smith prepared for a long trip to Southern Arizona and Old Mexico. Flying first to Los Angeles, he went by train to Safford in the Gila Valley in southeastern Arizona. There he was met by the forty-eight-year-old president of the Mount Graham stake, Spencer W. Kimball. A native of Salt Lake City, Utah, President Kimball had moved to "the valley" as a little boy when his father, Andrew Kimball, was called by the Brethren to provide leadership in this remote outpost of the Church. There Andrew Kimball had served as the president of the St. Joseph Stake, which then included all of the Church units in the Gila Valley. And for many years, he also served as the president of the Indian Mission, whose jurisdiction extended to Indian tribes throughout the United States. From his father, Spencer Kimball had acquired a great love for the American Indians, a love that, in the years ahead, would extend to all those of Lamanite descent. This love was shared by Elder Smith, who, years before, had been especially assigned by President Heber J. Grant to work with the Lamanites. It was this charge that, in large part, accounted for Elder Smith's assignment to make the extended tour of the South Pacific Islands in 1938. And it was this charge that had taken Elder Smith on an extended visit to the Hopi and Navajo tribes in 1941. On that occasion, Elder Smith had visited the Indian villages of Oraibi, Tuba City, Hoteville, Moencopi, Keams Canyon, Indian Wells, Walpi, and Polacco. In these villages, he met with the Indian chiefs and with tribal members in their homes. There he administered to the sick and left his blessing on the families. It was this background that had given George Albert Smith the title of Apostle to the Lamanites among the leaders of the Church. And when he shook hands with stake president Spencer W. Kimball in Safford on February 27, 1943, little did either of them realize that within a few months President Kimball would be a member of the Twelve and that a few years later he would be given a special charge by the Prophet, George Albert Smith, to work with the Lamanites, a charge that would dominate the remainder of his life.

Elder Smith enjoyed his stay with the Kimballs. He was grateful for the treatment he received from President Kimball's wife, Camilla. "Sister Kimball welcomed us and served us a splendid supper," he wrote appreciatively. Later he confided to his journal gratitude for a "splendid bed." And on leaving Safford, he reported, "Spencer Kimball and family treated us fine and the conference was spirited."

From Safford, Elder Smith traveled across the border into Mexico, where he held meetings in the Mormon colony at Colonia Dublan. Here he found more of the descendants of the Latter-day Saint families who had sought refuge from the harassment of U.S. officials who had hounded the Mormon polygamists during the days of the underground. Nearby was the Latter-day Saint community of Colonia, Juarez, where his friend Marion G. Romney was born and from which he and his family had been driven during the Mexican revolution. The stamp of Mormon colonization lay upon these little villages, as it did upon dozens of others like them in the United States, with their wide streets lined with Lombardy poplars and the orderly arrangement of business, civic, and religious buildings in the central core and large lots in the residential neighborhoods for family orchards and gardens. And here he found the same spirit and attitude that characterized similar Latter-day Saint communities north of the border, where the members sang the same hymns, used the same instructional manuals, taught the same doctrine, and practiced the same religious rituals. Such uniformity and consistency was yet another testament to the effectiveness of the frequent conference visits of General Authorities like George Albert Smith who regularly monitored conditions in these communities.

On the return trip to Salt Lake City, Elder Smith

stopped in Phoenix, where he again was the guest of Delbert L. Stapley. There the apostle enjoyed another "good bed"; and during the quarterly conference of the Phoenix Stake, he called and ordained Orlando Clement Williams as a patriarch. On the way home, he also stopped in Los Angeles for a meeting of the board of Western Airlines.

There were occasional interludes during George Albert Smith's hectic life when the pace slowed and the crowded routine of meetings, interviews, ordinations, and blessings gave way to relaxed reflection and introspection. One of these occurred a few weeks after his return from the swing into Old Mexico. Having gone east to attend a meeting of the executive board of the Boy Scouts of America, he went to Cambridge to visit Albert and his family. Merely to be with this much loved and only son was enough to raise the spirits of the father, who had justifiable pride in his character and achievements. Albert had distinguished himself at Harvard, one of the most prestigious academic centers in the world. And that distinction had come from his own intelligence and industry, not from any reflected reputation from his famous Mormon ancestors. Indeed, in the cloistered halls at Cambridge, that ancestry would have been a hindrance rather than a help in the minds of some of Albert's less charitable colleagues. And so Elder Smith could take satisfaction in the fact that his son's eminence had come not because of but in spite of his name and ancestry.

Albert was good company. His intellectual bent and academic attainments had been tempered by his rearing in a home of faith and prayer. And the things he had learned there about spiritual influences had been magnified by his service as a young missionary. Albert was quiet and thoughtful, an interesting conversationalist and one who deeply loved his father and was proud to be descended from the Smith and Woodruff clans. All this, added to the love of the father for the son, the father's avid interest in historic sites, and his dedication to the Sons of the American Revolution combined to make March 29,

1943, a day of special significance for Elder George Albert Smith.

The day began with a brief visit to the New England mission home, where Elder Smith paid his respects to President Reeder. With that formality out of the way, the congenial pair drove northwest to Concord in the crisp coolness of an early Massachusetts spring. That sleepy town, with neighboring Lexington, is looked upon as the cradle of American independence. To one as dedicated to the SAR as was George Albert Smith, this was Mecca, the shrine of the revolution. Here the Minutemen met with the British at old North Bridge in a skirmish when gunfire was first exchanged between the Colonists and Royal British troops. That exchange was immortalized by Ralph Waldo Emerson in the "Concord Hymn" as "the shot heard round the world."

Elder Smith must have been excited to visit the Minute Men National Historic Park, where stands the reconstructed North Bridge and French's famous bronze minutemen statue. Here history came alive to the kindly man with the impaired eyesight. And we can be sure that his scholar son supplemented the information provided by the official guide. No less interesting to Elder Smith would have been visits to the Antiquarian Museum, which contains Emerson's study; Walden Pond State Reservation; and the old homes of Emerson, Nathaniel Hawthorne, and Louisa May Alcott.

While Elder Smith's visual limitations and Church duties had restricted his acquaintance with the writings of these and other early American authors, he had a genuine appreciation for good literature and its positive impact on the cultural development of a people. At the same time, he was conscious of the negative impact of some writings. As a result, he was more inclined in his sermons to emphasize and encourage the reading of the scriptures in preference to any other literature. "I admonish you, O Israel," he declared in a general conference address during World War II, when there was a flood of literature he considered questionable, "search the scriptures; read them in your homes; teach your families what the Lord has said, and let us spend less time in reading the unimportant and often harmful literature of the day and go to the fountain of truth and read the word of the Lord." (*Conference Report*, October 1917, p. 41.)

There were so many things of interest to see in and around Concord that two months later, during a mission tour, Elder Smith persuaded Albert to drive him there again. By this time the trees were all leafed out and these, with the well-tended grape orchards compliments of old Ephraim Bull who introduced the commercial cultivation of table grapes in the United States at this place, made Concord and its environs a veritable garden. And the Sleepy Hollow Cemetery, where Concord's famous sons and daughters lay buried, was a quiet reminder of the recurring cycle of life and death and of the transient nature of mortal existence.

The April 1943 general conference was pervaded by a somber air of uncertainty and sadness. Sixteen months of war, with its daily reports of far-flung battles, its shocking casualty lists, and its dislocations of family and community life had sobered America, for clearly the conflict would not be won speedily or easily. Despite the sacrifices that had been made, the men killed and wounded, the proliferation of the engines of war, and the daily toil of American warriors and workers, there was no end in sight. The British and Americans were still battling Rommel and his German panzer divisions in Tunisia; the United States naval and amphibious forces were island hopping in the Pacific; and Hitler's main army was locked in a death struggle with the Soviets on the eastern European front. The mood, therefore, was generally grim, and it was reflected in the sermons delivered from the Tabernacle pulpit. Elder Smith's sermon focused on the tragedy of war and the need for Latter-day Saint servicemen to preserve their integrity and moral purity. He reminded them that they not only had a duty to their country, but that they also had a duty to their wives and mothers to refrain from conduct that would violate the sacred covenants that bound them together. These and other similar admonitions of the Brethren were prompted by fear of the infidelity of some servicemen and of the resulting heartache and trauma of the offenders and their families. To provide an extra shield against temptations, Elder Smith and his Brethren had just approved the publication of a pocket-sized copy of the Book of Mormon and a compilation titled "Principles of the Gospel" for distribution in the armed forces. These were published a month after the conference.

Two weeks after the general conference, Elder Smith attended the stake conference in Weiser, Idaho; and on May 5, 1943, he again left for the East, where he remained for a month. En route to the Northern States Mission, which he had been assigned to tour, he held meetings in Ames and Des Moines, Iowa. The mission tour, which was interrupted to attend Boy Scout meetings in New York City and to visit Concord a second time, took him to twelve cities in Illinois, Michigan, Ohio, and Indiana. The trip was tiring, which must have reminded the seventy-three-year-old apostle that he was no longer young. It also brought on another siege of nervous tension accompanied by recurring nightmares. "Am weak and worried," he wrote on June 12; and the next day he was "weak and nervous."

Part of the strain on Elder Smith at this time was caused by the rapidly declining health of Rudger Clawson, president of the Twelve. Among the many ligaments binding this pair together was their service as young missionaries in the Southern States. Thirteen years older than George Albert Smith, Rudger Clawson served in the South in 1878, when he was twenty-one years old. Like Elder Smith, Rudger had experienced the bitterness and rage shown toward the Mormon elders by some Southerners during these early years. But his experience was more brutal and bloody than the ordeal George Albert and J. Golden Kimball suffered the night the mobbers fired into the cabin where they were staying. It occurred on July 21, 1878, when he and his companion, Joseph Standing, were surrounded by an armed mob at Varnal Station, Whitfield County, Georgia. As the elders were herded into the nearby woods, presumably to be beaten, Elder Standing, the senior companion, showed resistance and was shot in the head. When a leader of the mob ordered that Elder Clawson also be shot, the young missionary deliberately folded his arms and said "shoot."

This calmness under pressure, which apparently saved his life, also impressed Lorenzo Snow when he met Rudger Clawson in the Utah penitentiary, where they had both been imprisoned for practicing plural marriage. Later, after their release, Elder Snow recommended young Brother Clawson to succeed him as the stake president in Brigham City, Utah; and in 1898, after Lorenzo Snow became president of the Church, he called Rudger Clawson to the Twelve, the only person so called during his administration. On October 6, 1901, Elder Clawson was also sustained as the second counselor in the First Presidency, but he was never set apart because President Snow died four days later.

Following Elder Smith's call to the Twelve in 1903, he and Rudger Clawson served together for forty years, sharing the joys and trials of the apostleship. Such a lengthy association was the final cord binding this pair together, and their characters reflected the best qualities of their shared religion. We have already seen the saintly aspects of George Albert Smith's life. And Lorenzo Snow, himself a spiritual giant, once called Rudger Clawson the most Christ-like man he had ever known. This appraisal is extraordinary when considering that President Snow's acquaintance with Church leaders extended back to the early days in Kirtland, Ohio.

During the first week of June 1943, Elder Smith watched the life of his old friend slowly flicker out. It was finally extinguished on June 21, 1943. Immediately on learning of President Clawson's passing, George Albert went to the Clawson home to express his condolences to the family.

They needed no comforting because their husband and father had lived eighty-six fruitful years and had passed away as quietly and serenely as he had lived.

Later that same day, a meeting of the Twelve was held in the Salt Lake Temple. Elder Smith made special note of one item that came up for discussion: "Proposal to sustain me as President of the Twelve was considered pre-mature. I am the senior."

Chapter Nineteen

President of the Twelve

The guidelines and precedents established during the hundred and eight years of the existence of the Quorum of the Twelve obviated the need for immediate action to reorganize that body at the death of Rudger Clawson. Elder Smith's succinct statement "I am the senior" said it all. In this quorum, unlike any other quorum in the Church, the principle of seniority reigns. And the senior apostle in the quorum serves without counselors. He, of course, seeks counsel from his brethren; and because of the principle of unity enjoined upon members of the quorum, he seldom, if ever, takes action unless all are in accord. Yet, his alone is the final and controlling voice. While quorum action might be taken despite the dissent of one of its junior members, such action can never properly be taken without the consent of the president or senior member.

The position of the president of the Twelve is an anomaly in priesthood organization. The nearest thing to it is the priests quorum, where the bishop presides without counselors. But the bishop does not succeed to that position because of seniority in the quorum. He acquires it by appointment, even in the unlikely case of a direct descendant of Aaron. And while the formal act of setting apart the senior apostle as the president of the quorum might be regarded as an appointment, it is not an appointment in the strict sense. It is merely the confirmation of an inchoate right received when the senior member was first ordained to the apostleship.

This anomaly in priesthood organization preserves the structural integrity of the Church at the death of a president and provides for a smooth, predictable transfer of authority to a new leader. With the dissolution of the First Presidency at the death of a president, the Twelve becomes the governing body of the Church, subject to the ultimate control of its president who at that moment is the head of the earthly church. When, therefore, Elder George Albert Smith was formally set apart as the president of the Quorum of the Twelve on July 12, 1943, he was only one step away from becoming the presiding officer of The Church of Jesus Christ of Latter-day Saints.

There were two vacancies in the Twelve when Elder Smith was set apart, the first created by the death of Sylvester Q. Cannon on May 29, 1943, and the second by the death of President Clawson. Later that summer, Spencer W. Kimball and Ezra Taft Benson would be called to fill these vacancies, although they would not be ordained and set apart until the October general conference.

It was an interesting and diverse group over which the new president presided. At the time, exclusive of himself and the two unordained brethren, it included a farmer, George F. Richards; a historian, Joseph Fielding Smith; three lawyers, Stephen L. Richards, Charles A. Callis, and Albert E. Bowen; an engineer, Richard R. Lyman; and three educators, John A. Widtsoe, Joseph F. Merrill, and Harold B. Lee. Elder Richards was the eldest at eighty-two, and Elder Lee, the youngest, was forty-four. With the ordination of Elders Kimball and Benson, a business executive and an agricultural expert would be added to the group.

Elder Smith's administrative role in his new position was greatly simplified by his forty years of apprenticeship, and by the ability and dedication of the members of the quorum. Moreover, during the last months of Rudger Clawson's life, Elder Smith had handled most of the administrative details. So he fit very easily and quickly into the new routine. We can gauge his style of leadership as quorum president by this summary written by Elder Richard R. Lyman: "Under the direction of George Albert Smith the members of the Council of the Twelve are sure to be tied together by bonds of genuine affection, and unitedly and individually every member will have the freest possible opportunity, encouragement, and inspiration to do his best." (*Improvement Era,* September 1943, p. 529.)

Because of limitations on their number and the increasing demands on the General Authorities as the Church continued to grow, Elder Smith's new position did not diminish the number of his stake conference and other assignments. Indeed, it may have increased them because of the new president's desire to lead by example and to bear his full share of the load. So in July, during the recess, he attended special meetings in Preston, Idaho. And in August he was in Los Angeles for a stake conference. While there, he tended to his duties as a member of the board of Western Airlines. Meanwhile, in Salt Lake City, he accepted a government appointment to serve on the War Finance Commission.

Even as his new calling did not change Elder Smith's work patterns, neither did it change the recurring cycles of illness he had suffered through the years. In late August, he was stricken with a painful attack of lumbago. By September 8, he was able to report that his back was "not quite as lame." But the lingering effects slowed him down for weeks.

Although Elder Smith was still below par at the time of the October general conference, he was in robust health compared to President Heber J. Grant. The eighty-six-year-old Prophet had suffered a stroke months before that partially paralyzed his left side and slurred his speech. Determined to overcome this obstacle, as he had overcome many others during his long life, President Grant had faithfully followed a program of physical therapy to strengthen his left arm and leg. Not satisfied with the results, he had begun to carry a small rubber ball, which he squeezed with his left hand to strengthen his muscles. Since the Prophet's illness had limited his activity, the ceremony to ordain the two new brethren was held in the First Presidency's council room in the administration building rather than in the temple. There, on October 7, 1943, after the Prophet had given them the apostolic charge, first Elder Kimball then Elder Benson knelt before him with the counselors and the other apostles gathered around, to be ordained to the apostleship and inducted into the Twelve. Elder Smith reported that afterward all except President Grant went to the upper room of the Temple for the weekly council meeting and prayer circle.

Two weeks later, Elder Smith was in Pasadena, California, for a stake conference. On the day of the conference, he was driven to a Western Airlines board meeting by his nephew Gerald Smith, the son of his brother Nicholas, who at the time was in Southern California with his wife, Olive. Elder Smith took almost as much satisfaction in the achievements of his nephews as he did those of his own son; and this one, Gerald, was special. He had been an outstanding athlete at the University of Utah, was a promising business executive, and would later distinguish himself as a mission president. And his radiant, benign personality, so much like that of his father, undoubtedly gave President Smith a much needed lift, especially after the excommunication of Elder Richard R. Lyman.

The following Sunday, Elder Smith was at home for the conference of his own stake, which he commended for having a "splendid youth program." During the week, before leaving again for New York, he attended graduation exercises at the University of Utah, where his friend and neighbor Governor Herbert B. Maw delivered the commencement address.

The apostle left Salt Lake City December 12, 1943, for the East. He usually traveled light, depending on train porters or hotel employees to launder and press the few clothes he took along. On this trip, however, his bags were more bulky than usual because he planned to spend Christmas with Albert and had stuffed some presents among his clothing for the loved ones in Boston.

En route to New York City, Elder Smith stopped in Chicago to attend to affairs at the mission headquarters. When he was ready to go to the depot to leave, a young elder named Marion D. Hanks drove him there. Elder Hanks was a distant relative through the Lyman family; in less than ten years he would be called as a general authority by President David O. McKay.

Elder Smith speedily disposed of his business in New York City and hurried to Boston on the eighteenth to begin a relaxed eight-day visit with Albert and family. The next day, the pair left for Concord for the third visit in less than a year. The father seemed unable to absorb enough of the facts and the spirit of this special place. And he was probably anxious to be alone with Albert to discuss the recent events that had so affected the Church and the family. Duplicating the relationship that had existed between his grandfather and father and between his father and himself, Elder Smith treated Albert not only as a son but as a counselor and confidant. His journals and diaries reflect such a relationship. In times of special stress or anxiety, he expressed the wish that Albert were near to help and counsel him. And now, during this crisis, undoubtedly the father sought solace and spiritual strength from this sensitive son.

Calling again upon his family for support, Elder Smith convened a family council on January 2, 1944, after returning from Boston. "Had my family together and talked to them," he wrote of the event. It is one of the few times he ever did this. Given the trauma of Elder Lyman's recent excommunication, his relationship to the family, and Elder Smith's sense of moral rectitude and responsibility, it is unlikely that he failed to draw lessons from the incident for the guidance of his family. The most obvious of these is that high position in the Church does not suspend personal responsibility, nor does it provide immunity from the consequences of transgression. Two weeks later, he spent an hour and a half with the Lyman family, giving them counsel and comfort.

On Sunday, January 9, 1944, Elder Smith had occasion to rejoice again in the achievements of a nephew. "Robert Farr Smith spoke very well," he recorded on that day after attending sacrament meeting in the Yale Ward. Robert was the son of his deceased brother Nathaniel, who had tended George Albert so solicitously while he lay ill in the tent at St. George. The love and appreciation for his brother's kindness during that crisis had rubbed off on the son. This was especially true after Nathaniel died and his teenage son, Robert, was left fatherless. George Albert arranged housing for the widow and children across the gully from the Yale Avenue home. In that close proximity, they became part of Elder Smith's family. Later when Robert was called to the mission field, he was assigned to the Southern States, where his Uncle George Albert had served; and, like his uncle, he was appointed mission secretary.

Years after President Smith's death, Robert grew a beard and moustache exactly like those of his uncle, apparently out of a subconscious or a deliberate desire to imitate him. And this, coupled with his spare frame and balding head, has caused Robert Farr Smith to become a George Albert Smith look-alike. The resemblance is startling. A few years ago, Robert was persuaded to represent President George Albert Smith on the float of a July 24 parade. He later reported that as the float passed the reviewing stand in Liberty Park, President Spencer W. Kimball, who was seated there, did a double take on seeing this living image of his deceased friend. Bob also reported that he could scarcely restrain himself from calling out, "Spencer, we think you are doing a wonderful job."

Two weeks after Robert Farr Smith's homecoming speech, the pulpit of the Yale ward was occupied by Utah's governor, Herbert B. Maw. The governor, both a lawyer and a professor of speech, is an impressive orator, articulate and analytical with a commanding presence and flawless delivery. Elder Smith admired his friend's abilities and often attended meetings where he was to speak. But at this sacrament service, something other than the governor's eloquence drew his special attention. "Twelve uniformed men [were] present and passed the sacrament," wrote the apostle in his diary. Overshadowing everything George Albert did during these days and months was the specter of war. In ordinary times, most of these twelve young men would have been on missions, not in the military. Before 1944 would end, eighty thousand Latter-day Saints would be in uniform. Tragically, some of them would be pitted against each other in combat. And worse still, the civilian population would become subjected to the terrors of war to an extent never known before. One can imagine the feelings of Elder Smith, a former president of the European mission, when he learned on March 6, 1944, that 800 U.S. planes had made a daylight bombing raid on Berlin. In that city were Latter-day Saints whom he loved. And this raid was merely the beginning of round-the-clock bombings of Berlin and other German cities that would indiscriminately destroy and maim. The only consolation was that this deadly action was deemed necessary to hasten the end of the European war.

"The invasion is the talk of all," wrote Elder Smith on June 6 following the allied landings at Normandy, sounding a hopeful note that the end might be in sight. A meeting that night in Provo of a Brigham Young University alumni group was abuzz with the same optimistic talk, an optimism that carried over to the conference he attended in the Salt Lake Cottonwood Stake on June 18. With him was Elder Ezra Taft Benson, who was nearing the end of his first year as a member of the Twelve. "Glorious morning," wrote President Smith exultantly. And that same mood persisted into the summer recess, when on July 8 he wrote contentedly, "Puttered around home trimming shrubbery etc. Enjoyed my work at home."

By this time, the Quorum of the Twelve was again at full strength. At the previous April general conference, Elder Mark E. Petersen had been called to fill the vacancy caused by the excommunication of Richard R. Lyman. While the circumstances surrounding Elder Petersen's call could not mitigate the tragedy of Elder Lyman's fall, they could and did reaffirm the spiritual and revelatory powers at work in the call to service in the Twelve. Not long before Elder Lyman's difficulties surfaced, Mark Petersen, general manager of the Deseret News, had a vivid dream. In it he saw a garbled newspaper headline, "Lyman R. Richard Dies." The same newspaper also carried a story of his call to the Twelve. The next day, he sent a reporter to the Church Administration Building to inquire about the health of the Brethren, especially Elder Lyman. Advised that everyone appeared to be well, Elder Petersen still retained the feeling that some unforeseen incident would remove Elder Lyman from the Twelve and that he would be called to replace him. When the announcement of the excommunication was put in his hand for publication, that feeling was strongly confirmed and remained with him during the months before his call in April 1944. When President Heber J. Grant extended the call to him, Elder Petersen related the dream and his spiritual promptings to the Prophet, who confirmed that the Lord had taken this means to reveal the call to him in advance. (Peggy Petersen Barton, *Mark E. Petersen* [Salt Lake City: Deseret Book Co., 1985], pp. 85-86.)

Similar incidents, demonstrating the manner in which God reveals his mind and will to his servants, were common among Elder George Albert Smith and his brethren in the Twelve. Revelation was a continuing phenomenon to them. It came in different forms: by dreams, as in the case of Mark E. Petersen; by visions; by the spirit of prophecy and revelation; by visitations from the unseen world; or, more frequently, by inner whisperings or promptings. Often the revelations came instantly and dramatically, and the Brethren knew in a moment what they should do. At other times, it came as an indistinct impression or a feeling that something was wrong. Ordinarily in a case of this kind, the Lord would be sought in prayer for clarification, direction, or simply his blessing to resolve any difficulty that had prompted the feeling. Elder Smith once related to a Provo, Utah, audience a sacred experience of his grandfather, who was a member of the Twelve when a vague, troubling feeling came over him. Unable to discern what had prompted it or what he could do about it, he went to the Endowment House in Salt Lake City, where he put on his temple robes and knelt in prayer at the altar. "Heavenly Father," he prayed, "I feel that there is something seriously wrong with my family in Provo. Thou knowest that I cannot be with them there and be here. Heavenly Father, wilt thou preserve and safeguard them, and I will be grateful to thee and honor thee." George Albert Smith then told his audience that at the time his grandfather was praying, "just as near as it was possible to indicate by checking the time," his father, John Henry Smith, who was a young man at the time, had fallen into the Provo River. "It was at flood time," he explained. "Logs and rocks were pouring down from the canyon, and he was helpless. Those who were near saw his predicament, but they could not reach him. The turbulence of the water was such that nobody could live in it. They just stood there in horror. Father was doing everything he could to keep his head above the water, but he was being thrown up and down and being dashed against the rocks and logs. All at once a wave lifted him bodily from the water and threw him on the shore. It was a direct answer of the prayer of a servant of the Lord." (*Church News,* February 16, 1946.)

Elder Smith had attended another stake conference in Provo shortly before the general conference where Elder

Petersen was sustained as a member of the Twelve. It was there in the Provo Tabernacle forty-one years before that he had attended his first stake conference as a member of the Twelve. The next time he would speak there, it would be as president of the Church. Meanwhile, a year of constant travel, meetings, appointments, and interviews remained, intermixed with sieges of illness. The week after general conference, Elder Smith was in Los Angeles for Church business and a meeting of Western Air. Returning home the same day, he went to bed with a throbbing headache. "Neuralgia in my head and shoulders," he reported. "Use hot bottle and electric pad and bromo seltzer. . . . Didn't get up until 3 p.m." He felt well enough to attend the Pioneer Stake conference the following weekend; and a few days later, he left for a stake conference in Fresno, California. Afterward, he commenced what was supposed to be a five-day mission tour. The first meeting was in Oakdale. The following day, April 26, Elder Smith became ill in San Francisco and was in bed for three days, missing missionary meetings there and in Rosevale. He managed to recover sufficiently to join the mission president for the last meeting in Watsonville.

Two weeks later, the apostle was in New York City, where on May 14, 1944, he installed young Roy W. Doxey as the new president of the Eastern States Mission. The next day, he was driven to Boston in a car with no heater. "Car cold. Kept coat and hat on," he wrote. On the way home, he stopped in Ames, Iowa, to visit Robert Farr Smith, who had been inducted into the navy, and to speak to a group of servicemen who were in training there. Four months and seven stake conferences later, he again met this nephew, who had completed his training and been assigned to a naval unit in the San Francisco Bay area. "Robert Farr at meetings," wrote the apostle on September 17 of a stake conference in Oakland, California. "He spoke well."

After the October general conference, Elder Smith finished the year with the customary assignments, including another trip East, a tour of the Northern California Mission, and two trips to Los Angeles, the last on December 5 to speak at the funeral of relative Ida Smith. Despite a painful attack of lumbago, he fulfilled a speaking appointment the day before Christmas at the sacrament meeting of the University Ward near the campus of the University of Utah in Salt Lake City. "Had felt my inability," wrote he, "but the Lord kept me free from pain and gave me liberty." A week later, the last day of the year, the apostle visited his father's widow, Aunt Josephine, who was near death, and then called nine families of friends and relatives to wish them a happy new year.

The following day, the first of the most auspicious year in the life of George Albert Smith, did not begin well. He awoke after a restless night, having been plagued by pain from lumbago and "disturbing dreams." Later in the day, a grandson drove him to the state capitol building for the inauguration of governor Herbert B. Maw. President Smith occupied a place of prominence on the stand with other religious, government, and civic leaders. Held in the rotunda of the capitol building, the services were short and simple yet grandly impressive because of the vast expanse and marbled elegance of the rotunda. The occasion could not have failed to remind the apostle of his father and of their involvement in formulating the basic design for this striking structure.

President Smith's disturbing dreams seem to have been triggered by the uncertainties created by the war, the illness of his son Albert, and his own physical problems. "Worried about general conditions," he noted the day following the inauguration. A week later while traveling to San Francisco by train, he experienced a deep depression. "Wished could hear Albert improving," he wrote plaintively. And while staying in the Bay Area with mission president German E. Ellsworth, he suffered another painful attack of lumbago that put him in bed. While he was down recuperating, a steady stream of war news over the radio aggravated his nervous tension. The week before, he had been reminded

264

pointedly of the pervasive influence of the war, not only upon those directly involved in the conflict but also upon those at home. On January 4, during a trip to Los Angeles to attend a Western Air board meeting, he had spoken at the funeral of Ronald T. Bollinger, a Douglas Aircraft test pilot who had been killed while testing a military plane. The aviation industry, for which he had such high hopes as an instrument to bless and elevate humanity, now was dedicated in large part to destroying human civilization. The natural repugnance a person of peace like George Albert Smith had toward war was neutralized by his perception that the war served a higher purpose: to preserve institutions, such as the government of the United States, which guaranteed independence and freedom of choice.

Following his return from the two trips to California in early January, Elder Smith became immersed again in the continual round of meetings, interviews, and ceremonies that characterized his headquarters duties. On the eighteenth, he attended the weekly temple meeting of the First Presidency and the Twelve. After this, George Albert changed into a white suit to perform the sealing and marriage of a young couple who had sought his services. Such ceremonies were frequent. Indeed, the next day found him in the temple again for the same purpose.

Elder Smith's role as president of the Twelve brought with it additional duties beyond the scope of his ecclesiastical calling. His prominence and experience put him in demand as a corporate board member. In addition to his service on the board of Western Air, he regularly attended the meetings of the Utah–Idaho Sugar Company, the Heber J. Grant Company, and other Church corporations. While time limitations prevented him from becoming deeply involved in the daily activities of these businesses, his wide-ranging experience, good judgment, and creativity enabled him to make positive contributions to them in setting policy and charting a course for the future. At the same time, the stipends President Smith received for these services were essential in augmenting the modest living allowance he received for his service as a General Authority. It was only by the greatest frugality that he was able to maintain the standard of living his family reputation and responsibilities and his status in the community demanded.

During the last months preceding his elevation to the presidency of the Church, Elder Smith's role as a good Samaritan and comforter was greatly magnified. In early February, for instance, Elder Marion G. Romney and his wife, Ida, were involved in a terrible automobile accident that almost took their lives. George Albert repeatedly went to the hospital to inquire about their condition or to encourage or bless them. During the following weeks, he gave similar attention to three other General Authorities who were hospitalized, Elder Charles A. Callis of the Twelve and elders Rufus K. Hardy and Samuel O. Bennion of the First Council of Seventy. President Smith was frequently at their bedsides to administer to them or to speak words of comfort and encouragement. Elder Callis, who had suffered a serious heart attack, recovered and lived on for two more years. But elders Hardy and Bennion passed away on successive days, March 7 and March 8, 1945. Afterward, Elder Smith comforted the families of his deceased brethren and participated in their funerals, offering a eulogy and a prayer. A few weeks before these services, Elder Smith had traveled to remote Randolph, Utah, during the coldest part of the winter to speak at the funeral of an old friend. And following the death of President Franklin D. Roosevelt in early April, he attended a memorial service for the nation's president in the rotunda of Utah's capitol.

Intermittently throughout this period, Elder Smith was himself in need of a Good Samaritan. He continued to have spells when he was "weak" or "nervous," had occasional nightmares, was bothered with a trauma in his left eye, and suffered excruciating pain from lumbago that made him so lame that he began using a cane. The crowning agony came in mid-February, when he made four visits within a week to his dentist, Creed Haymond. With no apparent intention to disparage the skill of his friend and neighbor, the apostle noted following these visits, "Grateful for novocaine."

Amid all this, the normal flow of life continued unabated. Elder Smith spoke at the ninety-sixth anniversary of the organization of the Fourteenth Ward; attended the forty-fifth wedding anniversary of Stephen L Richards; welcomed Ezra Taft Benson into the neighborhood; set apart eighteen missionaries in a single day; attended two stake conferences; counseled with a Salt Lake City ministerial group that included Catholic Bishop Hunt and Episcopalian Bishop Moulton about a commemorative service on Good Friday; hosted the winning M-Man basketball team at a luncheon in the Hotel Utah; and received a courtesy call from Indian Chief Thunderbird of Canada.

As the April 1945 general conference approached, Elder Smith's normal anxieties about his participation were greatly magnified. He had been invited to give the Church of the Air talk over a national radio network in connection with the conference. George Albert was not a stranger to radio. Indeed, he had been an avid supporter of the medium from its inception, recognizing in it a useful tool to advance the work. Moreover, he had spoken over the radio numerous times, both at general conferences and on other occasions. But special circumstances removed this event from the ordinary and invested it with an apprehension he had not experienced before. It was the greatly expanded size of the audience, the prestige of the program, and the subject of his talk that made the difference. The national hook-up would carry his message to many times the number of people he had spoken to before. The Church of the Air had featured nationally known clerics and theologians of various denominations. Most intimidating, however, was the subject of his discourse — the origin of man. While Elder Smith understood the subject perfectly well, as also its significance and implications to the individual and society, it was contrary to his customary speaking style to deliver a deep, doctrinal discourse such as this. To him, the origin of man was a given that required neither demonstration nor explanation. Left strictly to his own choice, he likely would have preferred to discuss not the whence of man but the why and whither of man. George Albert Smith was much more concerned about personal conduct and the quality of life than about abstruse doctrines and concepts — and his teaching and preaching had always reflected this bias. So, to treat a subject so different from his customary format and under such unusual conditions was especially stressful. He struggled with the talk for days, seeking counsel from others. "At night, talked over Church of air talk with Emily and Edith," he noted on March 27. A week later, he sought the advice of Elder Richard L. Evans, the skilled narrator of the Tabernacle Choir broadcasts. "He helped me very much," wrote Elder Smith of the meeting. Only three days before the talk was to be given, he was "nervous"; and the next day, after struggling over it for hours, he was "not satisfied" with the results. These feelings of uncertainty and agitation seem to have persisted until air time. And then, after the ordeal was over, the speaker felt great relief and satisfaction. "The Lord helped me and I am grateful," wrote he. The experience confirmed again that the work never becomes easy or routine and that past successes are no guarantee of success in the future. Elder Smith was constantly dependent on the Lord for inspiration.

Two weeks after the general conference, President Smith accepted an invitation to speak at the sacrament meeting of the Valley View Ward, whose thirty-one-year-old Bishop, Rex C. Reeve, would later become a General Authority. And the following weekend found him in Vernal, Utah, on a stake conference assignment. On the day of his return from Vernal, April 30, Elder Smith received a telephone call from the home of President Heber J. Grant advising that the eighty-eight-year-old Prophet had asked that he come to give him a blessing. George Albert invited his brother Winslow, the president of the Prophet's stake, to go with him. The two brothers were driven to the Grant residence, a plain bungalow high on the avenues north of the city. For several years, President Grant had been handicapped by a debilitating stroke he had suffered in California after playing two vigorous rounds of golf on successive days. Afterward, he had been able to continue his work but on a greatly reduced schedule. For several weeks before the visit of the Smiths, however, he had been confined to his home; and the perception of those close to him was that his days were numbered.

The brothers found the bearded Prophet lying in bed. He seemed not to be in pain, but he was lethargic and restless. After President Grant weakly greeted his visitors, Winslow anointed him with consecrated oil, and George Albert sealed the anointing, pronouncing a blessing of comfort, peace, and freedom from pain. It was the last time George Albert saw his old friend and fellow apostle alive.

Walking to the front porch of the home, the visitors were greeted with the view that President Grant had enjoyed for years and that often, in the early morning hours, had inspired him to burst into song with the hymns of Zion. Below them, stretching south toward Provo, lay the verdant Salt Lake Valley, hedged in by the towering peaks of the Wasatch Mountains on the left and the Oquirrhs on the right. Across City Creek Canyon to the west stood the state capitol, etched against the background of the Great Salt Lake glimmering now in the late April sun. And in the valley below, slightly to the right at two o'clock, stood the spired temple where for forty-two years Heber J. Grant and George Albert Smith had spent countless hours together. Although unknown to him at the time, only a few days hence George Albert Smith would meet there again with his apostolic brethren, all except Heber J. Grant, when he would be ordained and set apart as the eighth president of The Church of Jesus Christ of Latter-day Saints.

Chapter Twenty

President of the Church

Nine days after administering to President Grant, Elder Smith left Salt Lake City with Stephen L Richards, Clifford E. Young, Bishop Legrand Richards, and George Q. Morris, with Chicago as the first destination. There, on May 13, 1945, Elder Smith installed John K. Edmunds as the new president of the Chicago Stake. Then the travelers separated, with Elder Smith and Brother Morris continuing on to New York City, where George Albert had business to transact. In the early morning hours of May 15, Elder Smith was aroused from sleep by a porter on the train, who advised him that President Heber J. Grant had passed away a few hours before. He arose immediately, dressed, and, with George Q. Morris, left the train at Buffalo, New York. Unable to arrange for a return flight to Salt Lake City, Elder Smith took the next train west while Brother Morris continued on to New York City to conduct the business George Albert had intended to transact.

At the moment of the passing of Heber J. Grant, George Albert Smith became, in fact, the president of the Church by virtue of his position as the president of the Quorum of the Twelve Apostles. To make the transition official, of course, required the formal action of the members of the Twelve, including President Grant's counselors, J. Reuben Clark and David O. McKay, who, on the dissolution of the First Presidency at President Grant's death, had automatically become members of the Twelve. In these circumstances, it was not improper for Elder Smith to begin planning for his presidential administration as the train sped toward Salt Lake City. "Puzzled about adjustments with brethren and office help," he wrote on May 16, 1945, after his train left Chicago.

At the windy city, he had been met at the depot by Bishop Richards and Elder Clifford E. Young, who had remained in Chicago. Also there were railroad officials who helped Elder Smith make connections with the westward bound Streamliner, which delayed its departure from Chicago to accommodate the Mormon leader. And there, too, George Albert found something that would soon become a routine aspect of his life—a group of newspaper reporters. The news of President Grant's death had spread rapidly as had the word of Elder Smith's status as his successor. And since the Church by now occupied a position of prominence in the United States, its highest leader was a newsworthy subject, especially the one who had suddenly been thrust into the spotlight by the death of the Mormon Prophet, Heber J. Grant.

At Ogden, Utah, Jack Thomas boarded the train to accompany Elder Smith to Salt Lake City. Brother Thomas assisted the Brethren with their travel arrangements and otherwise helped them expedite nonecclesiastical matters. When the two of them arrived at Salt Lake City's Union Depot, they found a welcoming party that included friends, family members, and elders George F. Richards and Joseph Fielding Smith of the Twelve. Elder Richards, next in line to George Albert in apostolic seniority, would soon be set apart as the president of the Twelve. And his

271

cousin, Joseph Fielding Smith, would himself become the president of the Church not many years hence.

Typically, George Albert's first action on arriving in Salt Lake City was to drive to the Grant residence to visit "Aunt Gusta" the deceased Prophet's widow. He extended his condolences and counseled with her and other family members about the funeral arrangements. The long and distinguished life of President Grant and the recent infirmities he had suffered left little room for genuine mourning at his passing. The general feeling was one of gratitude for his life of virtue and achievement, for an end to his suffering, and for the knowledge that the separation was only temporary.

These were the principal themes of the sermons and tributes at President Grant's funeral in the Salt Lake Tabernacle on May 18, 1945. The services were conducted by President George Albert Smith, who was also the principal speaker. "Had good liberty in speaking," he wrote of the occasion. President Smith also led the funeral procession to the cemetery high on the north bench of the valley where the interment took place. As the cortege slowly moved past Third East on South Temple, the bells of the Catholic Cathedral of the Madeleine pealed out in a demonstration of ecumenical brotherhood, a feeling that President Grant had done much to foster and that President George Albert Smith would augment and strengthen during his prophetic tenure. The demonstration was repeated at Tenth East on South Temple as the nurses in training at the Catholic-owned Holy Cross Hospital stood respectfully at curbside while the hearse passed by.

On Monday May 21, 1945, three days after the funeral, the Quorum of the Twelve Apostles met in the upper room of the Salt Lake Temple for a ceremony that had been held there only three times since the temple's dedication in 1893. These had taken place when Lorenzo Snow, Joseph F. Smith, and Heber J. Grant were ordained as the prophet, seer, and revelator and the president of The Church of Jesus Christ of Latter-day Saints. Actually, sixteen men assembled in the upper room that day: the twelve men who comprised the Quorum of the Twelve at the time of President Grant's death (George Albert Smith, George F. Richards, Joseph Fielding Smith, Stephen L Richards, John A. Widtsoe, Joseph F. Merrill, Charles A. Callis, Albert E. Bowen, Harold B. Lee, Spencer W. Kimball, Ezra Taft Benson, and Mark E. Petersen); President Grant's counselors, J. Reuben Clark and David O. McKay, who took their place in the circle in the order of their apostolic seniority, Elder McKay between George F. Richards and Joseph Fielding Smith and Elder Clark between Charles A. Callis and Albert E. Bowen; and two men who did not participate in the ceremony, Joseph F. Smith, the patriarch of the Church, and Joseph Anderson, secretary to the First Presidency, who kept the record of the meeting.

Five years later, Elder Harold B. Lee set the scene for what took place on this occasion. "The chairs usually occupied by the First Presidency were vacant," he wrote, "and for hours the members of the Twelve, each in his turn, expressed his feelings fully on the matter of the new appointment." (*Improvement Era*, 53 [December 1950]: 1007.) When each one had spoken, George F. Richards moved that George Albert Smith be appointed as the president of the Church. That motion having been seconded by Elder McKay and unanimously carried, a chair for Elder Smith was placed in the center of the room. Gathering around him in a circle, the other apostles placed their hands on his head and, with George F. Richards as voice, ordained him and set him apart as the eighth president of the Church. Taking his place in the Prophet's chair at the head of the circle, President Smith then designated J. Reuben Clark and David O. McKay as his counselors. These were then set apart and took their places at his side. In turn, George F. Richards was sustained and set apart as the president of the Quorum of the Twelve Apostles.

The impact of these simple yet impressive proceedings was expressed by Elder Lee. "There was something that happened to me in that meeting," he wrote. "I was willing

273

George Albert Smith with counselors David O. McKay and J. Reuben Clark, Jr.

then, as always, to listen to the brethren and to follow them, but as they took their places at the front of our council room, there came into my heart a testimony and an assurance that these were the men who had been chosen by God's appointment, and I knew it because of the revelation of the Spirit to my own soul." (Ibid.)

George Albert Smith came to this critical point fully prepared for the role he was now called on to play, a role that had been prophetically marked out for him by the old patriarch, Zebedee Coltrin. It is a role almost universally misunderstood by the world and barely understood by many members of the Church. The essence of it is to receive the mind and will of the Lord and to transmit that to the Church and its members. To do this does not require a vast knowledge of economics, philosophy, politics, science, or world conditions. Nor does it require special administrative skills or the vigor of youth. It requires only that the Prophet understands the spiritual processes by which the mind and will of the Lord can be ascertained. It is his primary responsibility to chart the course the Church is to follow; and this essential function can as well be performed, indeed, can be better performed, by an older man who has an intimate knowledge of the doctrines and objectives of the Church, a sure understanding of human nature, and, above all, a deep spiritual sensitivity. For forty-two years, President Smith had been trained and disciplined to play the prophetic role that came to him at age seventy-five. Having arrived at the pinnacle of Church leadership and having become invested with the operative keys of authority, it was within his power to do everything necessary to lead the Church.

His first act of leadership occurred at the sacred meeting where he was ordained and set apart as the head of the Church. The selection of J. Reuben Clark and David O. McKay as his counselors gave a clear signal about his purposes and his leadership style. His action was reminiscent of the counsel he had given to Herbert B. Maw when he became Utah's governor. "Surround yourself with wise men, good counselors," he had told the governor, "and then listen to their suggestions." The obvious criterion President Smith applied in naming his counselors was to select the brethren best qualified to help lead the Church. These two had served President Grant ably and faithfully for many years, were thoroughly acquainted with the complexities of Church adminstration and were men of absolute integrity upon whom he could rely. President Clark, an international lawyer and diplomat of note and an honor graduate of a prestigious Ivy League school, had served in the First Presidency for twelve years when he was selected by President Smith. Credited by James E. Talmage with having the brightest mind of any Utahn of his day, J. Reuben Clark was a mental giant whose vast intelligence, common sense, and single-minded discipline had made a lasting imprint on the Church. Once President Heber J. Grant had set the course and turned the key, President Clark ultimately became the directing, administrative force in the development of the Church welfare plan. In the process, he became the mentor and the father figure of a powerful group of younger leaders, Harold B. Lee, Henry D. Moyle, and Marion G. Romney, whom in private he often referred to affectionately as "kids." Beyond this trio of disciples, all of whom were ultimately elevated to the First Presidency, was a host of other leaders or administrative personnel who regarded President Clark almost with awe and who sought to emulate him. His counsel was listened to with avid interest, and his words were quoted as having almost scriptural authority. Such was the impact of his mind and character, and such was the delegated authority he exercised during the final years of President Grant's life when the Prophet was handicapped, that many had come to regard J. Reuben Clark as the controlling authority in the Church. Those who thought this did so in ignorance of the deferential attitude he always had toward the Prophet. Once he had given counsel and reasons for or against a proposed course of action, he was always prepared to yield to the decisions of his presiding officer. His careful training in jurisprudence, his keen sense of propriety, and his conviction that the president of the Church was a true prophet of God would not have allowed him to do otherwise.

The other counselor, David O. McKay, although very different from President Clark, was equally impressive and accomplished. He had served as President Grant's second counselor for eleven years and had held the apostleship for thirty-nine years, having been called to the Twelve only three years after President Smith. A university-trained educator by profession, this tall, handsome man, whose rugged physique hinted at his athletic skills and his agrarian upbringing, had first drawn the attention of the leaders of the Church because of his organizational innovations as a member of the Weber Stake Sunday School superintendency. There he had developed a system of teacher training and supervision that introduced an element of professionalism and an esprit de corps previously unknown to the

Sunday School. Later his ideas were extended Church-wide in the Sunday School and, with variations, in other auxiliaries.

Behind the ideas was a leader of unusual stature, both physically and spiritually. An extraordinary, well-publicized incident near the end of his mission to Scotland, in which spiritual powers were manifested to an electrifying degree, had prophetically identified David O. McKay as a future leader of the Church. Because of these prophecies, his youth at the time of his call to the Twelve, his robust health as he acquired apostolic seniority, and his many years of apprenticeship as a member of the Twelve and the First Presidency, there was a widely held perception that David O. McKay was destined to become the president of the Church. And that perception seems to have been reinforced by his physical appearance, which, as he matured with a flowing white mane and a benign, fatherly countenance, created an image strikingly similar to an artist's conception of an ancient biblical prophet.

There are few incidents in the life of George Albert Smith that better demonstrated his self-confidence, his good judgment, and his dedication to the work than did his selection of these two to be his counselors. That he was lacking in the high education they both possessed, that he lacked the genius of J. Reuben Clark and the physical strength and classic good looks of David O. McKay, and that he lacked the extensive public reputation these men had gained through such long service in the First Presidency seem not to have created any sense of inferiority in him or to have shaken in the least his basic sense of self-worth. He frankly recognized the strengths and achievements of his counselors, was humble in comparing them with his own, yet did not allow the unfavorable comparisons to dim his own strengths or overshadow him in his role as the Prophet. "The Lord has not made a mistake," he told a visitor who had raised a question about his role as the head of the Church. "He did intend for me to be here." It was the basic confidence that his call had come from God in fulfillment of prophetic promises that enabled George Albert Smith to lay aside any personal feelings and to base his decisions and actions on what was best for the Church.

In retrospect, there can be little doubt that under the circumstances the two men selected by President Smith as his counselors were the best the Church had to offer and were the best for the Church. Their experience and skills in helping to steer the work during the years President Grant was disabled guaranteed that there would be a smooth transition to the new administration. Their knowledge of past policies and practices would prove invaluable in charting a course for the future and in deciding issues as they arose. Their continued presence in the highest council of the Church would also provide an important sense of continuity and stability among the Church membership. And their selection would help to allay any concern within the hierarchy about radical shifts in direction or emphasis. Finally, the call to President McKay laid to rest any unfounded concerns that a rift existed between him and President Smith because of the old controversy between May Anderson and Emily Smith Stewart. More important, it laid to rest any unflattering suggestion that the new Prophet was so shallow as to allow such an incident to influence, much less to control, a decision of such vast importance.

There was little time for President Smith to savor the significance of his elevation to the highest office in the Church. There was too much to do and too many things to learn about his new duties to permit any deep reflection about the long road that had led from the old family home on West Temple to the Prophet's suite at 47 East South Temple. The day following the temple meeting provided a jolting hint of what lay in store for the new head of the Church. Early in the morning, he presided at his first meeting of the Church finance committee. There his eyes were opened to an aspect of the Church about which he had little knowledge. As a member of the committee on the disposition of tithes, on which he had served over the years as a member of the Twelve, he had known generally about the income and expenditures of the Church. But now as the chairman of the finance committee, he would be regularly briefed about the details of Church finances and would be called on to make decisions about many important matters that came before it. President Smith had had sufficient experience with committees and boards during his long life that he moved with assurance into this new world, guided by his good instincts and training and by the confidence that any defect in knowledge or comprehension could be readily cured by his counselors or staff personnel or by spiritual means. He was humble enough to ask questions when he did not understand something and tough enough to reject a proposal if he thought it was ill conceived. And in matters of great complexity, he had the good sense to rely on the recommendations of his counselors or the financial experts. These qualities brought a sense of unity and teamwork to the finance committee and the other committees and boards on which the new president served, giving assurance that decisions would not be hastily or arbitrarily made and that conflicting viewpoints would be respectfully heard.

Later in the day of this first finance committee meeting, the Prophet was elected president of the Utah–Idaho Sugar Company, set apart S. Dilworth Young and Milton R. Hunter as members of the First Council of the Seventy, and conferred with an attorney about the affairs of the Heber J. Grant Company. And as if to demonstrate that his administration would be characterized by an ecumenical spirit of love, that afternoon he attended funeral services of a prominent nonmember, Russel Tracy, held in the Masonic Temple. Later in the day, he went to the Tracy home to pay his respects to the family of the deceased business leader, showing the same loving concern he showed to the grieving families of Latter-day Saints who had lost loved ones.

The reports of such demonstrations of love by President

Smith traveled with lightning speed throughout the community. To many nonmembers who heard them, these reports doubtless were heartening, implying a melting of barriers to friendship. And to members of the Church, the reports doubtless served as a powerful incentive to go and do likewise, emulating the example of their prophet-leader. Knowing that the well-disciplined Latter-day Saints would react in this way, a devious person might have performed such an act of brotherhood merely for show, doing the right thing for the wrong reason. But such was not the way of George Albert Smith. His charity came from genuine love and concern for other people. The consequences of his actions, whether to improve relations between members and nonmembers, or to goad members into acts of friendship, were merely incidental to his basic aim, as in this case, of bringing solace and encouragement to a grieving family.

The postal flood began only two days after the Prophet's ordination. "Plenty of letters arriving," he wrote on May 23, "with good will and congratulations." It would continue for several weeks as messages poured in from around the world from members and nonmembers alike. And the flood of invitations to speak at special events or to perform temple sealings commenced at the same time. Whenever possible, he accepted, but the large number of requests made it necessary for him to pick and choose. Two speaking invitations he accepted in early June took him first to Logan and two days later to Provo. Preston Nibley drove him to Logan on June 2 to speak to the Institute students attending the Utah State University. Arriving in the afternoon, they went to the Blue Bird Restaurant, then Logan's best, for dinner. The only thing the Prophet ordered was a little bread and milk. And, presumably, his main fare for breakfast the next morning before speaking to the students was a serving of the grain concoction he usually carried around. June 5 found the Prophet at Brigham Young University in Provo, where he attended the president's reception and later spoke at an alumni banquet on campus. Spending the night with President Franklin S. Harris, in whose home he enjoyed a "good bed," the next day, the Prophet attended the graduation exercises, where he spoke and presented the diplomas to the graduates. Afterward, he drove home with Elder Joseph Fielding Smith and his wife, "Aunt Jessie." Between these two events at Logan and Provo, President Smith acceded to the request of his friend and dentist, Creed Haymond, to perform the sealing of his daughter Marie to Joseph Stobbe. The marriage took place on June 4 in the Salt Lake Temple.

The day after returning from Provo, President Smith attended the regular weekly meeting with his brethren in the upper room of the temple. During this meeting, the new Prophet defined the objectives of his administration. "I counselled the Brethren to love the people into living righteously," he wrote of the meeting. No one who knew him should have been surprised that George Albert Smith adopted this counsel as the theme of his administration. He had repeatedly expounded this philosophy during the long years of his ministry. "Let us love one another," he told the members of the Church at the October general conference in 1930. "Let us love one another that our Heavenly Father may be able to bless us; and he will bless us if we love one another and do good to all his children." (*Conference Report,,* October 1930, p. 69.) In an earlier sermon, he had elaborated on what he meant by this: "Husbands, be good to your wives," he said in April 1923. "Wives, be kind to your husbands; parents, treasure your children and safeguard them in every way; children, honor your father and your mother, that your days may be long in the land which the Lord your God giveth unto you." (Ibid., April 1923, p. 78.) And during his final message at the October 1945 conference, he specifically extended the admonition to include everyone outside the Church. "They are all my father's children," he said. "He loves them and he expects me and he expects you [to love them]. . . . Let us love them into doing the things that our Heavenly Father would have them do." (Ibid., October 1945, pp. 173, 174.)

These and many similar admonitions over the years were underscored by the way President Smith lived, by the way he treated other people. There was an exact correspondence between his words and his actions. Like a seamless garment, they were of one piece.

As the president of the Church, Brother Smith's activities were marked by a much greater variety than before. On two consecutive days following the important council meeting in the temple, he met with the executive committee planning for the Centennial celebration—Governor Herbert B. Maw, John D. Giles, and George Q. Morris. June 9 found him at a luncheon honoring the University of Utah football coach, Ike Armstrong. Typically, the Prophet had to speak for his dinner. Two days later, he was closeted with Spencer W. Kimball, Antoine R. Ivins, and Ralph Evans about Indian Mission affairs. And the crowded calendar on June 13 included board meetings of ZCMI, the Hotel Utah, and the Heber J. Grant Company; another Monument Committee meeting; and a meeting of the War Relief Committee at the USO Hall. On the three weekends that followed, he spoke at ward sacrament meetings. The one on June 24 was at Evanston, Wyoming, where he dedicated a new chapel, and the following Sunday found him at the Ogden Seventh Ward.

During these days of his administration, President Smith's staff support was still in flux. For years, only two full-time secretaries—Pearl Johnson and Jeanette Sorenson—handled all the work for the members of the Twelve. In the latter part of June, these two efficient and overworked sisters supervised the move of President Smith's personal effects into his new office in the northeast corner of the main floor of the Administration Building. A few days later, Bertha Irvine, who had been working in the office of the First Council of the Seventy, was assigned as the Prophet's secretary. President Smith also had access to the services of Joseph Anderson, who, assisted by a

George Albert Smith at his office

secretarial staff, had for many years served both as the personal secretary and assistant to President Heber J. Grant and as the secretary to the First Presidency. In addition, there were others at headquarters whom President Smith used periodically for chauffering or administrative assistance, such as Preston Nibley and Cannon Lund. And, of course, his sons-in-law, Murray Stewart and George Elliot, assisted in many ways and never failed to render help when it was requested or obviously needed. But all of these people had their own full-time responsibilities and were not always available at the moment of need. The increased demands of his office, his advancing age, and his single status required that President Smith have an assistant whose sole responsibility would be to assist him at any time, on call, whether to help plan his agenda, organize his papers, chauffeur or travel with him, or serve as his emissary or consultant in the numerous matters that confronted him each day. It would be two years before the ideal one to fill his needs emerged in the person of a young bishop, D. Arthur Haycock. Meanwhile, the Prophet called on whomever was available. So, on June 24 when he went to Evanston to dedicate the chapel, he pressed Cannon Lund into service as a chauffeur. He also took Preston Nibley, a skilled writer who worked in the Historical Department and who served as a literary assistant and consultant to President Smith and who sometimes filled in as an unofficial press agent. To make it a foursome, the Prophet also invited his son-in-law George Elliot to go along. Short trips such as this provided a welcome break in President Smith's crowded schedule. A good car, good roads, good companions, and good weather undoubtedly combined to make this four-hour drive enjoyable and profitable, especially since their route of travel paralleled the route followed by the pioneers as they wound their way toward the Salt Lake Valley. We can be assured that brothers Lund and Elliot heard several interesting anecdotes related by the monument marker and the writer-historian as the foursome traveled to and from Evanston.

As the president of the Church, Brother Smith found he could no longer take full advantage of the customary summer recess he had enjoyed for so many years as a member of the Twelve. Too many things demanded his attention. On June 20, for instance, he attended the annual outing for the "old folks" held at Liberty Park, where the seventy-five-year-old Church leader, who had just assumed the most challenging work of his life, spoke to 6,000 senior citizens, most of whom were retirees younger or not much older than he. And on July 21, he granted an audience to Herbert Brownell, the national chairman of the Republican party. While personally the Mormon leader shared many of the political views and aims of his visitor, he refrained from expressing them publicly in his role as the president of the Church. And when Democratic leaders sought an audience with him, permission was granted as readily as for the Republicans.

Three days after Mr. Brownell's visit, the Prophet celebrated Pioneer Day by leading the customary parade and by reviewing the various floats, bands, and marchers from a special stand set up in Liberty Park. Later in the day, he was driven to the mouth of Emigration Canyon. There, on a dusty knoll, beneath a hot July sun, with the Great Salt Lake shimmering in the distance to the west across the verdant valley below, George Albert Smith broke ground to commence the construction of his most famous monument—This Is the Place. It would be finished in time for the Centennial celebration two years hence.

Two weeks later, the Prophet hosted a lawn party for all of the General Authorities and their wives on the spacious grounds of his Yale Avenue home. Emily and Edith and their families joined to prepare the elaborate event, which seems to have been a deliberate effort by President Smith to create love and unity among the Brethren.

Intermittently during the summer, the Prophet found time to enjoy his family and to perform the acts of Christian charity that were such an ingrained part of his character. "Called on several including Rae Ellen and baby," he wrote on July 8; Rae Ellen was a the wife of his nephew Robert Farr Smith. The night before, a Saturday, he had looked in on a party hosted by a relative in the canyon cabin behind his home; and later in the summer he was involved in the already mentioned Canada outing for a granddaughter and the Scout encampment of grandson Tom Elliot. These family relationships and events loomed large in the Prophet's priorities. He also was pleased to receive a telephone call from Albert on July 3 announcing that he had become a full professor in Harvard's graduate school of business administration. And a month later, learning Albert had purchased a new home, the always concerned father sent him a check for $2,000 to help cover the moving and closing costs. One can only guess about the mixed feelings this turn of events created in President Smith. It is reasonable to surmise that he was proud of the son's achievement and of the fact that their shared name now stood enrolled among the permanent faculty of America's most distinguished university. It is also easy to conjecture that the incident created some sadness, since it sent a sure signal that Albert's future almost irrevocably lay at Harvard and that he would never build on the lot near the Prophet's home that had been reserved for him with such hopeful expectation.

The excitement created by Japan's defeat seemed to infuse everyone with a new optimism and enthusiasm. This was clearly evident in the tone of President Smith's diary entries. Freed from the grinding demands of war, the Church would now be able to move out again aggressively in its worldwide proselyting efforts. This undoubtedly was one of the topics of conversation the night after the surrender at a dinner party hosted by Elder Joseph Fielding Smith and his wife, Aunt Jessie, where President Smith was the guest of honor. Also present were elders Ezra Taft Benson and Mark E. Petersen and their wives. It was Joseph Fielding Smith who had had the melancholy task of closing out missionary work in Europe at the outbreak of World War II and of supervising the evacuation of the missionaries. And it was Elder Benson who, four months after this leisurely dinner party, would be appointed by President George Albert Smith to reopen the work in Europe. "A very pleasant evening," wrote the Prophet of the occasion. A few days later, President Smith, heeding the call of President Harry S. Truman, invited the members of the Church to join in a day of prayer and thanksgiving marking the end of hostilities. He also arranged for a V.J. (Victory over Japan) celebration in the Salt Lake Tabernacle on September 4. This was a community affair where a capacity crowd heard patriotic addresses delivered by the Mormon Prophet, several clergymen of other denominations, and Utah's governor, Herbert B. Maw.

Four days after the community meeting in the Tabernacle, President Smith again indulged his fancy for trekking. Donning his hiking gear, he joined some of his friends from the Pioneer Trails Association for a trip to Henefer, northeast of the Salt Lake Valley. The men apparently were surveying a route for a reenactment of the entry of the pioneers into the valley to be staged in connection with the Centennial celebration two years hence. "I walked part way up and all the way down Big Mountain," wrote the seventy-five-year-old Prophet with an ill-concealed sense of achievement. "Home feeling very well."

These were busy days for President Smith. In addition to his involvement in the duties and activities already mentioned, he was preparing, as time permitted, for two major events in the next few weeks. The first was the dedication of the Idaho Falls Temple. The second was the Solemn Assembly to be held as part of the October general conference. Notwithstanding his vigorous trek up and down Big Mountain, President Smith needed to husband his energy as much as possible. For many years, he had taken a little nap in the afternoon, when possible, as a pick-me-up. With the acceleration of his work schedule, he found it difficult to fit this into his daily routine, given the fact it usually took about forty minutes for the round trip to and from his home. As a solution, a room was made available to him in the Hotel Utah adjacent to the Church Administration Building so he could slip over there for a little snooze without taking too much time from his crowded schedule. "Am trying to rest an hour each day at the Hotel Utah," he wrote on September 13, 1945, "and it helps."

The Prophet needed all the help he could get at this critical time since his increased load as the president of the Church roughly coincided with another deterioration in his eyesight. "Eyes weak," he wrote on September 15, 1945, as he had done several times in the previous four months. On this same day, while he was busily preparing the dedicatory prayer for the Idaho Falls Temple, he noted, "Joseph Anderson read to me for an hour." This practice of having someone read to him was one he had followed intermittently over the years but that he would follow more extensively during the remainder of his life. Four days after

287

the reading session with Joseph Anderson, he completed the dedicatory prayer with some editing help from Murray Stewart and members of the Twelve. It was then typed on a machine with extra-large type so he would be able to read it without difficulty at the dedicatory service.

There was a touch of autumn in the air as President Smith prepared to leave for Idaho Falls on September 22, 1945. And there was an air of gaiety in the automobile as his two chattering daughters and their husbands joined him for the five-hour drive. Murray Stewart was at the wheel. It was harvest time, and their route of travel via Ogden, Brigham City, Malad, and Pocatello took the travelers through some of the finest agricultural land in the West. The orchards south of Ogden and near Brigham City were laden with ripe fruit, some of which was displayed invitingly at roadside stands. And northward through the Malad Valley, vast fields of alfalfa and golden wheat stretched for miles. It was a scene that could not have failed to remind them of the bounties of the good earth and the blessings of the Almighty upon a choice land whose people were again at peace.

The scene that greeted President Smith and his family on reaching Idaho Falls was the epitome of peace. On a slight eminence near the meandering Snake River stood the pure white, single-spired temple gleaming in the afternoon sun. It was a visual symbol of the Holy One, the Prince of Peace, whose house it was. Once the Prophet had been settled in his room and had freshened up, he went immediately to the temple for a final tour of inspection before the dedicatory service, which was scheduled to commence the following day, Sunday. There he found everything in readiness. The furniture and fixtures, the draperies and the carpeting were elegant in their tasteful simplicity. Everything had been cleaned, dusted, and scrubbed to remove any trace of the scuffings left by those who had previously visited or inspected the temple. And fresh-cut flowers adorned the hallways and rooms of the building. No expense or effort had been spared to make the temple as nearly perfect as possible.

It was in this tasteful setting that the Prophet met with the Saints the following morning for the first dedicatory session. President Smith conducted the meeting, was the principal speaker, read the dedicatory prayer he had worked so laboriously to prepare, and led in the Hosanna Shout. A selected choir with organ accompaniment provided the music, joining with the congregation to sing "The Spirit of God Like a Fire Is Burning" in a moving, emotional finale to the service. President Smith also read the dedicatory prayer at the other two sessions on Sunday, although he relinquished some of the other duties he had performed at the first one. And at the five remaining sessions, three Monday and two Tuesday, his counselors alternated in reading the dedicatory prayer. Several General Authorities spoke at each of the eight sessions so that all of them had the opportunity to participate, as did others, including the temple presidency and some of the stake presidents, who either spoke briefly or offered opening or closing prayers.

The dedication of this the tenth temple built by the Saints, including the temples at Kirtland and Nauvoo, was an occasion for celebration throughout the Church. But it was of special significance to the members of the Idaho Falls temple district, which included most of the stakes in Idaho and the Big Horn and Star Valley stakes in Wyoming. All the worthy members of the Church in the temple district, and selected others, had been invited to attend. The number of dedicatory sessions was determined by the number of those who accepted the invitation and obtained tickets of admission from their bishops.

Since there were only two sessions the last day of the dedication, President Smith and his party were able to return home on Tuesday. They left Idaho Falls in mid-afternoon, savoring the feelings the joyous occasion had created, feelings that were suddenly jarred when they came upon a terrible accident. A collision on the narrow highway had crushed and twisted the two cars involved into heaps of metal and torn fabric, surrounded with broken glass and sprinkled with blood. Police at the scene prevented passing motorists from stopping so that President Smith and his family were unable to learn how the accident occurred, who was involved, or the condition of the passengers. The next morning's paper carried the news that one of the wrecked cars belonged to President Smith's good friend Clarence Neslen, former mayor of Salt Lake City, whose wife and one other passenger had been killed. The Prophet conveyed his condolences to the grieving families, doubtless helping to ease their pain and bring some understanding of why their loved ones had suffered such a tragedy while returning home from the temple dedication. Neither the Prophet, who spoke at the funeral of Clarence Neslen's wife, nor anyone else could provide an entirely satisfactory answer except to repeat the comforting words spoken at the funeral that life is tenuous at best and is fraught with many hazards from which no one is immune, that departed ones live on in the spirit world, and that the separation will be brief.

President Smith confronted similar questions at a personal level a month later when his brother Nicholas, younger than he by eleven years and in apparent good health, suddenly passed away. President Smith "comforted all" at the unexpected death of this admired brother, whose genial countenance and friendly manner illustrated the message of love and brotherhood he taught. "A great loss has been sustained," wrote the Prophet. "Nicholas was a noble character."

Two days after President Smith returned from Idaho Falls, a senior member of the Twelve sought counsel about lapses of memory he had suffered, impliedly questioning whether he should be replaced by a younger, more vigorous man. The question was not new, nor was it the last time it would be raised. Neither was the assumed answer new: that the principles of life tenure and seniority control among the members of the Twelve, and that once one enters that circle, he will remain there for life, if worthy.

On September 30, a Monday, President Smith attended a reception to welcome home Matthew Cowley from his mission to New Zealand. The Prophet's forty-eight-year-old friend and protégé had been laboring in the Pacific for seven long years. Unknown to the other guests at the time, Elder Cowley would stand at the Tabernacle pulpit five days later to accept his call to the circle of the Twelve. The Prophet, of course, knew of the call. And Elder Cowley knew of it, but only because of the prediction of his Maori brother. The prophecy was confirmed after the council meeting in the temple on Thursday, October 4, when President Smith formally extended the call. As Matthew Cowley faced the Tabernacle audience the following day, he reminisced about his long association with President Smith and his family. "I have known President George Albert Smith all the days of my life," began the new apostle. "I have had the arms of his father about me in my childhood and early youth. I have had his arms about me in my maturity. I think it was he who set me apart for my first mission. He married me to my good wife. He took me upon my second mission — and now this!" (*Conference Report,* October 1945, p. 50.)

The close relationship between the Smith and Cowley families existed chiefly because for many years both families had lived as neighbors on West Temple Street. The home of Matthias Cowley where his son Matthew was born and reared was on the west side of West Temple Street almost equidistant from the home to the south where George Albert Smith was born and reared and the home to the north where Nicholas G. Smith was born and reared. It was a secure, sheltered, and closely knit neighborhood where lines marking blood relationships almost disappeared, merging in a common family relationship where one and all were familiarly called and genuinely regarded as brothers and sisters.

Elder Cowley was the last speaker at the afternoon

session of the conference on Friday October 5, 1945. The morning session was the Solemn Assembly, where George Albert Smith was sustained "as Prophet, Seer, and Revelator, and President of the Church of Jesus Christ of Latter-day Saints." The other General Authorities were sustained at the same time according to the usual pattern, with the various priesthood quorums and groups voting separately, starting with the quorum of the First Presidency, followed by the vote of the whole congregation. With the completion of this procedure, President Smith was finally and officially installed in the position foreshadowed by the venerable patriarch. How does one respond when given such vast power and authority? President Smith's first words following the sustaining provide the answer and reveal the key to his character. "I wonder," said he, "if anyone else here feels as weak and humble as the man who stands before you." (Ibid., p. 18.) But, it was in his humility that the Prophet found his greatest strength. In acknowledging the superiority and preeminence of God, and his own dependence on Him, President Smith was able to invoke heavenly power that gave authority and conviction to his words and actions.

The words of the Church's leader on this occasion were both brief and comprehensive. He traced the origin and growth of the Church, quoting the foundational scripture in James 1:5 that had prompted Joseph Smith to seek wisdom in the Sacred Grove. He described the events surrounding the translation of the Book of Mormon by the Prophet Joseph and summarized the organization of the Church, its initial development in the eastern United States, and its exodus to the Rocky Mountains. He commented on the essential role of the priesthood and its various quorums in the governance of the Church, while acknowledging the vital role of women, not only in advancing the work but also in nurturing children and strengthening the foundations of Latter-day Saint homes. He alluded generally to the prophecies and revelations in the Doctrine and Covenants, and specifically to the 89th section, which had been emphasized repeatedly by his predecessor, Heber J. Grant. He expressed gratitude to the members for their sustaining vote to "help the humble man who [had] been called to preside over [the] church as he [sought] to carry on by the inspiration of the Almighty." Finally, he invoked the blessings of the Lord upon the people, praying that "peace, comfort and satisfaction" would abide in the homes of the Latter-day Saints and that the Spirit of the Lord would continue with them "today, henceforth and forever." (Ibid., pp. 18-25.)

While President Smith's keynote address at the Solemn Assembly was directed almost exclusively to the members of the Church, his final sermon was directed in large part to nonmembers, or to the responsibilities Latter-day Saints have toward nonmembers. "As representatives of the church," said he, "we have the responsibility to go among them with love, as servants of the Lord, as representatives of the Master of Heaven and Earth." He acknowledged there is good in other churches and that "it is the good that is in these various denominations that holds them together." He admonished the Latter-day Saints to be wise and diplomatic in their dealings with nonmembers, citing some of his own experiences as examples. "It has been my privilege," said he, "to be in the homes of many people of various denominations of the world, both Christian and Jew. I have been with the Mohammedans; I have been with those who believe in Confucius; and I might mention a good many others. I have found wonderful people in all these organizations, and I have the tremendous responsibility wherever I go among them, that I shall not offend them, nor hurt their feelings, nor criticize them, because they do not understand the truth." Yet, he emphasized that the representatives of the Church should teach the principles of the gospel without restraint or fear, even though this might produce some negative reactions. "They may not altogether appreciate that," he said, "they may resent that as being egotistical and unfair, but that would not change my attitude." (Ibid., p. 168.)

In these and in many other of his words and actions are reflected an interesting aspect of the character of George Albert Smith. While he was kind and charitable to all, democratic and ecumenical in his attitude toward others and the churches to which they belonged, he was unyielding and unequivocal in his views that The Church of Jesus Christ of Latter-day Saints is the only church on earth that teaches correct gospel doctrine and whose leaders have binding authority to speak and act in the name of God. Beneath his mild, affable exterior was a man firm in his ideas and loyalties. He would yield on unimportant points, concede on an irrelevant issue or maintain a discreet silence to avoid offending or embarrassing someone. But touching anything related to his Mormon beliefs or his apostolic calling, he was positive and immovable. Yet even then, he exhibited the qualities of a good diplomat, disagreeing without being disagreeable, and usually with a smile and genuine friendliness.

Whatever may have been the faults of this kindly Prophet, they were never evident to his family and friends, especially his family. The close-knit love and unity in the Smith clan has already been noted. These feelings appear to have been especially strong between President Smith and his brother Nicholas. This was indicated by the brief but significant allusion Nicholas made to his brother's elevation to the presidency of the Church during his talk at the Saturday morning general session on October 6, 1945. "When President Joseph F. Smith was first voted upon as president of the church in solemn assembly," said he, "I had the privilege of sitting here and voting for him. When President Grant was chosen, I was in Africa and missed that opportunity. Yesterday, as my own brother was voted upon, I thrilled to the very finger tips." (Ibid., p. 57.) Three weeks later, Nicholas G. Smith was gone. There was no hint of impending death as he stood before the Tabernacle audience. With an athletic build and a ruddy, smiling face this sixty-four-year-old younger brother seemed to be in robust good health, while the Prophet, eleven years older, seemed frail by comparison and the one most likely to go first. Yet George Albert Smith lived on for another six years, fulfilling the destiny that had been prophetically marked out for him.

Chapter Twenty-one

Prophetic Initiatives

With the war at an end, the main focus of President Smith and his brethren was to help bind up the wounds of war and speed the transition to peace and normalcy. Of special concern were the Saints in Europe, many of whose cities had been devastated by saturation bombing and whose economies had been ruptured. To assist the Saints in Europe during the transition, the Brethren decided to ship food, clothing, and other commodities from the Church's welfare storehouses. This involved making complicated arrangements with the governments of the United States and Europe. Since Elder John A. Widtsoe of the Twelve had been designated to spearhead this work, he and his assistant, Thomas E. McKay, accompanied President Smith to Washington, D.C., to meet with U.S. officials. With them as they left by train on October 31 was Joseph Anderson. En route, the Brethren laid plans for a whirlwind visit of six days in the nation's capital.

Arriving on Friday, November 2, they checked in at their hotel, and Joseph Anderson made telephone calls to

*George Albert Smith
with Church and
government officials
near Washington, D.C.
chapel*

confirm the two appointments for the following morning.
The first was with the secretary of agriculture, Clinton
Anderson, who gave helpful advice about exporting agricultural products to Europe. This friendly Democrat, who
years later as a senator from New Mexico would be a strong
ally of his Republican successor, Ezra Taft Benson, was
well acquainted with the Church and its leaders and gave
warm encouragement to the plan to aid the European
Saints. In mid morning, the Utahns visited the White
House, where President Harry S. Truman received them
cordially. Only a few months before, President Truman
had visited Salt Lake City and met with President Smith
and other Church leaders. During the interview, where

297

representatives of the press were present, the Prophet related a little-known story about President Truman's grandfather, who, after the invasion of Johnston's army, brought
a wagon train of supplies to Utah intended for sale among
U.S. troops. On arriving, however, he found that the army
was preparing to abandon Camp Floyd, located southwest
of Salt Lake City. With the loss of his intended market,
the merchant was faced with financial ruin until he sought
the assistance of Brigham Young, who helped him dispose
of his goods to the Latter-day Saints. (*Salt Lake Tribune,*
June 27, 1945.) Now the head of the Church was seeking
the cooperation of the merchant's grandson to ship supplies to the needy Saints in Europe. On learning of the
Church's plan, the outspoken Missourian warned that European money was scarce and that what there was of it
wasn't "any good." As he had previously met President
Smith and knew of his charitable reputation, the nation's
chief executive likely was not surprised by the answer.
"Our people over there need food and supplies," said the
Mormon Prophet, "much more than we need money. We
want to help them before winter sets in." When President
Truman asked how long it would take to gather the commodities for shipment, the Mormon Prophet, reflecting his
political bias, answered good-naturedly, "When the
United States government was advising people to kill their
pigs and refuse to plant grain, we were building ware-
houses and granaries and root cellars, and during the war
we have been filling these until we have plenty on hand."
Mr. Truman, who was accustomed to a constant barrage
of political invective and insult, spoken in earnest and with
malignant intent by his partisan enemies, smilingly passed
off this friendly quip. "We will help you all we can," he
assured the visitors. "We will put nothing in the way."
Before leaving, the Prophet, who rarely missed an opportunity to plant a gospel seed, handed President Truman a
personalized, leather-bound copy of *A Voice of Warning*,
one of the Church's widely used proselyting pamphlets.
In doing so, he informed the president that the Latter-day

Saints regularly prayed for him. The chief executive promised to read the pamphlet, whose author, Parley P. Pratt, had been intimately involved in the Church's turbulent history in Mr. Truman's native Missouri.

On Sunday, the Prophet attended church services at the Chevy Chase Ward, where he complied with the usual request to speak. Present were many members from Utah and other western states who had been attracted to the nation's capital by employment or educational opportunities. Among them was Edgar B. Brossard, a member of the U.S. Tariff Commission, whose wife, Laura, a sister of Matthew Cowley, was an old neighbor from West Temple in Salt Lake City. The following day, the Prophet joined Edgar Brossard, who had succeeded Ezra Taft Benson as the president of the Washington, D.C., stake, and others for picture-taking near the impressive chapel that had become a landmark in the city.

After the picture-taking, President Smith and his party paid courtesy calls on the U.S. commissioner of reclamation, the president of the War Relief Control Board, and Harold Ickes, the secretary of the interior. Mr. Ickes, a crusty, outspoken individualist and self-styled curmudgeon, had a scholarly knowledge of western history and lore. He engaged President Smith in a discussion about the origin of the American Indians. While a transcript of the meeting is not available, we can be assured that the subject opened the door to pertinent comments about the Book of Mormon.

On Tuesday, President Smith accompanied Elder Widtsoe to the passport division of the U.S. State Department, where Ruth B. Shipley agreed to expedite the processing of Elder Widtsoe's papers. Because of Elder Widtsoe's Scandinavian origins and the expectation that his role in coordinating Church relief efforts in Europe would bring him in contact with their governments, the pair also paid courtesy calls on the ambassadors from Norway and Sweden. The last day in the capital was equally busy. The representatives met with native Utahn Marriner Eccles, chairman of the board of governors of the Federal Reserve System. Later, they called on Admiral William Thomas, chief of chaplains of the navy, and Luther D. Mills, chief of chaplains of the army. The Prophet was concerned about how the plans for demobilization of the armed forces would affect the thousands of Latter-day Saints who were then in the service. And he was eager to maintain a close relationship with the chiefs of chaplains to ensure that there would be enough LDS chaplains to care for Latter-day Saint needs in the future.

Later in the day, President Smith took a commuter train to New York City. There he counseled with Boy Scout leaders at national headquarters, accompanied Harvey Fletcher to a mid-week meeting in the chapel of the Manhattan Ward, and, on the afternoon of the ninth, left for Boston for a three-day visit with Albert and his family.

President Smith's church duties usually made it difficult to devote himself exclusively to the family. It was so on this occasion. While in Boston over the weekend, he sandwiched in a long meeting with sculptor Mahonri M. Young to mediate a misunderstanding the artist had had with Church representatives over his fee for a sculpture. The matter was resolved amicably when the sculptor agreed to a fee of $10,000. The Prophet also attended and spoke at a Relief Society conference and later at a sacrament meeting in the Cambridge Ward, where he discussed the Apostasy. That night, he spoke at a fireside to which students from Harvard and other nearby universities flocked in large numbers. President Smith never lost the appeal to youth that he first demonstrated on his MIA mission to southern Utah.

President Smith arrived home on November 15 in time to report the results of his trip to the weekly temple meeting. The next morning, he flew to Los Angeles for a Western Air board meeting, returning by plane in the afternoon. And a few days later, he added variety to his customary duties by speaking at the annual dinner of the newsboys of the Deseret News. "They are a fine lot of youngsters," he wrote of the sixty-seven boys in attendance.

The following day, the Prophet was asked about an issue that was then being raised with greater frequency because of the relaxed racial policies that had been followed by the military during World War II. It was raised on this occasion by his friend Andre Anastasian, who with his wife and daughter came to visit him. "We talked about the equality of the negro and [the] association of races," wrote President Smith. Specifically, the visitors were interested in the policy of the Church that withheld the priesthood from blacks. The Prophet could add little to what had been said on the subject by his predecessors. All were in essential agreement that the policy would remain in effect until it was changed by revelation. What is of special interest is the wording used by President Smith in explaining this to his visitors. It reflects at once his resignation to the existing policy, his personally held Democratic views that extended to all irrespective of race, and his submission to Divine will. "The Lord has the last decision," he wrote on November 22, 1945, "and if we will be fair to all, he will bless us." Little did he know that this "last decision" would be made known thirty-three years later to his young associate, Spencer W. Kimball, who shared with him a special love for the Indians and other so-called minorities.

President Smith enjoyed a brief respite from his duties over the Thanksgiving holiday, relaxing with his family and savoring the traditional feast and the serenity and beauty of his home. He was at peace, but he was also tired. The excitement of the conference, the death of Nicholas, and the long trip East with its many meetings, followed immediately by the trip to California, had taken their toll, lowering his resistance and making him susceptible to an attack of the "flu." On November 30, he went to bed, where he remained for almost three weeks, fighting against the virus that had invaded his system. He finally wore it out

301

a week before Christmas when he got out of bed to keep an appointment to speak to the Rotarians at the Hotel Utah.

Three days later, Elder Widtsoe contacted the Prophet to report that he was not well and that he doubted his ability to perform the arduous mission in Europe to which he had been called. "J.A. feels too shaky to go," wrote President Smith, "high blood pressure and hardening of the arteries." This unexpected development required prompt action because the elaborate machinery for shipping relief supplies to Europe had already been set in motion, and an active director of the operation was vital if the commodities were to reach the needy Saints before winter. After hurriedly conferring with his counselors, President Smith convened a special meeting of the First Presidency and the Twelve three days before Christmas. It was then that Elder Ezra Taft Benson was designated to replace Elder Widtsoe. Hindsight suggests that his appointment was almost inevitable. Elder Benson was young and vigorous and a superb executive. But what apparently tipped the scales toward him in preference to other members of the Twelve who had similar qualifications was his rich background in agriculture and his Washington, D.C., experience and connections. During his four years as the executive secretary of the National Council of Farmer Cooperatives, Elder Benson had learned his way around the nation's capital. He was, therefore, in the best position of any of the Brethren to expedite the issuance of the documents necessary to clear his travel to Europe. And he knew the key executives in the Department of Agriculture whose cooperation would facilitate the smooth flow of commodities.

Demonstrating that President Smith had selected the right man, Elder Benson flew to Washington after the holidays and in three days solved the visa problems for himself and Frederick Babbel, the young man who would be his secretary and traveling companion. The predictions of insiders had been that this would take three months because civilians had not yet been cleared to enter the parts of

302

Europe occupied by Allied troops. Later in January, the young apostle left for his overseas assignment, where he supervised the distribution of 127 forty-ton carloads of food, clothing, bedding, and medicines to the destitute Saints in Europe. He also reestablished the line of priesthood authority and communication among the Church members, which fostered self-help within the European community. A notable example of this occurred when the Saints in Holland raised and shipped a crop of potatoes to the members in Germany, the land of their erstwhile enemies and oppressors. Meanwhile, in the United States, President Smith and his brethren organized a special fast for European relief that generated over two thousand dollars in cash, which was used to buy needed commodities not produced within the Church's welfare system.

With the project for the relief of the European Saints in capable hands, President Smith turned to other duties connected with his new calling. Although he had had a close relationship with the presidents of the Church and members of the First Presidency from his boyhood on, their role looked much different from the inside than it had from the outside. To begin with, he was hardly prepared for the love and support that members of the Church lavish upon their president. "As the cards and gifts pour in," he had written on his first Christmas in office, "I am embarrassed. Our people are very kind and generous." Nor was he quite prepared for the wide variety of matters that came before him for decision, counsel, or merely information. The area of Church activity that now claimed his attention more than ever before was in the temporal field. The explanation for this lies in the division of responsibility between the Aaronic and the Melchizedek priesthoods. At the general level of the Church, this division is most clearly seen in a comparison of the duties of the Twelve and the Presiding Bishopric. As a member of the Twelve, President Smith only rarely became involved in the Church's temporal affairs. The exception usually occurred when a member of the Twelve was asked for recommendations about a proposed chapel or when the Twelve annually joined the First Presidency and the Presiding Bishopric as members of the Council on the Disposition of the Tithes. But these exceptions gave the Twelve only minimal exposure to the Church's temporal affairs. And since the Twelve had little to do with the preparation of Church budgets, their involvement in the work of the Council on the Disposition of Tithes was quite perfunctory. Moreover, there was no mechanism to keep the Twelve advised of the activities of the temporal arm of the Church since the Twelve and the Presiding Bishopric never met together except at the annual meeting of the Council. On the other hand, the Presiding Bishopric met weekly with the First Presidency to coordinate the temporal affairs of the Church. Apart from these weekly meetings, the First Presidency also met regularly with the expenditures committee to supervise the appropriations and expenditures of Church funds. Here again, the members of the Twelve had no knowledge of these actions except when occasionally one or more of them received assignments to serve on the expenditures committee. Therefore, when George Albert Smith became the president of the Church, there was opened to his view a vast area of Church activity about which he had had little knowledge during his forty-two years as a member of the Twelve. But more important, he found that his was now the controlling voice in decisions affecting matters about which he had previously had only a vague knowledge.

Aside from his new role in directing the temporal affairs of the Church, the Prophet also found himself voted into the leadership of various businesses. These included The Utah–Idaho Sugar Company, The Beneficial Life Insurance Company, The Hotel Utah, ZCMI, Zion's First National Bank, and other Church-owned or controlled companies. And, as already indicated, he continued his role with Western Airlines.

President Smith's involvement with so many businesses was not entirely to his liking. But, it was an inherited role that traced back to an earlier day when the Latter-day

Saints were under heavy attack from many sources and fought back at the economic level by organizing cooperatives or Church-owned companies. The president of the Church usually took a key leadership role in these companies. And it was this practice, which by 1945 had become a tradition, that propelled President Smith into positions he would just as soon not have held.

His escape from the potentially crushing burden of these and of his official Church responsibilities was in delegation. There were many able people on whom he could rely to fulfill any duties delegated to them. And President Smith was an adept administrator who delegated extensively but wisely. The skills that had enabled him to organize and direct a Young Men's Board of such diverse abilities and interests were now used to direct the Church and other organizations.

There were some temporal duties that President Smith was unwilling to delegate. One was the final approval of temple sites. When it was reported that Church representatives had found a site for a temple in Los Angeles, the Prophet wanted to check it out personally. Instead of flying there as he ordinarily did, President Smith chartered a private railroad car and took his counselors and Presiding Bishop Legrand Richards with him. "Visited and exchanged ideas during the day," he wrote of the trip. The following day, February 9, 1946, he examined the proposed site, which had once been the private estate of movie star Harold Lloyd. He found it to be "well situated" and acceptable as the location for the sacred building, which was later constructed there during the administration of his successor, David O. McKay. While he was in Southern California, President Smith went to nearby Long Beach, where he held two special meetings.

President Smith also took an interest in the purchase of mission homes. Having served as a mission president and having stayed in most of those owned by the Church during his years in the Twelve, the Prophet had fixed ideas about the physical accommodations and the appearance

305

of these buildings. So when it became necessary to purchase a new mission home in New York City, he sent a member of the Twelve there, instead of a representative of the Presiding Bishop, to locate a site and conduct negotiations. The Church president's instructions were precise: "We ought to have one of the finest places in New York—if we can afford it." The result was the purchase of an impressive residence at Fifth Avenue and Seventy Ninth Street opposite Central Park. Its owner, a French woman who had been negotiating with the Russian government for the sale of the home, accepted a much lower offer from the Church because she wanted it to be used for the best possible purpose. Later when President Smith stayed in the home, he pronounced it "very elegant and beautiful, . . . well suited to the New York area."

As the head of the Church, President Smith's ceremonial responsibilities were greatly enlarged. When dignitaries visited Salt Lake City, they routinely sought an audience with him. And social events took on a new meaning and importance. The presence or absence of the president of the Church at these events was significant, not only to those directly involved but also to the Church members and others who read meanings into his attendance or nonattendance. Ordinarily, he took one of his daughters with him to social events where the guests attended as couples. And so, on January 4, 1946, he took Edith with him to a "statehood dinner" at the governor's mansion. Afterward, a program celebrating Utah's fiftieth anniversary was held in the Salt Lake Tabernacle. In a gesture of ecumenical friendship, the Mormon Prophet drove Catholic Bishop Duane Hunt home following the program. And later that month, Edith and Emily helped him prepare and host a dinner in the Lion House for all the General Authorities.

Meanwhile, George Albert Smith's elevation to the Prophetic office did not alter the habits of kindness he had practiced all his adult life. He continued to make unsolicited, surprise calls on the sick or despondent, to speak at funerals, and to be an advocate for the underprivileged and the minorities, especially the Indians. He continued to increase Spencer W. Kimball's involvement with the Indians, turning over to him many administrative duties affecting the Lamanites. So on March 8, 1947, he held a meeting with Elder Kimball, Albert Lyman, and the stake president from Monticello, Utah, about the needs of the Navajo Indians in that area. The Navajo-Zuni mission that existed at the time was later enlarged to create the Southwest Indian Mission with more than a hundred missionaries who worked among the Navajos, Zunis, Utes, Piutes, Hopis, Walpais, Apaches, and Yumas. Because of Elder Matthew Cowley's long association with the Maoris in the Pacific, President Smith also assigned him to work with the Indians. On one occasion, the Prophet joined elders Kimball and Cowley to visit the Navajo reservation for a conference with other religious leaders. Some of the ministers of other churches complained because Mormon missionaries had visited hospital patients other than Latter-day Saints. Speaking at President Smith's funeral, Elder Kimball reported on the Prophet's response to these charges. "My friends," said he, "I am perplexed and shocked. I thought people went to the hospital to rest and get well. If I were ill, it would please me very much if any good Christian missionary of any denomination would be kind enough to visit me and bind up my wounds and pour on the sacred oil." The Prophet went on to recite how the Latter-day Saints had helped other denominations get a foothold in Utah. He mentioned specially that the Catholics were once permitted to conduct mass in the St. George Tabernacle. The Prophet's appeal was greeted with warm applause, and the issue of interdenominational visiting in the hospital was never raised again.

In addition to appointing a committee of General Authorities to work with the Indians, President Smith took other important steps to give special help to them. A paid, full-time supervisor was appointed to coordinate work among the Lamanites. The Sunday School, Relief Society, and Primary were asked to organize special recreational and other programs for Indian groups, where feasible.

The General Authority committee on Indian Affairs already mentioned was formally organized by President Smith on September 13, 1946. In addition to Elder Kimball as chairman and Matthew Cowley, it included Antoine R. Ivins of the First Council of Seventy, who had had a long association with the Polynesians in Hawaii. Elder Kimball later related the circumstances under which President Smith delegated to him the chief responsibility for working with the Lamanites. "I went down to the office of President George Albert Smith at his request," reported Elder Kimball, "relative to the Indians. We talked about the Navajos in the mission. He then said, 'Now I want you to look after the Indians — they have been neglected. You watch all the Indians. I want you to have charge and look after all the Indians in all the world and this includes those in the Islands also.' I told him I would do my best. I told him that this commission . . . fulfilled my patriarchal blessing literally. . . . He indicated that he wished me to lead this committee in a vigorous program for all the Indians in all the world." (Boyd K. Packer, "President Spencer W. Kimball: No Ordinary Man," *Ensign,* March 1974, p. 12.) The statement in Elder Kimball's patriarchal blessing declared: "You will preach the gospel to many people, but more especially to the Lamanites. . . . You will see them organized and be prepared to stand as the bulwark 'round the people.' " (Ibid.) Elder Kimball waited forty-two years for the fulfillment of this part of his patriarchal blessing. During his two-year mission in the Central States as a young man, he did not see one Indian. "Can I have failed," he asked himself, "or did the patriarch err, and then, forty two years after the promise, President George Albert Smith called me to that mission, and [the] blessing was fulfilled." (*Improvement Era,* 50 [May 1947]: 291-92.)

George Albert Smith's principal duty as the head of the Church was to preside among the people. The patriarch had told the unknown boy that he would "become a mighty prophet in the midst of the sons of Zion." These words found literal fulfillment as President Smith stood to open the April 1946 general conference, the first one following the Solemn Assembly where he was initially sustained. It was a special time for President Smith. The joy he always felt in mingling with the Saints was heightened, not only by the new role that had recently come to him but also by the presence of his son Albert, who had arrived from Boston with his family for a two-week visit. There was a special chemistry between father and son that transcended their filial relationship. President Smith derived strength from Albert's presence and yearned to have him live on the lot next door, which still stood invitingly vacant. He trusted the son's judgment and would have taken joy in an easy, neighborly relationship of the kind that had existed between him and his father and between the father and the grandfather. And while President Smith's strong feelings against nepotism make it unlikely that he ever would have called his son to the Twelve, yet there is sufficient evidence that had Albert lived nearby, his influence with the Prophet would have been as great or greater than that of many who occupied official Church positions. Albert overtly reciprocated his father's love and confidence. He welcomed his counsel, and while the father lived, he relied on him for support and direction. Although there appears to be no convincing evidence of it, the supposition is that Albert shared President Smith's strong feelings against nepotism. Assuming this to be true, he likely would have been uncomfortable living next door to his father. Such proximity, given the ancestral pattern of apostolic service and communal living, could have given rise to distasteful speculation that the pattern would be repeated in Albert's case or, worse still, that Albert aspired to office. So, it was fated that the father and the son would live a continent apart and would have to be content with periodic visits of the kind that occurred during the April 1946 general conference.

A month after the conference, President Smith prepared for a lengthy trip to Mexico City via Denver and Louis. In Denver, the Prophet met with Governor Varian, not only to pay his respects but also to seek his support for a Mormon Trails project. The governor required little persuasion to endorse the construction of a fitting monument at Pueblo, Colorado. It was here that sick and disabled members of the Mormon Battalion spent the winter of 1846–47. And it was from here that John Brown led a group of Mississippi Saints to join Brigham Young's pioneer company at Fort Laramie in early June 1847. One can imagine the happiness that reigned among the board of the Trails Association to learn that George Albert Smith's elevation to the Church presidency had not dimmed his enthusiasm for historical markers.

President Smith spent two days in St. Louis attending Boy Scout meetings; and on May 17, he and Joseph Anderson, who, he wrote, was "a good travelling companion," entrained for Mexico City. The Prophet's purpose in visiting the Mexican capital was to lay to rest an ecclesiastical controversy involving a group of dissident Saints called the Third Convention. For ten years this group had been in rebellion. Their chief complaint was that the Church in Mexico should not be directed by North American missionaries but by Mexican Saints. The leaders of these dissidents were articulate and persuasive and had drawn away about twelve hundred Latter-day Saints. Unwilling merely to go their own way, they seemed impelled by a missionary fervor to agitate among other members of the Church to join them in rejecting the duly called branch and mission leaders. It was this explosive turmoil that President Smith hoped to defuse.

En route, Brother Anderson read to the Prophet excerpts from the voluminous file on the controversy. These revealed that after the dissenters originally demanded that the Church appoint local leaders over the Mexican units, several officials were sent from Utah to try to resolve the conflict. Their approach, however, lacked diplomacy and therefore failed. Indeed, it strengthened the hand of the chief agitator, Margarito Bautista, who began to broaden the scope of the dissent. For one thing, he advocated a return to polygamy, a plank that proved his undoing. When the Third Convention came together later, Bautista was rejected for his extremist views, and Abel Paez was elected in his place. Although more moderate than his predecessor, Paez was also adamant in demanding a change in local leadership. This obstinacy and the shrill manner in which their dissent was expressed finally resulted in the excommunication of eight ringleaders. Predictably, this action exacerbated the turmoil, raising it to the level where only the president of the Church could resolve it.

The approach President Smith took is a model in diplomacy and tact. He first softened the blow against the eight leaders by reducing their judgments from excommunication to disfellowshipment. He took this action on leaving Salt Lake City so that word of his conciliatory attitude would precede him to Mexico City. On arriving there, he verified his understanding of the facts and assessed local feelings. He also conferred at length with the mission president, Arwell Pierce, who had laid the groundwork for his visit. And he conducted interviews with other knowledgeable members to get their views. With his preparations completed, the Prophet was ready to meet with the dissidents.

A series of meetings was held in the chapel of the Ermita branch. Several hundred people crowded into the small building for each session, eager to see or hear the first head of the Mormon Church to visit Mexico during the term of his presidency. Arwell Pierce conducted under the direction of President Smith. During the first sessions, the Prophet was content merely to listen to the complaints of the dissidents and the responses of some Mexican Saints who had remained loyal to the Church. As the Prophet did not speak or understand Spanish, Harold Brown interpreted for him. When all had had their say, the Prophet rose to speak. Those in the audience who were unacquainted with George Albert Smith's character and speaking style were probably surprised by what they heard. Instead of a profound doctrinal sermon or a stirring call to repentance, they heard a calm, friendly, nonaccusatory talk about love, patience, and forgiveness. Typically, the talk was interspersed with pertinent anecdotes, some amusing, others touching or tragic. All were woven around the same theme, that the dissidents, as well as those who had remained faithful to the Church, were brothers and sisters, spiritual children of the same Heavenly Father, who should be charitable toward each other and reconcile their differences in love and forgiveness. The effect on the audience was startling. After the Prophet had finished, Arwell Pierce stood and asked for a vote to sustain the General Authorities of the Church. All except Margarito Bautista and a few other die-hards raised their hands in approval. The typical reaction was expressed by one of the leaders of the dissidents who said, "There is only one president of The Church of Jesus Christ of Latter-day Saints, and he is here today." (Joseph Anderson, *Prophets I Have Known* [Salt Lake City: Deseret Book, 1973], p. 107.) Afterward many in the audience crowded forward to shake the Prophet's hand, wish him well, or seek a blessing. Later, President Smith met with other groups of dissidents in small communities near Mexico City with the same results. At Tecalco, where word of his reception at Ermita had been received, the Prophet was serenaded by the people before the meeting began.

While a few of them never became reconciled to the Church, the great majority of those who had rebelled returned in full fellowship. Moreover, the influence of the few recalcitrants was destroyed so that they were never able afterward to mount a serious threat to the stability of the Church in Mexico. This is the only instance in Church history when a large group of dissenters became reconciled and returned to the fold en masse.

President Smith took advantage of his ten-day stay in the Mexican capital to visit the nearby pyramids and other

312

archaeological sites that stood as mute testimony of the skill and industry of the ancient people who had built them. And his avid interest in the Book of Mormon gave special significance to the things he saw. Despite the protests of his hosts, the seventy-six-year-old leader struggled up the steep steps of the Pyramid of the Sun to see a spectacular view of the fertile valley of San Jaun Teotihuacan. Concerned that he might stumble on the way down, two members of the party each took one of his arms to steady him. It reminded him of a similar experience of his grandfather, who, in being helped up a hill by two volunteers, told them he probably would be able to help one of them go up but doubted he could help both.

The Prophet's good humor carried over to a shopping spree that followed. President Smith, wanting to take some keepsakes back to his family, began to shop among the sidewalk vendors, whose leather goods, jewelry, blankets, and shawls were displayed on outdoor stands. His old competitive instincts surfaced as he sought to drive the prices down through good-natured bargaining. But ultimately his conscience prevailed, and he ended up paying more than was originally asked. Obviously, his enjoyment came from the crossing of wits and the verbal contest, not from any expected monetary gain. Later, during a photo session, he joked with one of the party who had his picture taken on a burro, asking whether his friends would be able to tell who was who. The joyful outing brought to the surface the fun-loving and carefree qualities so evident during George Albert Smith's youthful experiences as a traveling salesman and MIA missionary. The boy was still inside the man, but the burdens and cares of office rarely allowed him to escape.

President Smith also visited other places of historic or cultural interest, including the Institute of Anthropology and History, the Maximillian Castle, and the Guadalupe Cathedral. He also paid courtesy calls on Mexican President Manuel Camacho and the secretary of economy, Gustavo Serrano, giving to each a leather-bound copy of the

Book of Mormon. On leaving the presidential palace, the Prophet met and visited briefly with his old friend, Herbert Hoover, the former president of the United States.

Two days before leaving Mexico City, President Smith received word of the unexpected death of John H. Taylor of the First Council of the Seventy, who was five years younger than he. This vacancy would be filled at the following October general conference when the Prophet called thirty-one-year-old lawyer Bruce R. McConkie to replace him. In returning home, President Smith retraced his steps, clearing customs at San Antonio, Texas, where he declared the prized purchases made during his Mexican shopping spree. He then traveled by train through St. Louis and Denver to Salt Lake City.

After returning from Mexico, President Smith remained home for only five weeks before leaving on another lengthy trip that was a prelude to the Pioneer Centennial Celebration of 1947. Accompanied by friends from the Trails Association, the Prophet left Salt Lake City on July 11, 1946, on the Denver & Rio Grande. The first stop was in Pueblo, Colorado, where, on the twelfth, a monument was dedicated marking Pueblo as the first white settlement in the state of Colorado. In the beginning, it was settled principally by members of the Church. The next day found the travelers in the Kansas City–Independence area. There the Prophet spoke at a special meeting in the chapel in Independence before traveling a few miles upriver to old Fort Leavenworth. It was here in 1846 that the members of the Mormon Battalion were mustered in, equipped, and trained for their historic march to San Diego. During the next two days, President Smith's party visited places of historic interest in Missouri — Richmond, where Joseph and Hyrum were once incarcerated and where David Whitmer and Oliver Cowdery are buried; the jail in Liberty where the Prophet and his brother had been imprisoned; Haun's Mill, where several members of the Church had been massacred by a mob emboldened by Governor Boggs's callous extermination order; and Adam-ondi-Ahman, identified by the Prophet Joseph as the place where, in the last days, Adam, or the Ancient of Days, will come to visit his people. From Adam-ondi-Ahman, the Prophet and his friends traveled to Quincy, across the Mississippi in Illinois, the small river town to which the Mormons fled in early 1839 to avoid the wrath of Governor Boggs and his militia. President Smith and his party then drove to nearby Carthage, inspecting the jail where Joseph Smith and his Brother Hyrum were murdered. At Nauvoo, a brief memorial service was held at the grave sites of the two martyrs before ferrying the river to visit Montrose and Fort Madison on the west bank of the Mississippi. Here the Brethren found no evidence of the old barracks in which many of the early leaders of the Church and their families had lived while Nauvoo was being developed. The party then headed west in an automobile caravan, following as closely as possible the trail of the Latter-day Saints after their expulsion from Nauvoo. Since 1946 was the centennial of the exodus from Illinois, the travelers held special commemorative meetings with members or local civic officials at such places as Sugar Creek, Richardsons Point, Garden Grove, Mount Pisgah, and Kanesville. The history buffs in the party told stories along the way to give the trekkers a vicarious sense of what the Mormon Pioneers had experienced. Crossing the Missouri River at Council Bluffs, President Smith and his party inspected the area on the outskirts of Florence, Nebraska, once occupied by Winter Quarters, and they visited the Memorial Cemetery where the bodies of many Saints lie buried, victims of the harsh winter of 1846-47 and the diseases that ravaged the Mormon community.

After leaving Omaha, the group traveled on the north side of the Platte River to old Fort Laramie, roughly paralleling the route followed by Brigham Young's pioneer company, selected to avoid the heavier immigrant traffic on the south side of the river. Later Mormon immigrant companies followed the same route for the same reason, so it was named "The Mormon Trail." Along this trail, the party stopped to pay their respects at the lonely grave of

315

Rebecca Winters, one of the many pioneers who never made it to the Valley.

Saturday night, July 20, was spent at the Gladstone Hotel in Casper, Wyoming; and the next morning, after worship services, the party traveled to Independence Rock, one of the most famous and visible pioneer landmarks. After passing through Lander, Wyoming, the party went on to the Wind River Indian Reservation, where they visited the grave of Sacajawea, the Indian "bird woman" who had helped guide the Lewis and Clark expedition on its historic trek to the Northwest. The Prophet later helped promote the erection of a monument there to honor this intrepid woman.

At Rock Creek Hollow, the party paused to hold a brief prayer and testimony meeting surrounding the common grave of the fifteen members of the Willey Handcart Company who had perished there. Perspiring under a hot July sun, President Smith recalled the tragic circumstances under which these unfortunate ones had died from fatigue and the biting cold of an early snowstorm that had howled in from the northwest. He cited their example of faith and fidelity to their religion as being worthy of emulation by modern-day Saints. This same theme was interwoven throughout the songs and speeches of a bonfire meeting at Fort Bridger on the night of July 23, 1946, their last night on the trail. Up early the next morning, the Mormon Prophet led his motor caravan through Evanston, Wyoming, to Henefer, Utah where they joined with Governor Herbert B. Maw, who had driven there from Salt Lake City, in this small community's annual pioneer parade and celebration. The caravan, augmented by the governor's group from Salt Lake City, then drove to Coalville for a brief meeting at the home of Frank Evans before traveling on to the Salt Lake Valley, where, in the afternoon, President George Albert Smith laid the cornerstone of the This Is the Place Monument, a year to the day following the groundbreaking ceremony. A year hence, all would be ready for the formal dedication of the monument as the key event of the Pioneer Centennial celebration.

Chapter Twenty-two

The Year of the Pioneer Centennial

P resident Smith's well-publicized jaunt in the summer of 1946 to commemorate the centennial of the Mormon exodus from Illinois was an appropriate prelude for the Utah Pioneer Centennial, which would be celebrated the following year. After having been on the road for two weeks, sleeping in a different bed each night, traveling long distances by train or automobile each day, holding meetings, giving interviews, and counseling with associates and local leaders and dignitaries, President Smith was relieved and happy to return to the comfort and quiet of his home at 1302 Yale Avenue. "If heaven is anywhere near to being as nice as Yale Avenue," he had been heard to say, "I'll be happy to be there." Since the Brethren were in recess at the time, he spent a few quiet days at home, going downtown only to check on the mail or to take care of matters needing immediate attention. One of these was to pay a courtesy call on his old friend John Fitzpatrick, the nonmember publisher of the *Salt Lake Tribune*. In past years, this daily newspaper had been a constant irritation and embarrassment to the leaders of the Church,

317

seldom missing an opportunity to criticize the Brethren. President Smith could remember only too well the days when apostate Frank J. Cannon was writing editorials for the *Tribune,* openly insulting the Church and its leaders with blunt, unrestrained rhetoric. Because of his own sensitive feelings about nepotism, the Prophet could not forget the embarrassing articles the *Tribune* had published during the years President Joseph F. Smith called so many of his relatives to high positions. Frank Cannon had begun to call the Church "the church of relations" rather than the "church of revelations." His most scathing criticisms were made following the general conference in April 1910 when George Albert's father, John Henry Smith, was called as a counselor in the First Presidency and his cousin, Joseph Fielding Smith, was called to fill the vacancy in the Twelve. "Joseph F. is losing no time unnecessarily in his well defined purpose and process of Smithizing the Mormon Church," trumpeted the *Tribune.* "The Smiths are increasing in numbers in the hierarchy, there now being seven of the royal gentry in the governing body. . . . One may turn to the right or to the left, move to the front or back up, and one will bump into an official Smith. Gaze where one may in the hierarchy and the sight taken is a front or a rear elevation of a Smith. There isn't a single Mormon pie but there is a Smith finger in it. . . . It is a system of nepotism seldom witnessed in history — everywhere the omnipresent, robbing, non-accounting, lawbreaking Smiths, until the Mormon people actually begin to look and feel Smithy."

With the ascension of John Fitzpatrick to the helm of the *Tribune,* such unbridled and distorted attacks on the Mormon leaders had ceased. While he rejected the claims of the Church to a divine origin and differed with its leaders on many issues, Mr. Fitzpatrick's criticisms were expressed in civil, nonaccusatory language, thereby avoiding the bitter polarization that had divided the community at an earlier time. President Smith appreciated this new atmosphere of friendship, which he wanted to cultivate and strengthen.

So, on this hot summer day, he had gone, hat in hand, to the office of the *Tribune*'s publisher to wish him well and thank him for his "consistent attitudes." John Fitzpatrick was undoubtedly well enough acquainted with his visitor to know that this was a genuine gesture of goodwill and not merely a self-serving tactic, executed in the expectation of benefits to come.

Two days after his unprecedented visit to the office of John Fitzpatrick, the Mormon Prophet accepted the invitation of another non-Mormon friend, Russell Tracy, to use his cabin on the South Fork of the Snake River near Mack's Inn, Idaho. President Smith enjoyed the restful seclusion of this rustic hideaway for almost two weeks. Here in solitude, amid an almost pristine forest, he was able to engage in an unhurried contemplation of his duties that was not possible in Salt Lake City, even in his beloved home, where he was always the prisoner of the telephone or of friends and neighbors who popped in unannounced for a visit or for counsel.

The Sunday after returning home from Mack's Inn, President Smith resumed his lifelong habit of reaching out to others. "Made calls on aged friends and relatives," he noted on August 18, 1946. And since this date marked the end of the so-called summer recess, he resumed the quickened pace of his headquarters responsibilities. With the quantum leap in these duties that had accompanied his ordination as the head of the Church, President Smith found that even when he had delegated broadly, there was more on his plate than he could efficiently handle alone. Bertha Irvine was an exceptionally skilled secretary who ably and satisfactorily handled the normal flow of correspondence and receptionist duties. But what the Prophet urgently needed was someone in whom he had implicit confidence to help organize his agenda and assume responsibility for many routine tasks that consumed more and more of his precious time. "I wish I had a competent private secretary," he confided to his diary on September 27, 1946, "to keep track of my affairs and do a lot of detail work." The Prophet continued to look for someone to fill this critical need, as did his counselors. Ten more months would pass, however, before a solution would be found.

Meanwhile, President Smith continued the course, using whomever was available to assist him. He was now busily preparing for the October general conference. In doing so, he perceived a laxity and carelessness in spiritual matters that had spread in the world during the year following World War II. This same spirit had also crept in among the Latter-day Saints. To help counteract this, the Prophet had made an unusually strong statement on the need for the Latter-day Saints to keep the commandments, which was published in the September 8, 1946, issue of the Church Section of the *Deseret News*. "I say to you," wrote President Smith, "that unless the members of this Church keep the commandments of God, and turn to the Lord, the war we have just passed through will be nothing compared with what is yet to come." Then, as if to make it plain that this admonition was a prophetic warning in the long tradition of those who had preceded him in the Prophetic office, he added: "These words are not said in unkindness. They are not said in the way of a threat. They are not said to find fault, but my voice is raised in warning and to encourage all of our Father's children to turn to him." And in the true Prophetic spirit, his warning was coupled with a promise to those who heeded it. "Honor him and keep his commandments," added President Smith, "for he has promised us if we will do that, he will be our King and Law Giver, and will eventually give us our inheritance in the Celestial Kingdom."

Aside from the customary pressures of preparing talks and coordinating the numerous elements that make up a conference, he was faced with two important organizational matters. The first, already referred to, was the call of a replacement for John H. Taylor of the First Council of the Seventy, who had died while President Smith was in Mexico. In selecting Bruce R. McConkie as Elder Taylor's successor, the Prophet came close to crossing the barrier of nepotism about which he was so sensitive. Elder McConkie's wife, Amelia, is one of the daughters of President Joseph Fielding Smith, which made the new General Authority a quasi cousin of President George Albert Smith. However, because of the remoteness of the relationship and the lack of any blood ties, only President Smith's most ardent detractors would accuse him of nepotism on this account. And, there is an implication that President Smith was unaware that Bruce McConkie was married to a Smith, or, at least, that the Prophet's prior relationship with him was not close. "Bruce McKonkey came in office," President Smith wrote on November 7, 1946, "and I talked to him about his responsibility." The Smith clan was sufficiently large that the Prophet could not have been expected to know all the in-laws of the various branches of the family, nor the correct spelling of their names. But even if a case for nepotism could be made here, one might ask, "so what?" As it turned out, this obscure young man eventually became a member of the Twelve and one of the most prolific writers in the Church, exerting an influence far beyond that entailed in his ecclesiastical callings.

The other action taken at the October 1946 general conference was the release of Joseph F. Smith, patriarch to the Church. While he was only forty-seven years old, the patriarch was sick and had to be released. This cleared the way for the call of Eldred G. Smith six months later. The Prophet's blood relationship to Eldred Smith created no problem for him because by tradition and doctrine the office of patriarch to the church ordinarily descends through the lineage of Joseph Smith, Sr., and his son Hyrum.

In his major conference addresses, President Smith took up the same theme he had developed in the *Church News* editorial of September 28, 1946. In his keynote address on the opening day of the conference, he drew attention to unsatisfactory world conditions that fostered misery, loss of hope and a deterioration of morals. England, Europe, Russia, Japan, and the Philippines still showed the terrible scars of the recent war. And the cold-war mentality had begun to seep into the consciousness of the world, creating fear and uncertainty about the future. These, in turn, lowered the faith and resistance of the people, producing the conditions that had prompted the Prophet's editorial. In his concluding sermon on October 6, President Smith again admonished the Saints to keep the commandments, and he ended with a warning and testimony that disobedience would bring distress and sorrow.

But, the Prophet also wove a positive theme into his instructions to the Saints, a theme that seemed to be his antidote for the poisonous conditions that gave him such concern. This was the theme of missionary work. In his keynote address, he had extolled the uplifting spirit and rewards of missionary service. Implying that an effectual door might soon be opened to preaching the gospel in the orient, he mentioned the shortwave broadcast of the conference that was being carried to Japan. This became a reality the following year when, during the Centennial, the Japanese mission was reopened. This was part of a general revival of proselyting worldwide when missions were reactivated or created in North and South America, Europe, the Orient, and the islands of the sea. This revival resulted in an increase of the missionary force from 386 in 1945 when the war ended to over 3,000 by the end of 1946. And by the time of President Smith's death in 1951, this force had almost doubled to 5,800.

In January 1947, President Smith tightened up the administration of missionary work in the Pacific by creating an umbrella organization called the Pacific Mission, similar to the European Mission. Elder Matthew Cowley was called to preside over this new Church unit with jurisdiction over the Hawaii, Central Pacific, Samoa, Tonga, Tahiti, New Zealand, and Australia missions. In addition to overseeing Church work generally in this vast area, he was given the specific responsibility to increase the use of the Hawaii Temple, to study the impact of the war on the

Church and its members, and to ascertain the need and feasibility of establishing Church schools in the area.

The Prophet's intense interest in proselyting also resulted in an increased emphasis on stake missionary work with improvements in the training and supervision of the local workers and an increased awareness of the important role of the general Church membership in the conversion process. With all this, President Smith also encouraged the improvement of techniques in welcoming and informing the nonmembers who visited Church history sites. The most popular of these was Temple Square in Salt Lake City, where, following the war, the number of visitors skyrocketed as people generally had more leisure and more money to travel.

Following the October 1946 general conference, President Smith's round of duties continued unabated. On October 8, he received Chief Red Fox, who made him an official member of the Indian Association of America. A special certificate was given to the Prophet, signifying his commitment to Indian causes and expressing appreciation from the Indian community for his continued support. Three days after the chief's visit, the Prophet was again closeted with Spencer Kimball about Indian matters. The Prophet's young protégé, heedful of the charge to keep his eye on the Indians in all the world, was brimming with ideas about how to bring the Lamanites into the mainstream of Church life, thereby helping to elevate the whole Indian nation. High on the agenda was increased educational opportunities for Indians, an initiative that ultimately led to the development of the Indian Placement Program.

Meanwhile, whenever possible, the busy Prophet continued to respond to personal requests to perform marriages or speak at funerals. In the midst of his planning for the October general conference, for instance, he performed the temple sealing for a promising young couple, Homer Ellsworth and Mary Lucille Madsen; and in mid-November, he responded to the family's request to speak

323

at the funeral of another old friend who had passed away, Gertie Michelsen. "I had good liberty," wrote President Smith of the occasion, a phrase he often used to signify that his thoughts and words had flowed smoothly and that his purpose in speaking had been satisfactorily achieved, whether to bring solace and comfort, as in this case, or to speak words of warning and admonition as he had at the general conference. And President Smith, seemingly heedless of the need to conserve his strength for the more significant aspects of his calling, sometimes yielded to requests of the most trivial kind, as when, on November 23, 1946, he cut the ribbon marking the opening of ZCMI's new escalator! "Quite interesting," was his reaction to the event, which, on reflection, may not have been so trivial to the former ZCMI salesman.

In mid-December, President Smith planned another trip East, principally to attend Boy Scout Meetings in New York, but also to enable him to spend Christmas with Albert and his family. Shortly before leaving, he welcomed home the president of the European Mission. "Ezra T. Benson looks well and has performed a splendid mission," wrote the Prophet of his friend and neighbor, who, by this time, had completed the most critical phase of his assignment abroad.

President Smith's traveling companion on this trip east was Cannon Lund, one of the sons of Anthon H. Lund, a former president of the Twelve and counselor in the First Presidency. Cannon, who had been reared around General Authorities, understood their needs and the protocol that governed their relationships with others. He was steeped in Church history and lore, was a skilled storyteller, and was routinely cheerful. He was, therefore, as good a traveling companion as he was a versatile worker around Church headquarters, efficiently performing various administrative chores. One of his little-known skills was the ability to write in beautiful script. Of the old school that stressed good penmanship, he took pride in this skill and was frequently asked to letter special invitations, announcements, and certificates. And sometimes, under careful restrictions, he was authorized to affix the signatures of the Brethren to correspondence or documents.

The pair left the Salt Lake Union Pacific Depot on December 15, amid the usual good-byes from family and associates. Checking in at New York's Waldorf-Astoria two days later, President Smith was busy with Boy Scout meetings on the eighteenth when he received an unexpected wire from Washington, D.C., advising that President Truman wanted to see him. He immediately canceled his remaining appointments in New York and entrained for Washington, where he was met by stake president Edgar B. Brossard. The following day, accompanied by President Brossard and his counselors, Ernest L. Wilkinson and J. Willard Marriott, President Smith went to the White House for the interview with the chief executive. It turned out that President Truman had no special reason to meet with the Mormon Prophet but apparently only wanted to shake his hand and wish him a merry Christmas while he was in the East.

Following the presidential interview, the Utah visitors were shown around the city by members of the Washington stake presidency, native Utahns who had succeeded in the nation's capital. In time, the names of the two counselors would attain international recognition, J. Willard Marriott through the far-flung food services and hotel chain that bears his name, and Ernest L. Wilkinson as the president of Brigham Young University. They were examples of the "Mormon boys" of whom George Albert Smith was so proud, who had followed his admonition not to be a "scrub" and had risen from the obscurity of small Mormon towns to international prominence through hard work and integrity.

President Smith spent an enjoyable Christmas in Boston with Albert and his family, who were now comfortably situated in their new home. "Am glad to be with this part of my family," wrote the father appreciatively on Christmas day. "They are very kind to me." President Smith

George Albert Smith, 1947

returned home in time to ring in the new year with members of the Salt Lake City branch of his family who treated him with equal kindness and respect.

The appreciation President Smith had for his family and his Brethren found expression in his remarks at the general priesthood session of the April 1947 general conference. "I do not know of anybody who has ever had a happier life than I have had," he told the Brethren on that occasion. "I have not had very much money—maybe that is the reason I have been happy—but I want to tell you that I have had the comforts and necessities of life and the companionship of the best men and women and boys and girls that have lived upon the earth. And I have lived in an atmosphere of peace and happiness and stand here today to thank my Heavenly Father in your presence of that fact." (Proceedings in Church Archives.)

The ranks of the General Authorities were so thin that the Prophet found it necessary to continue to accept stake conference assignments. So on January 19, 1947, he drove

to Idaho Falls for stake conference there. With him was
Joseph L. Wirthlin, first counselor in the Presiding Bishopric, his former stake president. While in Idaho Falls, the
Prophet and his companion held a special fireside with the
M-Men and Gleaners in the area. The following Thursday
was a solemn time for President Smith and his brethren
as they assembled in the upper room of the temple for
their weekly council meeting. Two days before, January
21, 1947, Elder Charles A. Callis of the Twelve had passed
away suddenly in Jacksonville, Florida. On the previous
weekend while President Smith was in Idaho Falls, Elder
Callis and Elder Harold B. Lee had organized the first stake
in the southeastern United States at Jacksonville, Florida.
This had fulfilled a cherished dream of Elder Callis, who
had served as president of the Southern States Mission for
many years. Two days after the organization, Elder Callis
was riding in an automobile driven by A. O. Jenkins, a
wealthy Florida businessman and faithful member of the
Church, when suddenly, without warning, the eighty-two-
year-old apostle stopped speaking and quietly passed
away. Elder Lee, who after the conference had driven to
South Florida with mission president Heber Meeks, was
summoned back to Jacksonville and on Thursday, January
23, 1947, presided at a memorial service for Elder Callis in
Jacksonville. Because of the time differential, the service
took place at the same time President Smith and his brethren had met in the temple. During the memorial service,
Elder Lee, filled with emotion at the passing of his brother,
was unable to continue and asked President Meeks to carry
on. At about the same time, President Smith had called
on Elder Stephen L Richards to offer the prayer at the altar
as the apostles were gathered in their prayer circle in the
upper room of the temple. In that prayer, Elder Richards
especially remembered Elder Lee, who was far away in
Florida, invoking the blessings of the Lord upon him as
he presided at the services honoring their departed
brother, Charles A. Callis. Soon after, a sense of comfort
and peace settled upon Elder Lee, who was able to resume

the direction of the memorial service with complete composure. Elder Lee later cited this as an illustration of the power generated by the sacred prayers of the apostles in their council meetings in the upper room of the Salt Lake Temple. (As related to the author by Harold B. Lee.)

President Smith not only derived strength and direction from these prayers offered by his apostolic brethren, but he also sought special guidance as he prayed alone in the temple. "To office to work and to Temple to be alone for prayer," he recorded on Sunday, February 23, 1947. At the time, the Prophet was heavily involved in preparing for the culminating events of the pioneer centennial and the arrangements for the April general conference, where the vacancy in the Twelve caused by the death of Elder Callis would be filled. These and other matters, whether official or personal, were doubtless put before the Lord as the Prophet prayed alone in the Holy Place. It is in such a setting that one glimpses the solitary nature of the role played by a Prophet, God's mouthpiece, holding the ultimate keys of authority on the earth and answerable only to God.

It is not unlikely that President Smith's secret prayers on this occasion included a petition for an improvement in his health. During this period, he continued to suffer from weakness in his eyes and occasional nervousness. He also spent four days in bed with a cold the last of January and the first of February. A few days later, although not fully recovered, he attended a stake conference in Roosevelt, Utah. With him were John D. Giles and Preston Nibley. He was so "exhausted" by the strain of the conference meetings that he sent his traveling companions to Vernal, Utah, to represent him at a special meeting scheduled there. On returning home, he went to bed again.

To preserve his muscle tone and help ease his nervousness, President Smith occasionally went to the Deseret Gym for a massage. At the time, this facility was located between the Church Administration Building and the Hotel Utah. It was very easy, therefore, for the Brethren to slip over for a swim; a game of handball, basketball, or volleyball; or a jog around the indoor track. And many of the Brethren took advantage of the gym for this purpose. Considering President Smith's competitive instincts, he probably would have joined in the fun had his impaired eyesight and frail health not prevented him from doing so.

But while the Prophet's physical disabilities prevented him from participating in competitive sports, they enhanced his interest and involvement in sports as a spectator and fan. Because the Church basketball tournaments originated during the time he was a leader in the YMMIA, he seemed to prefer that sport. And so on March 24, 1947, when the University of Utah played the University of Kentucky in Madison Square Garden for the national basketball championship, the Mormon Prophet was glued to the radio. "Listened to the Utah-Kentucky basketball game," he wrote in his diary. Then with ill-concealed pride he added, "Our boys won 49-45." It was not enough for the fan merely to record that Utah had won. The score was important and therefore deserved special mention.

It was fitting, though certainly not planned, that Utah won the national basketball championship during the Centennial year. It focused the attention of the entire country on the beehive state, but not as much as would occur later in the year. Given President Smith's long involvement in sports, drama, and dance as an MIA leader, his flair for staging media events, his avid interest in monuments and markers, and his key role in planning the Centennial agenda, it is no wonder that the celebration included events featuring sports, drama, dance, and the spectacular unveiling of a monument, all orchestrated so as to gain the maximum media coverage. Later in the year, the NCAA track championships would be held in Salt Lake City, attracting top athletes from all over the country. Their exploits would be publicized in newspapers across the land with the dateline "Salt Lake City, Utah." The University of Utah stadium where these athletes would perform would also be the site of the state's most ambitious outdoor dramatic production when an original play with an original score, "Promised Valley," would be presented nightly for several weeks during the summer. And as part of the Church's June Conference events, a mammoth centennial dance festival would be staged in the same stadium, featuring dancers from all over the state. And, of course, the keystone event would be the unveiling of the heroic monument at the mouth of Emigration Canyon. All these events, and many more that would take place during the Centennial, indelibly bore the imprint of George Albert Smith's genius.

But all this lay in the future as President Smith continued the course. In mid-March he authorized the Relief Society general presidency to launch a campaign to raise funds to construct the society's own office building. The result was the classic structure that now stands on the corner of Main and North Temple Streets across the street east of the Salt Lake Temple. Two weeks later, the Prophet traveled to Pocatello, Idaho, for a stake conference. Joseph Anderson was at the wheel of the car. With them was Elder Spencer W. Kimball, President Smith's General Authority companion for the conference. Welcoming the visitors in Pocatello was the stake president, William P. Whitaker, whose tall, powerful physique belied the fact that he was a florist by occupation. His avocation was politics, which had once led him to be an Idaho gubernatorial candidate. In this gentle but dominant giant, the Salt Lake brethren found still another of the many leaders throughout the Church who had been tutored in the skills of priesthood leadership while serving as a missionary under their recently departed associate, Charles A. Callis.

The trip was a pleasant interlude for the Prophet. It marked the first time he had shared a stake conference assignment with Spencer Kimball. President Smith first met this young apostle when he was a boy in the home of his father, Andrew Kimball, the president of the St. Joseph Stake in southern Arizona. Since Andrew Kimball also served as the president of the Indian Mission and therefore shared George Albert Smith's interest in the Lamanites, there was a special bond between them that, with Andrew Kimball's death, had been transferred to the son, Spencer. The two apostles who shared the pulpit with William P. Whitaker in Pocatello that weekend also shared the bond of being the grandsons of men who had served as counselors in the First Presidency of the Church, Elder Kimball being a grandson of Heber C. Kimball, and President Smith a grandson of his namesake, George A. Smith. Although they did not know it at the time, they would later share the bond of being two of the small handful of men to preside over the Church.

The following weekend was general conference, which was distinguished by the call of a new Church patriarch, Eldred G. Smith, and a new apostle, Henry D. Moyle, who filled the vacancy in the Twelve caused by the death of Elder Callis. During the conference, on April 4, President Smith celebrated yet another anniversary, marked by a birthday dinner with his family. "Seventy Seven years old today," he wrote in his diary. "The Lord has been kind to me." The culminating event of the conference was a meeting in the assembly room of the Salt Lake Temple, where the General Authorities, stake presidents, mission presidents, and bishops gathered under the direction of the Prophet. "A splendid spirit prevailed," he wrote of the unusual meeting, whose purpose was to tighten the lines of priesthood authority and responsibility, to more accurately define the objectives of the Church, and to generate more enthusiasm and dedication among the principal leaders.

The week after conference, President Smith was driven to St. George by Governor Maw, who joined the Prophet in a special meeting during which a marker commemorating the Daughters of the Utah Pioneers was unveiled. "Governor and Sister Maw most kind to us all," wrote President Smith appreciatively. Repeatedly during the Centennial year, this pair, representing the highest ecclesiastical and civil authority in Utah, joined in honoring the Mormon pioneers and others who had played vital roles in the founding and development of the state.

The mounting pressure on President Smith as events moved toward the finale of the Centennial celebration in July is suggested by his cryptic diary entry on April 30. "Rush, rush, rush," wrote he on that day. The volume and variety of his various commitments and activities continued unabated. Everyone seemed to want the Prophet's ear, to press a special request, to receive counsel or advance some private or public purpose. Such was his temperament and dedication that he seldom declined any request. And as yet, there was no one in his office empowered to use discretionary authority in sorting out who should be given personal access to him, someone who could also help organize his agenda. On this account, trips out of the city were a welcome diversion, notwithstanding the inconveniences of travel, not the least of which were the frequent changes in beds and diets. He could control his diet to an extent by taking along a supply of his grain concoctions, but he was never able to find a bed that quite measured up to the one at home.

Under these circumstances, President Smith looked forward to a three-week trip to the East he had planned for May. He left on the ninth with Cannon Lund. A Pullman drawing room provided adequate space to enable him to lay out his papers to work during the day without interruption. After stopping in Ames, Iowa, where he visited the campus of Iowa State University, President Smith went on to Chicago, where, on Sunday, he spoke at a conference of the University Ward. He then traveled to Huntington, West Virginia. His main purpose there was to attend a national congress of the Sons of the American Revolution. During this three-day stay in Huntington, however, he also sandwiched in a special meeting with the Saints in their small chapel and spoke to missionaries from the East Central States Mission.

Because of the heavy demands on his time, President

*George Albert Smith in
a jovial mood at
Huntington, West
Virginia, May 13, 1947*

Smith had reluctantly decided to step down as vice-president general of the SAR. By prearrangement, he nominated Salt Lake attorney Franklin Riter to replace him at the general session of the congress on May 15. His long acquaintance with the national leaders of the SAR made the occasion especially poignant for President Smith, and perhaps even more so for his associates. They had come to appreciate his buoyant leadership and doubtless recognized the diminished prestige that would be caused by the loss from their executive ranks of a person of such prominence. But President Smith's severance from the leadership of the SAR did not end his lively interest in its affairs. This he retained to the end of his days, and he remained available to add his voice and influence in aid of its objectives.

At Washington, D.C., the Prophet presided at a quarterly stake conference. And during a four-day stay in the nation's capital, he followed a whirlwind agenda that included visits to the consular offices of Switzerland, Norway, Brazil, and Argentina to check on missionary visas; the customary contact with the Department of Indian Affairs; and attendance at a session of the United States Senate, where he offered the invocation, the first president of the Church to do so.

Leaving Washington, the Prophet made a quick trip to Boston to visit Albert and his family. While there, he also conferred with S. Dilworth Young of the First Council of the Seventy, who was then serving as president of the New England States Mission. Going on to New York City, the Prophet presided at a stake conference on May 24 and 25; and during the two days afterward, he attended National Boy Scout meetings. One of these was a worship service where noted Protestant minister Norman Vincent Peale was the speaker. President Smith was called on to pray at the service.

While in New York City, President Smith stayed in the Plaza Hotel, whose manager was Frank G. Wangeman, a son-in-law of Elder Henry D. Moyle. Seven weeks earlier, Elder Moyle was in New York City on an important legal matter. Since he was then chairman of the General Welfare Committee and as such was expected to attend general conference, he had conferred with President Smith before leaving Salt Lake City, and the president had excused him from attending. During Elder Moyle's New York visit in early April, his daughter asked him who was going to replace Elder Callis in the Twelve. Answering that he did not know, she responded with a mixture of inspiration and daughterly prejudice that her father would be called. Assuring her this was not possible because President Smith had excused him from the conference, he soon after received a telegram asking him to call the Prophet at his home. Assuming the purpose was to advise him of his release from the General Welfare Committee, he telephoned President Smith only to learn with surprise that he had been called to the Twelve and that his name would be presented for sustaining vote the next morning. There was barely time for the Wangemans to drive him to the airport, where, without baggage, he boarded a plane that was waiting on the tarmac with its motors running. The red-eye flight arrived in Salt Lake City in time for Elder Moyle to take a short nap, shave, shower, change clothes, and drive to the Tabernacle in time for the 10:00 a.m. session, where he was sustained as a member of the Twelve.

As we shall see, the unusual way in which Elder Moyle was called to the Twelve was repeated, with variations, when Elder Delbert L. Stapley was called. And this seems to have been a common practice of President Smith. When, for instance, Elbert Curtis was called as the superintendent of the MIA, he was serving as a stake president. He had visited President Smith's office to discuss matters about his stake. During the conversation, the Prophet, after inquiring about President Curtis's financial status, merely said that some of the Brethren had been discussing him for the MIA. A month later, the office of the First Presidency called for his picture. When he asked why it was needed, he was told it was to accompany the announcement of his call as the general superintendent of the MIA! Those who may have thought President Smith was unorthodox in the way he extended calls were probably unaware of how he learned of his calls to the Twelve and as the superintendent of the Salt Lake Stake MIA. At least he provided some advance notice to those whom he called.

On returning from his three-week trip East, President Smith went directly from the train depot to the pioneer monument on First Avenue to help the Young family celebrate the 146th anniversary of the birth of President Brigham Young. Even then, plans were under way to further honor the second president of the Church with memorials at the place of his birth and in the nation's capital. These were projects President Smith had long had in mind to memorialize the Church's modern Moses. And the following month, of course, the heroic monument would be unveiled at the mouth of Emigration Canyon whose name came from Brigham Young's exclamation when he first saw the Salt Lake Valley, "This is the place."

Aside from Brigham Young's key role in the exodus and his leadership in establishing the Church in the west, George Albert Smith had good reason for a special interest in Brigham Young. His grandfather and namesake, George A. Smith, had served as President Young's first counselor for seven years. And George Albert was over seven years old when President Young died and therefore was mature enough to have remembered him. Brigham Young was, therefore, a personal link George Albert Smith had both to the early history of the Church and to his own family heritage. It was a genuine pleasure, therefore, for him to join the Young family in honoring their ancestor on his birthday, June 1, 1947. And two days later, he went south to the university that bears Brigham Young's name to preside at the BYU commencement.

The excitement and stress of the June Conference exhausted President Smith and put him in bed for several days. And the same thing happened following the Independence Day celebration when he went to bed "ill and exhausted." He managed to pull himself together sufficiently to begin the flurry of events that led up to the Big Day. On the thirteenth, the Prophet attended a reception, hosted by Governor Maw at the Executive Mansion, for the forty-six governors and their wives who had accepted invitations to join in the pioneer centennial celebration. The following night, a governors dinner was held at the Hotel Utah; and on the fifteenth, President Smith hosted a buffet dinner on the spacious grounds at his home, where four hundred guests, including the governors and their wives, were in attendance. Emily and Edith joined to plan this memorable event, which was the most elaborate social undertaking of President Smith's administration. And just to make sure the governors didn't leave Salt Lake City hungry, they were the guests of the local chapter of the Sons of the American Revolution at a dinner in the Hotel

Utah on the sixteenth. Earlier that day, the Prophet received a thoughtful call from his cousin Wallace Smith of the Reorganized Church congratulating him and the Church on their celebration.

On July 20, the Prophet addressed a Daughters of the Utah Pioneers luncheon meeting and participated in a round-table discussion over the radio. The next night found him at the Newhouse Hotel for a dinner meeting with the association of United States County Officials, who held their annual convention in Salt Lake City that year. During the day, President Smith had Cannon Lund take the Church car to the garage to have a huge buffalo head attached to the radiator in preparation for the parades to come. On the twenty-second, Cannon drove the Prophet in the buffalo car to Little Mountain to meet a caravan that was reenacting the last leg of the pioneer entry into the Valley a hundred years before. The following day was the most hectic of all for President Smith, who by now was so caught up in the excitement of the Centennial events that he seemed not to notice his advanced age or the physical frailties that had troubled him earlier. In addition to riding in the children's parade honoring the pioneers, he participated in three different luncheons, staggered in time to enable him to attend each one and to speak briefly. The first was with a group of bankers who were in Salt Lake City for a convention; the second was hosted by the national officers of the Daughters of the Utah Pioneers; and the third consisted of Post Office officials who had also scheduled their national convention in Salt Lake City. President Smith still found time later in the day to go to the mouth of Emigration Canyon to check out the monument and make certain that everything was ready for the unveiling.

The Big Day dawned clear and cool, although it turned hot later. The organizers of the mammoth parade had stretched the limits of their ingenuity to provide a spectacle worthy of this once-in-a-century occasion. There were dozens of bands and floats, interspersed with marching groups

George Albert Smith
at garden party,
July 24, 1947

and limousines carrying Church and government dignitaries. Leading this colorful column in his distinctive Buffalo Car was the smiling, bearded Mormon Prophet,
decked out in a white, western-style Stetson that he waved
intermittently to acknowledge the waves of applause that
greeted him along the route. It was a genuinely joyous
occasion for the man who reveled in pageantry, who loved
the pioneers and the heritage they had left, and who delighted in honoring and memorializing them for their lives
of faith and devotion.

But the parade, dramatic as it was, was merely a prelude to the culminating drama to be staged later east of
the city at the entrance to the Salt Lake Valley. The details
of the unveiling of the heroic monument and its dedicatory
ceremony have already been given. It is sufficient here
merely to add that, in a sense, the events of this day cap-
sulized the life and ministry of the man who conceived

George Albert Smith with Boy Scout at This Is the Place Monument

them and brought them to fruition. They demonstrated his love for the lives and deeds of those who had gone before. They demonstrated his love and concern for those who would follow by providing physical symbols of their heritage that would stand as constant reminders of the qualities of character they should emulate. And because he had insisted that the This Is the Place Monument recognize and memorialize all groups and individuals who had contributed to the development of the area, whether members of the Church or not, they demonstrated his universal love for all people, regardless of race or religion. "A great day" was George Albert Smith's simple summation of the key events of the celebration for which he had planned, prepared, and prayed for so long.

During the crush of events connected with the Centennial, President Smith received an answer to fervent prayers he had offered during the first two years of his administration. The first hints of fulfillment were tentative. "Arthur Haycock helped me," he wrote of the young bishop who had worked in different offices at Church head-quarters for several years. Five days later, on August 4, after carefully appraising the newcomer's performance, the Prophet wrote half approvingly, "Arthur Haycock is quite helpful." And after another five days of trial, the young man had proven himself to be the one. "Arthur Haycock is a splendid help at the office. I am encouraged." And before the month was over, Arthur was *in*. Thereafter, throughout the balance of President Smith's life, this devoted man was as intimately acquainted with the Prophet as was any other living person. He not only helped the president prepare his agenda and direct the affairs of his office, but he also became his traveling companion, his confidant, his personal emissary, and, on occasion, his spokesman on non-Church matters. And later when President Smith became ill and was unable to go to his office regularly, Arthur Haycock was a daily visitor in the Prophet's home and was accepted and treated as if he were a member of the family. Indeed, the relationship was almost that of father and son. And no son was ever more thoughtful and solicitous of a father than Arthur Haycock was of President George Albert Smith. Nor was a father ever more considerate of a son than was President Smith of him.

While the major events of the Centennial ended in July, others were staged later in different parts of the state, and even outside the state. So on September 6, President Smith and Governor Maw traveled north to Brigham City to attend the annual Peach Day Celebration, whose theme honored the pioneers. And in early October, President Smith, accompanied by Arthur Haycock, traveled to San Bernardino on the new Streamliner. There the Prophet participated in a pioneer parade and attended a pageant commemorating the Mormon pioneers and especially those who had established the community there in 1851. The event gained wide publicity, not only because of the presence of the Church president but also because of the participation of the Salt Lake Tabernacle Choir. Later, on Sunday, President Smith spoke at two public meetings.

Aside from his participation in the diminishing number of Centennial events, President Smith ended 1947 as he had begun it, with a variety of Church and business meetings, interviews, and public relations events. On September 13, he represented the Church at a meeting at Judge Memorial High School in Salt Lake City commemorating Mexico's independence. A month later, he received a contingent of Republican politicians headed by General Patrick J. Hurley, a former secretary of war under President Herbert Hoover and a former ambassador to China. General Hurley and others of like mind were highly critical of the Far East policies of the Democratic administration in power, which, he charged, had tipped the scales in favor of the Communist revolutionaries in China, who were then engaged in a civil war with the Chinese Nationalist forces. This group was the forerunner of other politicians of both parties who would be calling on the Prophet in increasing numbers as the 1948 presidential election heated up. As always, the Prophet listened courteously without indicating either approval or disapproval of the views advanced by his visitors.

A few days later, President Smith was reminded again of the tragedy and turmoil created by the recent war when he attended a graveside service where the remains of Captain Mervyn Bennion were reinterred in Salt Lake City. Captain Bennion, a son-in-law of President J. Reuben Clark who commanded the USS *West Virginia*, the flagship of the Pacific Fleet, was killed in the Japanese attack on Pearl Harbor, December 7, 1941. The captain was originally buried in Hawaii but, at the request of the family, his body was returned to Utah for reburial in his native soil. The occasion was especially poignant for President Clark, who loved the captain as his own son.

A few days later, the Prophet's focus shifted from the dead to the living when he attended sacrament services at the Stadium Village Branch in Salt Lake City where his nephew Robert Farr Smith presided. Obviously impressed with the fertility of the University of Utah students who comprised the branch, President Smith wrote with amazement, "There were over forty babies in the audience and more in a nursery in another room." Later the same week, he flew to Los Angeles with Arthur to attend a Western Air board meeting. Afterward, he again visited the temple site and then was driven down the coast to San Diego for a special meeting where he shared the pulpit with California mission president Oscar W. McConkie, the father of Elder Bruce R. McConkie.

Back in Salt Lake City, the Prophet ended his official activities for the year by speaking at funeral services for a relative, Uncle Elias Smith, in the Assembly Hall on Temple Square. Sharing the pulpit was Bryant S. Hinckley, the former president of the Liberty Stake in Salt Lake City and the father of President Gordon B. Hinckley, at present (1989) the first counselor in the First Presidency.

Chapter Twenty-three

Continuing the Course

T he next year, 1948, was essentially a replay of the previous one but without the pressure and excitement of the Centennial celebration. This lack was compensated for in part by the excitement over the presidential election, which was in the forefront of the news much of the year. In an apparent effort to get a jump on the competition, perennial presidential candidate Harold E. Stassen came visiting in mid-January. The major candidates would come later. The Prophet continued to accept a few stake conference assignments. Two weeks before the April general conference found him at the Hurricane Stake in Southern Utah. And later, he and Elder Harold B. Lee were together at the Alberta, Canada, stake conference. However, other responsibilities made it necessary to curtail and ultimately eliminate this activity, which President Smith enjoyed immensely as it brought him closer to the people.

Meanwhile, President Smith's official and personal duties continued without interruption. He watched the finals of the all-Church basketball tournament; attended the BYU leadership week; inspected construction on the Los Angeles Brentwood Ward chapel, which he pronounced "very lovely but expensive"; attended the seminary graduation in the little town of Beaver, Utah; broke ground for a new science building on the BYU campus; attended services at Clarkston, Utah, commemorating the restoration of the Aaronic Priesthood; presided at the BYU baccalaureate and commencement services; dedicated new chapels in St. George and Newton, Utah; attended a reception at the Lion House for the outgoing YWMIA presidency of Lucy Grant Cannon, Verna W. Goddard, and Lucy T. Andersen; spoke at the annual old folks party at Liberty Park, excusing himself from a temple meeting to do so; joined Governor Maw and General Mark Clark at a reinterrment ceremony in Tremonton, Utah, honoring the four sons of Mr. and Mrs. Alben Borgstrom who were all killed within six months during World War II; joined some of his missionaries from the British Mission at a midsummer gathering in Liberty Park; interviewed released mission president Heber Meeks and outgoing mission president George Q. Cannon; spoke at funeral services for Winifred Andrew, whom he had met in England, "a lovely and faithful soul"; spoke at a student-body assembly on the BYU campus; and attended the thousandth broadcast of the Salt Lake Tabernacle Choir, commending the singers and their conductor, the organists, and their narrator, Elder Richard L. Evans of the First Council of the Seventy. Interspersed with these events were trips to the Pacific Northwest and to Minneapolis, Minnesota, for meetings of the Boy Scouts and the Sons of the American Revolution, and to Northern California, where he dedicated a new chapel at Santa Rosa. And during the summer, Albert and his family spent two months in Salt Lake City. "It seems so good to see them," the Prophet wrote of an early July party in the canyon behind his home where Albert and his wife and children were present.

The presidential pot heated up in the fall. On September 21, 1948, President Harry S. Truman, the battling underdog, arrived at the Salt Lake D&RG depot, where he was met by President Smith and Governor Maw. These three were then the centerpiece of an impromptu parade up Main Street to Temple Square, where President Truman's "give 'em hell, Harry" rhetoric was muted by the restraining influence of the venerable Tabernacle and the presence on the stand of the benign Mormon Prophet. Nonetheless, the spunky speaker made it plain to the capacity audience that if he went down to defeat, it would be with all guns blazing. Given President Truman's weak standing in the polls at the time and the conventional wisdom that he didn't have a chance, it must be assumed that the prevailing feeling among the Tabernacle audience was that they were witnessing the valiant but fruitless effort of a sure loser. And the feeling was undoubtedly enhanced when the confident, well-oiled campaign of the Republicans rolled into town. Their candidate, Thomas E. Dewey, gave a convincing speech in the tabernacle about the cosmic changes to be made when finally a Republican president would take office after sixteen years of Democratic misrule. President Smith, like most other voters, was stunned by President Truman's victory. "Truman political upset" was all he could manage for his diary entry on November 3, 1948.

President Smith presided at a meeting of all the General Authorities during the first week of 1949. "All bore their testimonies," he wrote of the special meeting held in the upper room of the temple. "And the spirit of the Lord was present in rich abundance. An inspirational meeting enjoyed by all." Nine days later, he left for Southern California, traveling overnight on the Streamliner rather than by air. He arrived in Los Angeles on Sunday, January 16, in time to speak briefly at the last session of the Los Angeles stake conference in the Wilshire Ward chapel. The next day, the Prophet inspected the Los Angeles temple site with President David O. McKay and Elder Spencer W. Kimball, who had accompanied him from Salt Lake City. With them was the Church architect, E. O. Anderson, who was then working on the drawings for the sacred building. That evening, the visiting brethren held a special meeting with all the stake presidencies and bishoprics in the area to lay plans to raise the money needed to build the temple. A committee of local leaders was then appointed to carry out the approved plans.

Having finished the principal work that had brought him to Los Angeles, President Smith decided to stay on for a few days to enjoy the mild weather. Before leaving Salt Lake City, he had been troubled by the old nervousness, which was aggravated by a frigid arctic air mass that lingered over the intermountain area. During most of the Christmas holidays, Salt Lake City had shivered from sub-zero temperatures. So it was a welcome relief to bask in the warmth of the California sun for a few days. He used the time profitably by renewing the acquaintance of some of his California friends. On Tuesday, he visited the offices of the Braille Institute of America and later met with transplanted Utahns Noble Warrum, Sr., an editor and historian, and actress Connie Woodruff, whose stage name was Edwina Booth. The next day, he called on Mayor Fletcher Bowron to brief him on the plans for the temple, and he visited with Norman Chandler, publisher of the *Los Angeles Times,* and Edward Carter, president of the Broadway-Hale department stores. On Thursday, the Prophet was the luncheon guest of H. D. Ivey, president of the Citizens National Bank, at the exclusive California Club. He did not feel well during the meal and later, after suffering from "stomach distress," he canceled an appointment he had made with a group of local educators. When his condition worsened at the home of Preston Richards, where he had gone to rest, Doctor E. Conway Stratford was called; the doctor recommended that the Prophet check into the California Lutheran Hospital for tests and diagnosis. There medical specialists concluded that he had suffered a thrombosis in his right temple and recommended that he remain in the hospital for a few days for further tests and observation. A few days stretched into almost three weeks while the doctors and nurses hovered over the bearded figure who seemed more concerned about their welfare and that of his family and friends than about his own. And the family and friends of the patient flocked around in droves, either personally or through letters, get-well cards, telegrams, or flowers.

There was a certain apprehension about the Prophet's condition on this occasion that had not existed since the early days of his ministry when he had struggled so long against death. He would soon be seventy-nine years old and therefore had lived far beyond the three score and ten traditionally defined as a normal lifespan. He was frail and weak. And his resistance to disease and infirmity had been dangerously lowered by the way he had driven himself since becoming the president of the Church. All these combined, coupled with the gravity of a thrombosis that threatened a stroke and paralysis, caused genuine concern that perhaps President Smith's time had come, or that he might become seriously impaired as had President Grant before him. On this account, Emily and Edith were at his side the day after the doctors had made their diagnosis. Albert came a few days later. If this were the end, those nearest and dearest to him wanted to be present when the mortal curtain descended. But the end was not yet. Faith, prayers, priesthood blessings, and the Prophet's indomitable will to live worked a miracle. By February 8, his condition had improved to the point that the doctors felt comfortable releasing him from the hospital. But they felt that a period of quiet recuperation was necessary away from the pressures of the office at Salt Lake City. For this purpose, his three children and Arthur Haycock accompanied President Smith on the short drive down the coast to Laguna Beach, where David I. Stoddard had made his oceanside cottage available for the Prophet's use. Situated on a bluff overlooking the Pacific, the beach house commanded a spectacular view of the sea, which rhythmically pounded night and day. Here President Smith settled down for six weeks of restful convalescence. After a few days, the children returned to their homes, leaving the Prophet in the competent care of Arthur Haycock, who remained to cook, keep house, provide companionship, and assist with correspondence. With no schedule to follow and relieved of the daily duties of office, which he had temporarily delegated to his counselors, the Prophet began to mend. With this came a calming sense of well-being and confidence. "It is very interesting and relaxing," he wrote on February 16, "to sit at the window and look out over the expanse of the ocean and the broken shore line."

To this secluded hideaway came occasional visitors from Salt Lake City, his counselors and others, merely to chat, to brief him about events at the office, or to receive any instructions President Smith felt disposed to give. As his strength returned, he took short walks with Arthur, who also took him on frequent rides for a change of scene. Late in the convalescence, the Prophet began to handle some Church matters that required his personal attention.

The only interruption in a steady progress toward recovery occurred on March 11. On that morning, President Smith awoke in physical distress with a sensation he could describe only as making him feel "terribly warm" inside and "freezing cold" outside. This was accompanied by a vague, dreadful impression that he was going to die. Arthur immediately called Dr. Stratford, summoned Emily and Edith from Salt Lake City, and gave the Prophet a rubdown to stimulate the flow of blood, thereby counteracting the sensation that he was freezing. From a careful examination, the doctor concluded that the episode was merely a nervous reaction, unrelated to the thrombosis, and that it was not life threatening.

By late March, President Smith was sufficiently recovered to return home. The officials of the Union Pacific Railroad Company made a private car available to him and his party. At the depot to meet him in Salt Lake City were his counselors and other General Authorities and co-workers and members of his family. The Prophet's illness had stirred world-wide interest and concern, especially among the members of the Church, so that representatives of the news media were also present to take pictures of the Church leader and to obtain statements about his condition and a prognosis of the effect of the attack on his future activity.

Questions such as these raised by the press were partially answered at the opening session of the general conference on April 3, 1949, when President Smith spoke for a half hour. He seemed a little more restrained than usual, which was understandable, but he spoke forcefully and with good liberty. After expressing his joy at being present, he confided to the audience, "I started praying about two and a half months ago that I might be here, and I am grateful to the Lord that he has heard not only my prayers, but also your prayers, and I take this occasion to thank every one of you for the interest you have had in me and for the kind words that have been written and the prayers that have been offered."

In a later sermon during the conference, the Prophet turned again to the basic themes that had dominated his discourses since the beginning of his apostolic ministry — his love for all, his joy in life, and the need to keep the commandments. "I want every one of you to know," he told the Tabernacle audience, "there is no one in the world I have an enmity towards. All men and all women are my father's children, and I have sought during my life to observe the wise direction of the redeemer of mankind, to love my neighbors as myself. I have had much happiness in life, so much that I would not exchange with anybody who has ever lived. . . . And I take this occasion to say to my brethren, the counselors in the presidency of the church, and those other men who are here on this stand: 'You will never know how much I love you. I have not words to express it.' And I want to feel that way toward every son and every daughter of my Heavenly Father, and I can feel that way if I observe his laws and commandments and follow his advice." (*Improvement Era*, May 1941, p. 302.)

On April 4, 1949, his seventy-ninth birthday, the

Prophet was in a mellow mood, reminiscing with the Tabernacle audience about his early life and ancestry and his call to the Twelve. And on April 6, at the last session of the conference, the Prophet again repeated his oft-mentioned conviction that America is choice above all other lands to those who keep the commandments and that the Constitution of the United States was written by men inspired of God.

There were a few repercussions from the thrombosis President Smith suffered in California. The most troublesome of these was a mild dizziness, as well as permanent damage to his hearing, which later made it necessary for him to use a hearing aid. His sense of humor was not impaired, however, as he was heard to say after getting his hearing aid that he could hear all right but that people didn't talk as loud as they used to.

After the April general conference, the Prophet accelerated his pace back to presidential speed. He was visited by former president Herbert Hoover to discuss his study of the possible reorganization of the United States government, traveled to Brigham City to inspect the facilities of the large Indian School there, and presided at the MIA June conference. In early July, troubled by reports of what was going on there, the Prophet took President McKay with him to meet with Utah's governor at This Is the Place Monument. This was Governor J. Bracken Lee, a Republican, who had defeated the Prophet's friend Herbert Maw at the November 1948 election. There these three, with several others who joined them, found earth-moving equipment chewing away at the nearby mountainside, clearing a path for an access road to a planned residential and commercial development. The completion of this project would have destroyed the vision President Smith had of a Pioneer Park near the monument that would not only provide space for the display of pioneer artifacts and structures but also help preserve much of the natural appearance of the area as found by the Mormon Pioneers upon their arrival in the Salt Lake Valley. As the group conferred about what could be done to stop the work, the gardener inadvertently turned on the sprinkling system at the monument; and before he could be alerted to turn it off, President Smith and the others were soaked. But the day was warm and comparatively free of humidity, so the clothes soon dried on their backs as they planned their strategy for stopping construction.

The group decided that neither a personal appeal to the owners of the adjacent property nor a legal action would be fruitful. The only viable alternative was to seek legislative authority to condemn the property as a state park. While the prospects for success were good because of the support of both President Smith and Governor Lee, there were many unforeseen pitfalls that would impede their plan. The issue was warmly debated in the legislature, where opponents argued in favor of the rights of the owners of the private property and questioned the wisdom of spending the large sums necessary to condemn the property and of losing the tax revenues, a loss that would continue forever were the property to be removed from the tax rolls. In the end, the Utah legislature passed a special act condemning a 177-acre tract adjacent to the monument to be developed as a state park. That this happened was chiefly the result of the efforts of President George Albert Smith. It was to be his last and perhaps most significant victory in his role as a conservationist and marker of historical sites and monuments.

President Smith rode in the pioneer parade as usual this year. The customary luncheon followed. And that evening he attended the pageant, "This Land Is Ours" at the University Stadium, which used the special staging and sound equipment purchased for *Promised Valley* during the Centennial celebration. Afterward, he was again the guest of Harold Fabian at Jackson Hole, Wyoming, flying there in a private plane.

When he returned later from a trip to Kansas City and St. Louis, where he dedicated new chapels, President Smith was surprised and upset to find that an anti-Mormon tract had been published by a group affiliated with the Catholic Church. It depicted Utah as a "black spot" in the United States and called for outside help to change the situation, presumably by diminishing the influence of the Latter-day Saints and their leaders. Instead of answering publicly through the press, the Prophet went quietly to his Catholic friend, John Fitzpatrick of the *Salt Lake Tribune,* to learn the source of the pamphlet and why it had been distributed. Mr. Fitzpatrick, in turn, conferred with Catholic Bishop Duane Hunt, who advised that the pamphlet had been prepared without official sanction during his absence from the state by a group of lay extremists. Bishop Hunt quietly took steps to silence them, and a potentially explosive situation was controlled behind the scenes without public rancor and without polarizing the community.

Not long after this incident, President Smith hosted the archbishop of York, Cyril Forster Garbett, who was also a member of the British House of Lords. In another show of ecumenism, President Smith made the Salt Lake Tabernacle available to his visitor for an Episcopalian service and even authorized the use of the Salt Lake Tabernacle Choir to provide the music. He then sat quietly on the stand throughout the meeting. Indicating that he had some apprehension about the situation because of the visitor's dual role in religion and politics in Great Britain, he later wrote in his diary, "I am much relieved to find that everything went off as well as it did."

Shortly before the October 1949 general conference, the president of Brigham Young University, Howard S. McDonald, advised President Smith that he had received a lucrative offer to become the president of the Los Angeles State College of Applied Arts and Sciences. Before responding, President McDonald wanted to know the attitude of the Church Board of Education, of which President Smith was the chairman. When the board signaled its approval, steps to find a replacement were initiated. A search committee was appointed, chaired by President Joseph Fielding Smith. Other members were elders Stephen L

George Albert Smith with archbishop of York

Richards, John A. Widtsoe, Joseph F. Merrill, and Albert E. Bowen of the Twelve. To remove pressure from the committee to find a replacement immediately and to enable President McDonald to complete his negotiations without concern about affairs at BYU, Professor Emeritus Christian Jensen was appointed acting president.

Both the search committee and President Smith were put in an awkward position when a groundswell developed in favor of George Albert Smith, Jr., as the replacement. It started when Howard McDonald publicly made the suggestion. Several deans and department heads at the university picked it up, petitioning President Smith directly that his son be appointed. The search committee, knowing that the Prophet's word would ultimately control, delayed making a recommendation. Apparently they questioned the wisdom of a son of the president of the Church occupying such a position, regardless of his qualifications. Yet they were reluctant to nominate someone else if the Prophet felt Albert was the one. They need not have wor-

353

ried. President Smith's attitude toward nepotism had not changed. And Albert had no desire to leave his secure circumstances at Harvard only to be put in an uncomfortable position. The speculations and uncertainties ended when Albert went directly to Elder Joseph Fielding Smith to tell him he was not interested. This left the committee free to nominate their choice, Ernest L. Wilkinson. When the board approved and installed him, the new president, serving without salary, set the university on a course to vastly expand its physical facilities.

At the October 1949 general conference, President Smith focused on the welfare program of the Church in the context of economic conditions in the United States. "There is plenty for all and to spare," he told the Saints in the Tabernacle. Yet he was troubled by certain emerging attitudes that were creating controversy and class distinctions. "There is growing in our country," said he, "a conflict between capital and labor, or may I say between the rich and the poor." He had words of counsel and caution for both groups. "I hope we are not going to become bitter," said he to the poor, "because some men and women are well-to-do." And to the rich he said, "If we are well-to-do, I hope we are not going to be self centered and unconscious of the needs of our Father's other children. If we are better off than they are, we ought to be real brothers and sisters, not make-believe." Turning again to the poor, he warned: "We must not get into the frame of mind that we will take what the other man has. Refer back to the ten commandments, and you will find one short paragraph, 'Thou shalt not covet.' That is what is the matter with a good many people today. They are coveting what somebody else has, when as a matter of fact, many of them have been cared for and provided with means to live by those very ones from whom they would take away property." (*Improvement Era,* 52 [November 1949]: 788.) Earlier, just before the conference, President Smith, addressing himself to all people, rich or poor, member or nonmember, gave the formula for happiness and serenity that he had cited repeatedly through the years. "All the happiness that is worthy of the name" wrote he, "all the real happiness there is in the world, comes from living in accordance with the commandments of God— whether men know it or not. And the only thing for us to do, if we want to be happy, is to live righteous lives; and if we will do that, the Lord will see that we are made happy." (Ibid., 52 [October 1949]: 621.)

During his administration, President Smith continued to hold out the olive branch to his cousins in the leadership of the Reorganized Church. He was determined to avoid any conduct that would drive a wedge further between branches of the generic family of Asael Smith, from whom both he and the president of the Reorganized Church had descended. So after Israel Smith succeeded to the presidency of the Reorganized Church, George Albert called on him in Independence, Missouri, whenever he was in that area, to cement good relations. And when Israel Smith was in Salt Lake City, he reciprocated by visiting his cousin George Albert Smith in the Church offices. But the Prophet never allowed such feelings of amity to obscure the basic differences between the two organizations. So when newspapers in the Independence–Kansas City area referred to Joseph Smith as the founder of the Reorganized Church, President George Albert Smith made it emphatically clear that the Reorganized Church came into existence more than fifteen years after Joseph Smith was martyred. He never allowed considerations of family unity to override historical fact or to minimize the organization of which he was the earthly head.

President Smith commenced the last complete year of his life, 1950, by dedicating the new Institute of Religion on the campus of the University of Utah. After a sojourn at the Laguna Beach cottage, he later returned to the campus to receive an honorary degree. Dressed in the medieval robes of academia, President Smith marched in the long procession of gowned and cowled scholars, led by University President A. Ray Olpin. Along to add words of commendation as the Prophet received his well-earned degree was Utah Governor J. Bracken Lee. No more appropriate academic recognition could have been given the great humanitarian, George Albert Smith, than was conferred on him that day when he received an honorary Doctor of Humanities degree.

As President Smith approached his eightieth birthday, he was asked to prepare an article for the *Improvement Era*. In it he affirmed the powerful testimony he had borne so frequently throughout the years, although it was now tinged with a special fervency and urgency. "I know today better than I ever knew before," wrote he, "that God lives; that Jesus is the Christ; that Joseph Smith was a Prophet of the Living God; and that the church he organized under the direction of our Heavenly Father, the Church of Jesus Christ of Latter-day Saints, the church that was driven into the wilderness—is operating under the power and authority of the same priesthood that was conferred by Peter, James and John upon Joseph Smith and Oliver Cowdery." Then, to lend powerful emphasis to what he had just written so eloquently, he added: "I know this as I know that I live, and I realize that to bear this testimony to you is a very serious matter and that I shall be held accountable by my Heavenly Father for this and all other things I have taught in his name. Realizing this and knowing that if I were to mislead you that I would be held accountable for it, with love and kindness in my heart for all, I bear this witness in the name of Jesus Christ, our Lord." (Ibid., 53 [April 1950]: 263.)

In March 1950, President Smith traveled to Los Angeles to participate in a ceremony commemorating the long trek of the Mormon Battalion. There, on the steps of the City Hall, the Prophet joined California Governor Earl Warren and Utah Governor J. Bracken Lee to recognize a group of men who had reenacted this historic march.

And after the April general conference, President Smith fulfilled the commitment he had made years before to memorialize President Brigham Young. In late May, he traveled to Whittingham, Vermont, President Young's birthplace. Assembled there on the twenty-eighth was a large group of people, including Church leaders and members, government officials, members of the press, and 160 missionaries from the New England States Mission. The speakers were United States senator from Utah Arthur V. Watkins, mission president S. Dilworth Young, and Elder John A. Widtsoe of the Twelve. The monument was then unveiled by descendants of the Great Colonizer, following which President George Albert Smith dedicated it.

The Prophet then traveled to Washington, D.C., for the unveiling of a statue of President Young in Statuary Hall of the Capitol, scheduled for the pioneer's birthday on June 1. Arriving early, President Smith called at the White House to visit President Truman, giving him a specially bound copy of Preston Nibley's biography *Brigham Young, the Man and His Work*. Predictably, he also visited the commissioner of Indian affairs, Dillon S. Meyer, to check on any new developments that might affect the Church's initiatives to help the Lamanites.

The dedicatory service was held in the rotunda of the Capitol with a distinguished group of church and government officials, civic leaders, and members of the family and press. The music for the occasion was furnished by the United States Marine Corps Band, the Utah Centennial Chorus, and the Manhattan Stake Choir. Utah Senator Elbert D. Thomas, Governor J. Bracken Lee, and Vice-President Alben W. Barkley were the speakers. The statue was unveiled by three of the pioneer's descendants: a daughter, Mabel Young Sanborn; a grandson, Mahonri Young, the sculptor; and a great-grandson, Orson Whitney Young. President Smith then offered the dedicatory prayer, following which Senator Carl Hayden of Arizona accepted the statue in behalf of the United States Senate.

On the surface, this ceremony seemed to go with silken smoothness. However, the Prophet's diary entry of that day paints a different picture. "I am fearful there was some politics involved," he wrote. "I am very much disturbed

357

over the situation." What troubled President Smith was that originally Republican senator Arthur V. Watkins was designated to accept the statue for the Senate, and announcements to that effect had been made. Then devious influences were exerted in the Democratic Party, which was then in power, resulting in the appointment of Senator Hayden. But even before this happened, the Prophet was irked at the Arrangements Commission. Weeks before the ceremony, the commission somewhat peremptorily advised that the dedicatory prayer should not be too long and that a copy of it should be submitted in advance for editing of grammatical errors. When Arthur advised him of these demands, President Smith showed an understandable irritation. The fact is, he was mad. He told Arthur to tell the commission that if they wanted someone to compose a prayer long before the event, without relying on the inspiration of the moment, they should get someone else to do it. The commission relented, of course, and President Smith prayed extemporaneously at the dedication, as he always did, uttering the feelings of gratitude, praise, and thanksgiving that came to him at the moment. Formal, hackneyed, and institutional prayers were not for him.

While in Washington, President Smith renewed some of his many acquaintances. He visited with Vice-President Barkley; John W. Snyder, secretary of the treasury; and the secretary of the interior, Oscar L. Chapman. Also, at the urging of daughter Emily, he had lunch with her and Utah congresswoman Reva Back Bosone.

On the way home, President Smith stopped in Winston Salem, North Carolina, to dedicate a chapel. Earlier in the morning of the same day, he had breakfast in nearby Raleigh with North Carolina Governor W. Scott Kerr and the state banking commissioner, Gurney Hood.

For some time, President Smith had been planning a trip to Hawaii to participate in the centennial celebration of the beginning of proselyting in the islands. A strong inducement to go was to honor the many missionaries who had labored there in the early days. Among these was his kinsman and mentor, Joseph F. Smith, who went there as a young teenager to preach the gospel and who was later exiled in Hawaii during the dark days of the underground. A few days before the scheduled departure, the Prophet went to Laguna Beach to rest and to arrange his thoughts for the events ahead. A large group of Latter-day Saints on the ship had personal or vicarious ties to Hawaii and wanted to share in the excitement of the celebration. Those in President Smith's immediate party included Emily and Edith, Elder and Sister Henry D. Moyle, and D. Arthur Haycock and his wife. Once the ship had breasted the ground swells off the California coast, it moved into the open sea, which President Smith described as being as "calm as a mill pond." Away from the telephone and the constant flow of people and problems that were the daily fare at Church headquarters, the eighty-year-old Prophet settled into a comfortable and carefree holiday routine. In such a setting, the years seemed to melt away from the venerable leader, revealing the cheerful, happy-go-lucky personality that had charmed and entertained his friends in his youth. Although he was not quite prepared to return to his outrageous costumes of the past, he did relent to the extent of wearing a French beret that Elder Moyle purchased for him. With the beret at a jaunty angle, the affable octogenerian was the center of attention and the life of the party. Many passengers, especially the members of the Church, gathered to shake his hand, to wish him well, or, occasionally, to seek special instruction. One sister, who for years had pondered deep questions about the mysteries, put them to the Prophet, who told her he didn't know the answers and that she should ask Elder Moyle. Later at dinner, when someone suggested capon cooked in Burgundy, President Smith immediately acquiesced. When Emily, aware of her father's abstemious habits, reminded him it would be cooked in Burgundy, he insisted he still wanted some though it be cooked in Australia.

As soon as the ship entered Pearl Harbor, stake president Ralph E. Woolley and mission president Edward L. Clissold boarded her with a group of entertainers, who sang and danced for the visitors until the ship reached dockside. There they were met by hundreds of well-wishers who loaded them with leis made from ten thousand orchids provided by the Saints at Hilo. The joy and friendliness shown by the Hawaiian Saints set the tone for what the Prophet expected to be a peaceful time of reflection and renewal among his Polynesian friends. That mood was shattered, however, when he was informed that Elder George F. Richards had passed away early that morning. Thinking, perhaps, that their forty-four years of service together in the apostleship and Elder Richards's key position as the president of the Twelve required it, President Smith began to make inquiries about travel schedules to the mainland so he could attend the funeral. Only a telephone call from President J. Reuben Clark and the realization that to leave early would disappoint the Hawaiian Saints who had planned so long for his visit dissuaded him from returning home immediately. To compensate for his absence for the funeral, President Smith not only sent a loving message of condolence to the members of the family, but he also advised them that the centennial celebration would become a memorial to Elder Richards.

The two-week celebration included a full and varied agenda, so much so that the Prophet, burdened with his accumulated infirmities and the loss of Elder Richards, was unable to participate in all the activities. On the day after he arrived, he attended a gala reception where he greeted Saints from different areas of the Pacific, many of them dressed in the colorful costumes of their native islands — Samoa, Japan, the Philippines, Hawaii, and Tonga. To these were added members who traced their national origins to North and South America, Europe, or China. Being on his feet for many hours during the day, shaking hands, visiting, and posing for numerous photographs, President Smith was exhausted at day's end. He therefore stayed in bed the next day, leaving it to Elder Moyle to represent him and the Brethren at the scheduled events. He arose refreshed the third day, ready for the short flight to Maui. There he ascended part way to Haleakala, an extinct volcano, to Pulehu, the site where the first baptisms of native converts were performed. The little chapel there was too small to accommodate the large crowd that had gathered, so the commemorative service was held in the open amid the lush vegetation of the islands. This natural setting added a touch of realism to the service, whose aim was to memorialize the early converts and the missionaries whose work was usually performed in the open. It was only as the number of converts multiplied that it became necessary or desirable to build chapels. In his sermon, the Prophet lauded George Q. Cannon, who was among the first missionaries in Hawaii, and George F. Richards, whose funeral was being held about the same time in Salt Lake City. After the service, everyone went to Wailuku for an elaborate native feast whose menu seems to have included most of the in-season fruits and vegetables indigenous to Hawaii and a wide variety of meats, condiments, and desserts. Notwithstanding these tasty temptations, President Smith ate sparingly and with his usual discrimination.

Two days later, after an interval of rest, President Smith put on his white linen suit for the Sunday morning session of the centennial conference. At the door to the chapel, two attractive, smiling girls gave him a beautiful lei made of a hundred native orchids, each representing a year since the Mormon missionaries first arrived in Hawaii. During the service, the grandson and namesake of George Q. Cannon gave to President Smith for the Church archives President Cannon's personal copy of the Book of Mormon in Hawaiian. The setting, the sermons, the spirit present, and the outpouring of love from the Polynesian Saints impressed President Smith in an extraordinary way. This is evident from the long and descriptive entry in his diary, which was usually characterized by a rigorous economy with words. "Seldom have I seen a more attentive or magnificent congregation," wrote the Prophet. "As I arose to speak, all the congregation stood up on their feet almost as one man in what appeared to be a spontaneous expression of good will and fellowship. The Saints listened to every word, leaning forward so as not to miss a word, and with tears streaming down their faces very often, as it was recalled to their minds the blessings they have enjoyed during the past one hundred years that the gospel has been in this beautiful land."

Exhaustion and a stomach upset prevented him from attending the Sunday afternoon session of the conference or a ceremony on Monday to dedicate a historical marker prepared by the Daughters of the Utah Pioneers. But he was well enough on Tuesday to visit the governor of the Territory of Hawaii, Ingram M. Steinback, who made many complimentary remarks about the Latter-day Saints and their industry and dependability.

The Prophet later met with the full-time missionaries and counseled with the released Church patriarch, Joseph F. Smith, whose health was better and who directed a centennial pageant in the outdoor theater at the University of Hawaii.

The following Saturday, the Prophet attended another feast, this one on the island of Oahu. Again, President Smith was selective in his samplings of the sumptuous meal, not because of any distaste for the delicious food but because of his delicate health. The next day, the final meetings of the celebration were held in the Laie Ward chapel, where the Prophet bore his testimony and blessed the people.

Large crowds of Latter-day Saints gathered at the pier to send their beloved Prophet on his way home with the same demonstration of love they had shown on his arrival. He and his party were laden with fragrant orchid leis as their Polynesian friends bid them good-bye in song and dance and with tears and sad alohas. Most of those present knew they would never again in life see the beloved, bearded figure who waved at them smilingly as the ship slowly maneuvered into the harbor.

During the return voyage, President Smith received a cablegram advising of the death of Frank Evans, who had served as the financial secretary to the First Presidency. So, when he returned to Salt Lake City, his first acts were to call on the families of Elder George F. Richards and Brother Evans to extend his condolences at the passing of their fathers and husbands.

As President Smith prepared for the October 1950 conference, his principal concern was to fill the vacancy caused by the death of George F. Richards. As he thought and prayed about it, his mind began to focus on Delbert L. Stapley, prominent Church leader in Phoenix, Arizona. Delbert Stapley had been a seven-year-old boy when President Smith was called to the Twelve in 1903. President Smith had watched this young man grow to maturity as he visited in Phoenix and Mesa from time to time. Delbert had filled his mission in the Southern States, where President Smith had served, and, like the Prophet, was an avid Scouter and leader of youth. And he had later served with distinction, first as a counselor and later as the president of the Phoenix Stake. When, at last President Smith received the spiritual confirmation that Delbert L. Stapley was the one, his name was presented to and approved by the counselors in the First Presidency and the Quorum of the Twelve.

Elder Stapley had traveled to Salt Lake City for the October 1950 conference and was staying at the Hotel Utah. He had received spiritual promptings that he was to be called to the Twelve. The prospects of such a call were intimidating to him, however, and perhaps as a subconscious reaction to these concerns, he had deliberately tried to avoid meeting President Smith or other high leaders of the Church and, except for attending meetings he was required to attend, had stayed close to his room, venturing out only to eat or transact necessary business. As he was walking through the lobby of the hotel one afternoon, a

George Albert Smith receiving honorary doctorate degree from A. Ray Olpin, president of the University of Utah, November 1950

day before the General Authorities were to be presented for sustaining vote, President Smith entered. Greeting each other, the pair stood together, chatting in what an onlooker doubtless would have assumed was merely a passing greeting between two old friends. In fact, the Prophet was informing Elder Stapley that the Brethren wanted him to join them as the new member of the Twelve! A practiced observer might have detected that something out of the ordinary was going on from the look on the younger man's face as he came to realize that his spiritual promptings had just been confirmed and that his career had taken a sudden and irrevocable detour. The informal, almost off-handed way in which the call was extended was undoubtedly compensated for by its novelty and impact.

Chapter Twenty-four

The Mortal End

resident Smith may have had premonitions that this conference was to be his last. At the concluding session, after announcing that the conference would be adjourned for six months, he added, "But in six months, we do not know what may occur." (*Improvement Era*, 53 [December 1950]: 1023.) He left the Tabernacle feeling ill and went home to bed. In his journal, he attributed the feeling to the tension of the conference. It proved to be a warning sign that he did not read. The next day, Monday, he was back in his office working to wind up the many affairs connected with the conference. And three days later, President Smith met with his brethren at their weekly council meeting in the upper room of the temple. On this occasion, the Prophet ordained Elder Stapley an apostle and set him apart as a member of the Twelve after he had been given and had accepted the apostolic charge.

Despite being weak and tired, President Smith continued handling the usual flow of work until Friday, October 20, when his body rebelled. As he sat at the dinner table at home that evening, he fainted. The doctor, whom Emily summoned immediately, prescribed an indefinite period of bed rest. The Prophet remained at home for seven weeks convalescing from the fatigue that had overtaken him. During this period, Arthur went to the home regularly to take the urgent mail and to brief the Prophet on the affairs at the office. His counselors also went to the home periodically to hold First Presidency meetings or merely to visit him or bless him. By December 14, he felt well enough to go back to the office, but only for a few hours at a time. Before Christmas, he attended a party at the Primary Children's Hospital and later spoke to the Church employees at their annual Christmas party. It was the last time George Albert Smith spoke in public.

For a while after the first of the year, President Smith went to the office for a few hours a day. But it entailed too great an effort. He just did not feel well enough to go. January 9, 1951, was the last day he did so. He never returned. Soon after, his health deteriorated to the point that he required around-the-clock nursing care. He lost all appetite for food and intermittently ran a temperature that caused him to perspire heavily. On February 3, his condition worsened. To provide him with medical care not available at home, he was moved to the hospital, where he remained for three weeks. On February 14, while at the hospital, he dictated a statement to Arthur in the presence of his daughter Edith that hinted he was preparing for death. "Last evening and last night were the hardest for me," he said. "I felt that perhaps my time had come. If it has, it is alright. If not, I would appreciate the continued prayers and faith of the people. Tomorrow in the regular meeting in the temple, I would like the brethren to lay the matter before the Lord. George and Arthur and Albert, I think, know where all my account books are, and I think they know where there are papers identifying what may be done with finances. . . . I would like in the disposing of funds that those who are most in need will not be overlooked. You know what I would like to say: 'Father in

Heaven, I would like to do Thy will. I would like my family to do the same.' "

Back at home, his condition remained serious but not critical. He was lucid and responded understandingly to his nurses, members of the family, and visitors. He continued to dictate items to be included in his journal; and occasionally he sent messages, as he did on March 17. "From the top of the Rockies, I send my love and blessing," he wired the BYU basketball team, which was competing for the NIT championship. "Many thousands share my pride in your record. I have faith in your abilities. Play clean, play hard, play fair, play to win. God bless you." They won.

Three days later, the president suffered a mild stroke that paralyzed his right arm and slurred his speech. Despite these added handicaps, he continued to function. The next morning after suffering the stroke, he dictated this statement to Arthur. "I have been so grateful for the association and the assistance of my splendid counselors, President Clark and President McKay. They have been willing and helpful and have been devotion itself."

Later in the day after dictating these words of appreciation, the Prophet suffered a relapse. Albert was summoned, and he came immediately from the East. During the president's remaining days, he became progressively weaker. Knowing that death was imminent, the members of his family and his associates from Church headquarters stayed close by. On the morning of his eighty-first birthday, April 4, 1951, the Prophet suffered a "sinking spell" that seemed to signal that the end was at hand. All of the members of his immediate family and his brothers and sisters gathered to wish him a happy birthday and, in a sense, to bid him good-bye. "What a pleasure it is to have all my family at my bedside at this hour," he told them. Also present were his counselors; Brother Haycock; his doctor, J. Leroy Kimball; and the nurses, all of whom remained at the home throughout the day. During the afternoon, he began to nod off into unconsciousness but revived intermittently when troubled by discomfort or pain. Once when one of the nurses and Albert tried to shift his position in bed to enable him to rest more easily, he revived to say, "Be careful. Don't hurt yourselves." He never spoke again. At 7:27 P.M., he slipped quietly into death. All those dearest to him were in the room or nearby in the house. After Dr. Kimball pronounce him dead, President Smith's counselors stepped into the room, where they stood for a while in respectful silence. Later, when word of his passing spread, other friends and relatives came to the home to pay their respects, including many of the General Authorities. Under these circumstances, they found it difficult to adequately express their feelings toward President George Albert Smith. But these came later, at the funeral, during the conference, or in written tributes sent to the family.

Because of the timing of President Smith's death, it was necessary to rearrange some of the general conference sessions. The funeral was held in the Tabernacle on Saturday morning, April 7, in place of the general session. President McKay, in noting the Prophet's passing, gave the first of the many tributes that would be given during the conference and the funeral. "Though his chair is vacant," said President McKay, "let us hope that the influence of his Christ-like character will pervade every heart. . . . Truly, he was a noble soul, happiest when he was making others happy. In his daily life he strove sincerely to apply the teachings of Jesus 'to love the Lord thy God with all thy soul, and with all thy mind, and with all thy strength — and thy neighbor as thyself.' " This was the theme woven throughout all of the spoken or written tributes paid to President George Albert Smith following his death — his love of God and his fellow beings. "His real name was love," said President J. Reuben Clark at the funeral. "I think no man that we have ever had in the church had a greater love for humanity than President George Albert Smith. He gave his love to all . . . and the sense of the love which came from him . . . is what has brought to-

Mourners lined up to view the body of George Albert Smith at the Church Administration Building

gether this great gathering to pay tribute to his memory." In his funeral address, President McKay said that George Albert Smith had "lived as nearly as it is humanly possible for a man to live a Christ-like life." President Smith's protégé, Matthew Cowley, said that he was "the kindest, the most generous, the most appreciative, the most considerate, the most forgiving, the most loving neighbor I have ever known. . . . George Albert Smith is love. He is godly. God has taken him unto himself." And Elder Spencer W. Kimball had this to say about him: "It seemed to me that every act, every thought of our President would indicate that with all of his heart and soul he loved the Lord, and loved his fellowmen. . . . The Lord Jesus Christ told us, 'Be ye perfect, even as your Father which is in heaven is perfect.' And so to compare President George Albert Smith with our Lord and Master I do not count a sacrilege, for perhaps he came nearer than the great majority of his contemporaries to that perfection."

These expressions of his brethren represented the uniform judgment passed upon him by all his peers. They saw in him an almost complete correspondence between his Christian creed and his personal conduct. He lived as he taught.

His place of burial was symbolic of the way he lived, surrounded by members of his beloved family. There, next to his own, was Lucy's grave. Not far away were the graves of his father, John Henry Smith; his grandfather George A. Smith; and his great-grandfather Uncle John Smith. And ranged around the graves of these patriarchs were the graves of their wives and children. In a sense, it was a repetition of the Smith compounds on West Temple and Yale Avenue. They were together in life, and death did not separate them. And if the Smiths who preceded him in death had had their say, they doubtless would have given him a "well done" as his body was interred, echoing the sentiments of all who knew him in life and of all who would come to know him vicariously.

Bibliography

Primary Sources

Official Reports of the General Conferences of The Church of Jesus Christ of Latter-day Saints, 1903–1951.

Smith, George Albert. Journals, 1890–1892, 1903–1951. Copy in Special Collections, University of Utah Library, Salt Lake City, Utah. Originals in Archives of The Church of Jesus Christ of Latter-day Saints, Salt Lake City, Utah.

—————. MSS in Special Collections, University of Utah Library, Salt Lake City, Utah, 118 boxes.

—————. Scrapbooks, Special Collections, University of Utah Library, Salt Lake City, Utah.

—————. MSS in Archives of The Church of Jesus Christ of Latter-day Saints, Salt Lake City, Utah.

Smith, Robert Farr. Personal notes regarding George Albert Smith dated February 23, 1981; copy in possession of author.

Newspapers

Deseret News. Salt Lake City, Utah, 1903–1970.

Deseret News, Church News. Salt Lake City, Utah, 1903–1970.

Salt Lake Tribune. Salt Lake City, Utah, 1910, 1945–1951.

Periodicals

Improvement Era, **Salt Lake City, Utah, 1903–1963, including the following articles by or about George Albert Smith:**

November 1903: George Albert Smith made an apostle, vol. 7:75–76.

June 1905: "How to Secure Prompt and Regular Attendance," by George Albert Smith, vol. 8:634.

June 1919: "Mission Leaders," a short biography of George Albert Smith, President of the British Mission, by Edward H. Anderson, vol. 22:791–95.

September 1921: George Albert Smith: General Superintendent of the YMMIA, vol. 24:1051.

Bibliography

August 1924: "Progress of the MIA — Their Slogans," by Elder George Albert Smith at June MIA Conference, vol. 27:899–904.

August 1926: MIA June Conference, welcome address by George Albert Smith, vol. 29:920–25.

April 1930: "The MIA — Builders of Youth," by George Albert Smith, vol. 33:388–90.

March 1932: "Greatness in Men: Superintendent George Albert Smith, by Bryant S. Hinkley, vol. 35:269–72.

March 1934: Excerpts from remarks of George Albert Smith at Aaronic Priesthood Convention, vol. 37:170.

August 1934: Superintendent George Albert Smith awarded the Silver Buffalo, vol. 37:462.

May 1935: "Our MIA," by George Albert Smith, vol. 38:278.

February 1938: "Outward Bound," goodwill journey of George Albert Smith to the Pacific Islands, by Richard L. Evans, vol. 41:97, 119.

July 1942: "New Honor Accorded George Albert Smith" (director of Western Airlines), vol. 45:442.

August 1943: "President George Albert Smith of The Council of the Twelve," by Richard L. Evans, vol. 46:480–511.

August 1943: "President George Albert Smith," by John A. Widtsoe, editorial page.

June 1945: Address delivered during funeral services of President Heber J. Grant by George Albert Smith, vol. 48:332, 370–71.

July 1945: "Mission of the Mormon Church," by President George Albert Smith, vol. 48:387.

July 1945: "President George Albert Smith," by John D. Giles, vol. 48:388–89, 430–31.

July 1945: "George Albert Smith," vol. 48:404.

August 1945: "The Spirit of Forgiveness," by George Albert Smith, vol. 48:443.

September 1945: "Some Thoughts on War, Sorrow & Peace," by George Albert Smith, vol. 48:501.

October 1945: Dedicatory prayer of Idaho Falls Temple, delivered by President George Albert Smith, vol. 48:562–65.

December 1945: "The Great Commandment," by George Albert Smith, vol. 48:741, 780.

December 1945: "When the Grass Grows," brief story from life of George Albert Smith, by Vilate Raile, vol. 48:748–49, 784, 786.

February 1946: "Utah's Golden Anniversary of Statehood," address by George Albert Smith at meeting marking the 50th year of Utah's statehood, January 4, 1946, vol. 49:75, 126.

Bibliography

March 1946: "Our Full Duty," by George Albert Smith, vol. 49:141.

April 1946: "The Sacredness of the Sacrament," by George Albert Smith, vol. 49:206.

April 1946: Birthday tribute to George Albert Smith, by Richard L. Evans, vol. 49:224.

June 1946: "Concerning Gratitude," by George Albert Smith, vol. 49:365.

July 1946: "Give the Lord a Chance," by George Albert Smith, vol. 49:427.

August 1946: "On Searching for Family Records," by George Albert Smith, vol. 49:491, 540.

August 1946: "On Buying Bonds," President George Albert Smith's recommendations, vol. 49:521.

September 1946: "Speak Up," by George Albert Smith, vol. 49:555.

October 1946: "The Place of MIA in the Programs of the Church," address delivered by George Albert Smith during MIA June Conference, 1946, vol. 49:621, 668–70.

December 1946: "Inventory of our Blessings and Opportunities," by George Albert Smith, vol. 49:779, 838.

December 1946: "President George Albert Smith as Salesman," by Preston Nibley, vol. 49:780–81, 829–31.

February 1947: "The One Hope of All Nations," by George Albert Smith, vol. 50:75, 126.

March 1947: "Your Good Name," by George Albert Smith, vol. 50:139.

April 1947: "President George Albert Smith's First Mission for the Church," by Preston Nibley, vol. 50:206–8, 245.

April 1947: "The Lord's Side of the Line," by George Albert Smith, vol. 50:201.

June 1947: "The Story of a Generous Man," by George Albert Smith, vol. 50:357.

June 1947: "President George Albert Smith's First Mission for the Church," II, by Preston Nibley, vol. 50:358–59.

July 1947: "Centennial Heritage," by George Albert Smith, vol. 50:441.

August 1947: "1847–The Beginnings of Utah," by George Albert Smith on the Chicago Round Table, vol. 50:506.

August 1947: "President George Albert Smith's First Mission for the Church," by Preston Nibley, III—conclusion, vol. 50:511–12.

September 1948: "The Right & The Wrong Way," by George Albert Smith, vol. 51:553, 602.

September 1947: "This Is the Place Monument Dedication," introductory remarks and dedicatory prayer by President George Albert Smith, vol. 50:570–71, 627.

373

Bibliography

October 1947: "Seek Ye First the Kingdom of God," by George Albert Smith, vol. 50:638–39, 688–91.

December 1947: "To the Latter-day Saints Everywhere," by George Albert Smith, vol. 50:797.

January 1948: "Counsel for a New Year," by George Albert Smith, vol. 51:11, 37.

February 1948: "The Founders of Utah," by George Albert Smith, vol. 51:75 126–27.

March 1948: "The Importance of Preparing," by George Albert Smith, vol. 51:139.

April 1948: "The Family Hour," by George Albert Smith, vol. 51:201, 248.

June 1948: "What We Have Been Taught," by George Albert Smith, vol. 51:361, 382.

July 1948: Brief biographical sketch of George Albert Smith, vol. 51:420.

July 1948: "Some Warning Signs," by George Albert Smith, vol. 51:425.

August 1948: "Partaking of the Lord's Blessings," by George Albert Smith, vol. 51:489, 534.

October 1948: "The Path of Peace," by George Albert Smith, vol. 51:617, 650.

December 1948: "A Message for Christmas," by George Albert Smith, vol. 51:785, 837.

January 1949: "Obey the Commandments," by George Albert Smith, vol. 52:9, 56.

February 1949: "As to This Generation," by George Albert Smith, vol. 52:73.

March 1949: "Some Points of Peculiarity," by George Albert Smith, vol. 52:137.

April 1949: "Faith and Life," by George Albert Smith, vol. 52:201, 252.

April 1949: "A Salute to George Albert Smith," vol. 52:225.

June 1949: "A Story of Two Boys," by George Albert Smith, vol. 52:365.

July 1949: "Obedience to Law," by George Albert Smith, vol. 52:429, 477.

August 1949: "Blessings for Youth," by George Albert Smith, vol. 52: 493, 540–42.

September 1949: "Opportunities for Leadership," by George Albert Smith, vol. 52:557, 603–5.

October 1949: "A Formula for Happiness," by George Albert Smith, vol. 52:621.

December 1949: "At This Season," by George Albert Smith, vol. 52:801, 831.

Bibliography

January 1950: "Happiness and This New Year," by George Albert Smith, vol. 53:13, 43.

February 1950: "Perpetuating Liberty," by George Albert Smith, vol. 53:93–94.

March 1950: "The Testimony of Patriarch John Smith," by George Albert Smith, vol. 53:173–74.

April 1950: "President George Albert Smith's Creed," vol. 53:262.

April 1950: "After Eighty Years," by George Albert Smith, vol. 53:263–64.

April 1950: "The Era Salutes Its Senior Editor," by Richard L. Evans, vol. 53:265.

April 1950: "An Exemplar to All Men: A Birthday Greeting to President George Albert Smith," by David O. McKay, vol. 53:267.

April 1950: "George Albert Smith, Born of Goodly Parents," by Archibald F. Bennett, vol. 53:268–69.

April 1950: "George Albert Smith—Sharing the Gospel with Others," by Preston Nibley, vol. 53:270–71, 311–12.

April 1950: "George Albert Smith Administration—A Period of Progress," by Doyle L. Green and Albert Zobell, Jr., vol. 53:272–73.

April 1950: "George Albert Smith—Humor, a Way of Life," by Marba C. Josephson, vol. 53:274, 310–11.

April 1950: "George Albert Smith—Honorary Doctor of Humanities," vol. 53:277.

April 1950: "Service through Industry—George Albert Smith as a Businessman," by Bryant S. Hinkley, vol. 53:282–83.

April 1950: "George Albert Smith—Markers & Monuments," by George Q. Morris, vol. 53:284–85.

April 1950: "A Normal Day in the Home of George Albert Smith," by Robert Murray Stewart, vol. 53:286–87.

April 1950: "A Day with the President," by D. Arthur Haycock, vol. 53:288–89.

April 1950: "President George Albert Smith—Scouter," by D. E. Hammond and Horace Green, vol. 53:290–91.

April 1950: "George Albert Smith, Friend of the Lamanites," by John D. Giles, vol. 53:292–93, 335–36.

June 1950: "Priceless Prospects," by George Albert Smith, vol. 53:469–70.

July 1950: "Brigham Young—A Great Man," by George Albert Smith, vol. 53:545–46.

August 1950: "See What God Hath Wrought," by George Albert Smith, vol. 53:613–14, 673.

Bibliography

September 1950: "Dedicatory Prayers at Unveiling Ceremonies," by George Albert Smith, vol. 53:693–94.

October 1950: "Preservation and Repentance," by George Albert Smith, vol. 53:773–74.

November 1950: "For Law & Liberty & Salvation," by George Albert Smith, vol. 53:869–70.

January 1951: "A Message for the New Year," by George Albert Smith, vol. 54:13–14.

February 1951: "Lincoln and This Land," by George Albert Smith, vol. 54:77.

March 1951: "The Power and Importance of Sincere Singing," by George Albert Smith, vol. 54:141–42.

April 1951: "Living up to the Light," by George Albert Smith, vol. 54:221–22.

May 1951: "A Tribute to George Albert Smith," by John A. Widtsoe, vol. 54:317.

May 1951: "Benediction," a tribute to George Albert Smith by Richard L. Evans, vol. 54:318.

May 1951: "George Albert Smith – A Prophet Goes Home," by John D. Giles, vol. 54:320–23, 368–70.

June 1951: "A Daily Good Turn," recounts experience with George Albert Smith by G. Homer Durham, vol. 54:386, 471–72.

June 1951: "Tributes Paid President George Albert Smith," by Doyle L. Green, vol. 54:404–5, 459–63.

February 1953: "Sons of the American Revolution Citation to Honor George Albert Smith," vol. 56:83.

October 1957: "Explorers Dedicate George Albert Smith Arch," vol. 60:706–7.

November 1958: "George Albert Smith," biographical sketch by G. T. Allred, vol. 61:840.

December 1963: Experience of George Albert Smith related by Boyd K. Packer, vol. 66:1085–86.

***Relief Society Magazine*, Salt Lake City, Utah, 1919–1953, including the following articles by or about George Albert Smith:**

June 1919: "Mothers of our Leaders: Sarah Farr Smith," by George Albert Smith, vol. 6:313–15.

January 1925: "Vigilance, Loyalty to our Standards of Government," by George Albert Smith, vol. 12:7–12.

December 1932: "To the Relief Society," address delivered at Relief Society Conference, October 1932, by George Albert Smith, vol. 19:703–10.

Bibliography

September 1943: "Elder George Albert Smith," by Richard R. Lyman, vol. 30:529.

July 1945: "President George Albert Smith," by Preston Nibley, vol. 32:387–92.

April 1947: "Birthday Greetings to President George Albert Smith," vol. 34:224.

April 1950: "An Exemplar to All Men," a birthday greeting to President George Albert Smith by David O. McKay, vol. 37:220–21.

May 1951: President George Albert Smith," a tribute by Joseph Fielding Smith, vol. 38:292–94.

June 1953: "No Wonder We Love Him," by Edith Smith Elliott, vol. 40:366–69.

Books

Anderson, Joseph. *Prophets I have Known*. Salt Lake City: Deseret Book Co., 1973.

Cowan, Richard O. *The Church in the Twentieth Century*. Salt Lake City: Bookcraft, 1985.

Nibley, Preston. *The Presidents of the Church*. 13th ed. Salt Lake City: Deseret Book Company, 1974.

Pusey, Merlo J. *Builders of the Kingdom*. Provo, Utah: Brigham Young University Press, 1981.

Smith, George Albert. *Sharing the Gospel with Others*. Excepts from the sermons of President Smith, selected and compiled by Preston Nibley. Salt Lake City: Deseret Book Company, 1948.

Smith, Henry A. *Matthew Cowley, Man of Faith*. Salt Lake City: Deseret Book Company, 1954.

Stubbs, Glen R. *A Biography of George Albert Smith*. Unpublished Dissertation Presented to the Department of Church History and Doctrine, Brigham Young University, in Partial Fulfillment of the Requirements for the Degree of Doctor of Philosophy, August 1974.

West, Emerson R. *Profiles of the Presidents*. 3rd ed. rev., Salt Lake City: Deseret Book Co., 1974.

Index

Index